BILL OF WRITES

DISPATCHES FROM THE POLITICAL CORRECTNESS BATTLEFIELD

BY LLOYD BILLINGSLEY

A Centershot Book

Also by Lloyd Billingsley

Exceptional Depravity: Dan Who Likes Dark and Double Murder in Davis, California

Hollywood Party: Stalinist Adventures in the American Movie Industry

Shotgun Weddings: The Saga of Grandma Cokey, California's Serial Husband Killer

ISBN 978-0-9968581-1-3 (pbk.)

First edition 2016

Printed in the United States of America

1 2 3 4 5 6 7 8 9 10

For JMB

One should either write ruthlessly what one believes to be the truth, or else shut up.

— Arthur Koestler

Contents

Locked and Loaded

Foreword by Peter Collier

I MET LLOYD BILLINGSLEY IN 1987 AT THE SECOND THOUGHTS CONFERENCE, a modestly historic gathering of former 60s radicals like ourselves David Horowitz and I put together to talk about that low dishonest decade (Auden's phrase for the 1930s was brilliantly apropos) and how its toxic legacy continued to spill into the 80s—in support for the noxious Sandinistas and their evil twin, the murderous FMLN in El Salvador; in opposition to Ronald Reagan's decision to dump the Soviet Union on the ash heap of history; and in an ongoing addiction to the idea, still very much with us as the lasting legacy of the 60s, that America was not a good country and therefore should not be regarded as a great one.

Those who took part in this Conference—figures such as Ronald Radosh, Jeffrey Herf, Bruce Cameron, Joshua Muravchik, Stanley Crouch, Martha Bayles, and P.J. O'Rourke among them—differed on many issues. But they shared one central conviction – that the god of the New Left had failed them personally during its nihilistic strut on the stage of the 60s and that they were now ready to testify against the smelly little orthodoxies they had once affirmed. In the future, some of these Second Thoughters would go on to become conservatives; but they would always have a more profound identity as "ex-leftists" who knew that the utopia they (we) had once claimed to be building had really never been anything more than a Potemkin waste site and that while leftism might try to disguise itself as "liberal" or "progressive" totalitarianism by any other name would smell as rancid.

The Conference was filmed in its entirety by C-SPAN and covered by journalists from the *Washington Post*, the *Los Angeles Times* and other publications. One of these journalists was Lloyd himself, who was there as a participant but wrote a memorable piece on the event for the *San Diego Union*. He too had once also been seduced by the left and had a change of heart in the decades since, as he watched the chickens of the 60s revolution come home to roost in epidemics of drug abuse, criminality, and dependence, as well as defeatism in the face of Soviet advances around the world. Being in the company with other Second Thoughters showed him that he was not alone in his reevaluations and that there would be like-minded others in the trenches beside him as he got locked and loaded for the culture wars to come.

Lloyd and I (as Boswell says of himself and Johnson) assimilated to each other immediately. We have been friends in the nearly thirty years that followed—more or less the period when the pieces that comprise his *Bill of Writes* were written. The work in this collection is about many things. But while Lloyd is a fox in the breadth of his interests, he is a hedgehog too (in Isaiah Berlin's duality) in his commitment to one big thing—the destructive nature of the left and its central belief that it is necessary to murder to create.

The pieces in this book share certain qualities: an ironic tough mindedness; a brave heterodoxy (the name, incidentally, of a journal of the 1990s I edited and Lloyd wrote feature pieces for) in the face of the scurvy smugness of the left; a determination and even an existential brio in the face of "political correctness"—a dogma whose anodyne name does not convey the full extent of its intellectual brutality.

The subject matter touches on the virtuous POWs in Vietnam and villainous Sandinistas in Nicaragua, on Hollywood commies and PC thought police, on Hayden-Fondaism and scurvy stem cell entrepreneurship and everything in between. Lloyd's Bill of Writes contains pungent opinion pieces and reviews whose writ stretches far beyond the subject at hand; it also contains some hard-bitten investigative reporting.

What unites all the pieces in this virtuoso performance is that they are all part of an inner conversation aimed at the truth. The contents of this book are not merely picked up pieces, like many collections; they are a unique trip log of a writer who has been singularly engaged with the issues of his day.

Peter Collier is the author of many books, including *Political Woman: The Big Little Life of Jean Kirkpatrick*, *The Fondas: A Hollywood Dynasty*; and the novel *Downriver*. He is co-author with David Horowitz of *The Kennedys: An American Drama*; *The Fords: An American Epic*; and *Destructive Generation: Second Thoughts About the Sixties*. Collier was the founding editor of Encounter Books.

Introduction:

Does Journalism Matter?

"WORDS EXIST LIKE INSECTS IN THE TROPICS, BUZZING BRIEFLY AROUND A hurricane lamp then piling up in dead heaps on the ground." That comes from the late Malcolm Muggeridge (1903-1990), author of *Winter in Moscow* and *Chronicles of Wasted Time*. In that book, one of my favorites, the author said his own "Niagara of words" signified "a lost life, possibilities vaguely envisaged but never realized. A light glimpsed only to disappear," and "footsteps echoing ever more faintly down stone stairs." Yet, his own career confirms that his words signify much more than that.

As a correspondent for the *Manchester Guardian*, Muggeridge broke the story of Josef Stalin's forced famine in Ukraine in 1932-33, a mass atrocity that took millions of lives. At the same time, Walter Duranty of the *New York Times* wrote that not only was there no famine in Ukraine but such a thing was impossible under the scientific social-ism of Stalin's USSR. Duranty won a Pulitzer Prize for those articles, which played a role in U.S. recognition of the USSR.

So journalism matters very much indeed, and I drew inspiration from Muggeridge, with whom I briefly corresponded, and his friend George Orwell. Over several decades, I compiled a body of work, as it were, my own eclectic Bill of Writes. Now, as I hang more years on the line, as Paul Simon put it, I thought I might backpack through those scattered piles of words and put together a collection. I did not organize the pieces chronologically, or by publication, but many share a common theme.

Political correctness is a legacy of the Old Left, which allowed only one "correct" view on anything. A vanguard of wise leaders has somehow escaped the false consciousness that smothers the masses, and therefore always knows best. As Orwell had it, Big Brother is always right. This superstition lingers in the notion that, when someone is elected to public office, or gains employment in a government bureaucracy, they suddenly acquire deep wisdom.

As several articles in this collection show, political correctness is usually at odds with factual correctness. In 2009 at Ford Hood, Texas, U.S. Army Major Nidal Hasan, a self-described "Solider of Allah," yelled "*Allahu akbar*" while gunning down 13 unarmed Americans, twice as many victims as in the first attack on the World Trade Center. As a matter of fact that is terrorism, but politically correct politicians called it "workplace violence," as though Hasan had been a discontented postal worker.

As another selection shows, politically correct orthodoxy holds that Julius and Ethel Rosenberg were persecuted idealists and noble devotees of peace. When author Ron Radosh found that the Rosenbergs were actually Stalinist spies, he was accused of having "succumbed to the facts" and attacked. As the review of Peter Collier's *Political Woman* shows, the PC troops on campus do not want to exchange facts and ideas with people such as Jeane Kirkpatrick. Instead they want to ban her from speaking in the first place.

Political correctness dead-bolts the mind and rigs an alarm system that demonizes any challenge to orthodoxy. As the "All in the Family" selection on Jim Wade shows, it deploys a presumption of guilt, not innocence.

Political correctness divides society into an oppressor class and a victim class, and elevates group rights over individual rights. In this view, individuals have only the distinction of drops of water in a clear pond. So political correctness is also a form of identity theft. I speak as a member of the human race, a non-Asian Atlantic Islander, and a person of no color.

Politically correct superstition is now dominant, a veritable jihad of junkthought, and increasingly deployed by government. In these conditions, I thought readers might derive some benefit from my encounters.

Besides that, and *anno domini*, I find another reason to assemble this collection.

Barack Obama is the first counterrevolutionary president, shrink-wrapped in statist superstition and deploying the machinery of the state against political opponents and those journalists who dare speak the truth to power. See the "West of the Wall" and "American Stasi" entries for details. And with a president who confuses the nation's friends with its enemies, writers can easily hold reasonable doubt about the future.

As Ray Charles said, night time is the right time to be with the one you love. The right time to put out this collection is now.

Let readers be the judge of my work, but there's something they should know. It doubtless took a village to write Barack Obama's books and Hillary Clinton's *Hard Choices*, reviewed in the "What Does It Matter?" selection. On the other hand, everything in this collection I wrote my own self, and the vast majority ran exactly as I wrote it.

Selected Journalism by Lloyd Billingsley

1. Politically Correct Cinema

Hollywood Party: Stalinist Adventures in the American Movie Industry, released in 2014, first appeared in late 1998 with the subtitle *How Communism Seduced the American Film Industry in the 1930s and 1940s.* Reviews were generally good and one Los Angeles professor said the book completely changed his thinking on the subject. A National Public Radio interview followed, as did an appearance on C-SPAN and a Bookstar event in Studio City. Among other things, the book explains why Hollywood remains uninterested in stories about Communism. Kindly editor Nick Gillespie invited me to explore that theme.

Hollywood's Missing Movies
Why American films have ignored life under Communism
Reason, June 1, 2000

EVERY SO OFTEN SOMEONE IN HOLLYWOOD USES HIS POWER TO BREAK THE movie colony's rules. Consider this year's *Total Eclipse*. Odd as it may seem, this is the first serious American film set against the background of the 1939 Nazi-Soviet Pact, the deal that allied Europe's two totalitarian powers against the West and helped plunge the world into war. With an ally on the eastern front, Hitler sent his Panzers west while Stalin helped himself to the Baltic states and invaded Finland. A film like this could easily have turned out as big a didactic dud as the Rev. Sun Myung Moon's 1982 bomb, *Inchon*, with Laurence Olivier as Gen. Douglas MacArthur. But this time the verisimilitude of the script, carried by some outstanding performances, is the source of the film's dramatic power.

Dustin Hoffman's persuasive portrayal of Soviet dictator Josef Stalin obviously emerges from his close study of how power and perversity converged in the dictator. Likewise, Jurgen Prochnow sparkles as Hitler's foreign minister, Joachim Von Ribbentrop, and so does Robert Duvall as Vyacheslav Molotov, his Soviet counterpart. Duvall's delivery of Molotov's line that "fascism is a matter of taste" is a key moment, and deserves at least as much admiration as Duvall's famous quip from *Apocalypse Now* about the smell of napalm in the morning. The Molotov speech has drawn some objections for being over the top, but it was not invented by screenwriter William Goldman (*Marathon Man*); it's an actual quote.

The sheer unexpectedness of the film is almost as shocking as its content. In one of the film's more chilling sequences, the Soviets hand over a number of German Communists, Jews who had taken refuge in Moscow, to the Gestapo. Modern audiences may find this surprising, but that incident too is taken from the historical record. Indeed, former KGB officials are credited as advisers on the film, whose cast also includes some of their actual victims.

There has simply been nothing like it on the screen in six decades. It has taken that long for moviegoers to see Soviet forces invading Poland and meeting their Nazi counterparts. Audiences would likely be similarly surprised by cinematic treatments of Cuban prisons, the Khmer Rouge genocide, and the bloody campaigns of Ethiopia's Stalinist Col. Mengistu, all still awaiting attention from Hollywood.

Total Eclipse is rated PG-13 for violence, particularly graphic in some of the mass murder scenes, images of starving infants from Stalin's 1932 forced famine in the Ukraine, and the torture of dissidents. Director Steven Spielberg (*Schindler's List*) deftly cuts from the Moscow trials to the torture chambers of the Lubyanka. More controversial are the portrayals of American communists during the period of the Pact. They are shown here picketing the White House, calling President Roosevelt a warmonger, and demanding that America stay out of the "capitalist war" in Europe. Harvey Keitel turns in a powerful performance as American Communist boss Earl Browder, and Linda Hunt brings depth to Lillian Hellman, who, when Hitler attacks the USSR in September of 1939, actually did cry out, "The motherland has been invaded."

Painstakingly accurate and filled with historical surprises, this film is so refreshing, so remarkable, that even at 162 minutes it seems too short.

Never heard of *Total Eclipse*? It hasn't been produced or even written. In all likelihood, such a film has never even been contemplated, at least in Hollywood. Indeed, in the decade since the Berlin Wall fell, or even the decade before that, no Hollywood film has addressed the actual history of communism, the agony of the millions whose lives were poisoned by it, and the century of international deceit that obscured communist reality. The simple but startling truth is that the major conflict of our time, democracy versus Marxist-Leninist totalitarianism – what *The New York Times* recently called "the holy war of the 20th century" – is almost entirely missing from American cinema. It is as though since 1945, Hollywood had produced little or nothing about the victory of the Allies and the crimes of National Socialism. This void is all the stranger since the major conflict of our time would seem to be a natural draw for Hollywood.

Though of global dimension, the conflict encompasses millions of dramatic personal stories played out on a grand tapestry of history: courageous Solidarity unionists against a Communist military junta; teenagers facing down tanks in the streets of Budapest and Prague; Cuban gays oppressed by a macho-Marxist dictatorship; writers and artists resisting the kitsch of obscurantist materialism; families fleeing brutal persecution, risking their lives to find freedom.

Furthermore, great villains make for great drama, and communism's central casting department is crowded: Lenin, Stalin, Mao, Hönecker, Ceaucescu, Pol Pot, Col. Mengistu – all of cosmic megalomania – along with their squads of hacks, sycophants, and stooges, foreign and domestic.

A few English-language films have drawn on this remarkable material, especially book-into-film projects based on highly publicized works, among them *One Day in the Life of Ivan Denisovich* (a 1971 British-Norwegian production) and, of course, *Doctor Zhivago* (1965). But many other natural book-to-film projects remain untouched, from the story of Stalin's daughter Svetlana (who left Russia for the West) to works by such high-ranking defectors as Polish Ambassador Romuald Spasowski (*The Liberation of One*), KGB agent Arkady Schevchenko (*Breaking With Moscow*), and persecuted Cuban poets Armando Valladares (*Against All Hope*) and Heberto Padilla (*Heroes Are Grazing in My Garden*). In light of the most recent revelations concerning the espionage of Alger Hiss, Whittaker Chambers' *Witness* is another obvious candidate.

The reason this ample supply of stories remains unfilmed is not ignorance. Though its films may not often reflect it, Hollywood is filled with knowledgeable writers and producers. The reasons lie elsewhere, especially in Hollywood's own convoluted political history, a history that has passed through many stages. Perhaps the most pertinent of those stages involves the "back story" of communism's own largely uncharted offensive in the studios.

The cinema's great potential for persuasion excited Stalin and his wholly-owned American subsidiary, the Communist Party of the United States of America (CPUSA), which lived off Soviet cash until it criticized Gorbachev's reforms as "old social democratic thinking class collaboration." Correspondence between American communists and their Soviet bosses can now be perused in *The Soviet World of American Communism* (1998). Editors John Earl Haynes, Harvey Klehr, and Kyrill Anderson gathered newly declassified material from the Moscow-based archives of the Communist International (Comintern), the Soviet organization that controlled national communist parties. Members of the CPUSA made some documentary films in the 1930s, but nothing that could compete with the American commercial cinema, which the party set out to co-opt.

"One of the most pressing tasks confronting the Communist Party in the field of propaganda," wrote the indefatigable Comintern agent Willi Muenzenberg in a 1925 *Daily Worker* article, "is the conquest of this supremely important propaganda unit, until now the monopoly of the ruling class. We must wrest it from them and turn it against them." It was an ambitious task, but conditions would soon turn to the party's advantage.

The Depression convinced many that capitalism was on its last legs and that socialism was the wave of the future. In the days of the

Popular Front of the mid-'30s, communists found it easy to make common cause with liberals against Hitler and Spain's Franco. In 1935, V.J. Jerome, the CPUSA's cultural commissar, set up a Hollywood branch of the party. This highly secretive unit enjoyed great success, recruiting members, organizing entire unions, raising money from unwitting Hollywood liberals, and using those funds to support Soviet causes through front groups such as the Hollywood Anti-Nazi League. "We had our own sly arithmetic, we could find fronts and make two become one," remembered screenwriter Walter Bernstein (*Fail Safe, The Front, The House on Carroll Street*) in his 1996 autobiography, *Inside Out*.

During the period of the Nazi-Soviet Pact, for example, actor Melvyn Douglas (*Ninotchka*) and screenwriter-director Philip Dunne (*Wild in the Country*) proposed that the Motion Picture Democratic Committee, a conclave of industry Democrats, condemn Stalin's invasion of Finland in late 1939. But the group was actually secretly dominated by Communists, and it rejected the resolution. As Dunne later described it in his 1980 memoir, *Take Two: A Life in Movies and Politics*, "All over town the industrious communist tail wagged the lazy liberal dog."

"There was never an organized, articulate, and effective liberal or left-wing opposition to the communists in Hollywood," concluded John Cogley, a socialist, in his 1956 *Report on Blacklisting*. As former party member Budd Schulberg (*On the Waterfront*) put it, the party was "the only game in town." But even though the Communists were strongest in the Screen Writers Guild, influencing the content of movies was a trickier matter.

Communist cultural doctrine cast writers as "artists in uniform," producing works whose function was to transmit political messages and raise the consciousness of their audiences. Otherwise, movies were mere bourgeois decadence, a tool of capitalist distraction, and therefore subjugation. Party bosses V.J. Jerome and John Howard Lawson (a co-founder of the Screen Writers Guild and screenwriter of *Algiers* and *Action in the North Atlantic*) enforced this art-is-a-weapon creed in Hollywood, as they had done earlier among New York dramatists. Albert Maltz (*Destination Tokyo*) was to challenge the doctrine in a

1946 *New Masses* article, arguing that doctrinaire politics often resulted in poor writing. Responding to the notion that "art is a weapon," Maltz suggested, "An artist can be a great artist without being an integrated or logical or a progressive thinker on all matters."

As a result of such heresy, the party dragged him through a series of humiliating inquisitions and forced him to publish a retraction. Maltz trashed his original article as "a one-sided, nondialectical treatment of complex issues" that was "distinguished for its omissions" and which "succeeded in merging my comments with the unprincipled attacks upon the left that I have always repudiated and combated." Maltz was to defend that retraction until he died in 1985.

Dalton Trumbo (*Kitty Foyle*), a Communist Party member and for a time the highest-paid screenwriter in town, described the screenwriting trade as "literary guerrilla warfare." The studio system, in which projects were closely supervised, made the insertion of propaganda difficult if not impossible. Hollywood did not become a bastion of Stalinist propaganda, except as part of the war effort, when Russia was celebrated as an ally. Ayn Rand, then a Hollywood screenwriter and one of the few in the movie community who had actually lived under communism, was to point out that, in their zeal to provide artistic lend-lease, American Communist screenwriters went to extraordinary and absurd lengths. In such wartime movies as *North Star* and *Song of Russia* (both 1943), they portrayed the USSR as a land of joyous, well-fed workers who loved their masters. *Mission to Moscow* (also 1943), starring Walter Huston, went so far as to whitewash Stalin's murderous show trials of the 1930s.

But if Comintern fantasies of a Soviet Hollywood were never realized, party functionaries nevertheless played a significant role: They were sometimes able to *prevent* the production of movies they opposed. The party had not only helped organize the Screen Writers Guild, it had organized the Story Analysts Guild as well. Story analysts judge scripts and film treatments early in the decision making process. A dismissive report often means that a studio will pass on a proposed production. The party was thus well positioned to quash scripts and treatments with anti-Soviet content, along with stories that portrayed business and religion in a favorable light. In *The Worker*, Dalton Trumbo openly bragged that the following works had not reached the screen: Arthur Koestler's *Darkness at Noon* and *The Yogi and the Commissar*; Victor Kravchenko's *I Chose Freedom*; and *Bernard Clare* by James T. Farrell, also author of *Studs Lonigan* and vilified by party enforcer Mike Gold as "a vicious, voluble Trotskyite."

Even talent agents sometimes answered to Moscow. Party organizer Robert Weber landed with the William Morris agency, where he represented Communist writers and directors such as Ring Lardner Jr. and Bernard Gordon. Weber carried considerable clout regarding who worked and who didn't. So did George Willner, a Communist agent representing screenwriters, who sold out his noncommunist clients by deliberately neglecting to shop their stories. On a wider scale, the party launched smear campaigns and blacklists against noncommunists, targeting such figures as Barbara Stanwyck, Lana Turner, and Bette Davis.

These were among the many actors defying the party-backed labor group, the Conference of Studio Unions. The CSU, which was trying to shut down the industry and force through jurisdictional concessions that would give it supremacy in studio labor, clashed with the International Alliance of Theatrical Stage Employees (IATSE) and its allies, who were trying to keep the studios going. Katharine Hepburn stumped for the CSU, reading speeches written by Dalton Trumbo, while Ronald Reagan, then a liberal Democrat, headed the anti-communists in the talent guilds.

These were the true front lines of the communist offensive, and bloody warfare broke out in the streets outside every studio. The prospect of communist influence in Hollywood got Washington snooping, but in classic style, the politicians got it backward.

The first head of what eventually became the House Committee on Un-American Activities was New York Democrat Samuel Dickstein. As the recently declassified "Venona" documents (decrypts of Soviet cables) reveal, Dickstein moonlighted for Soviet intelligence – not out of ideology but for money. Initially concerned with pro-fascist groups in the late 1930s, the committee after the war was dominated by right-wing Republicans, though its most loathsome figure was Mississippi Democrat John Rankin, a sulfuric anti-Semite.

In 1947, while investigating Comintern agent Gerhart Eisler, whose brother Hanns was a composer in Hollywood, the committee found movie people coming forth with stories of Communist Party intrigue and decided that there was enough to justify hearings. They selected fewer than 50 witnesses of various job descriptions and political profiles, including party heavyweights John Howard Lawson and Dalton Trumbo.

Eager to exploit Hollywood for publicity, the committee stupidly made film content the issue, ignoring the party's vast organizing campaigns in the back lots despite convincing testimony from, among others, Walt Disney. More important, the committee ignored the reality that it wasn't what the party put into *North Star* and *Song of Russia* that really mattered but the anti-communist, anti-Soviet material it kept out.

While the committee welcomed the publicity, the beleaguered film industry circled the wagons. Studio bosses, although adamantly anti-communist, asserted defiantly that no congressman could tell them how to run their business. A celebrity support group, including such figures as Humphrey Bogart and Danny Kaye, journeyed to Washington to defend their own.

The hearings featured a series of angry harangues by Stalinist writers who came to be known as the Hollywood Ten. Dalton Trumbo, who joined the party during the Nazi-Soviet Pact and even wrote a novel, *The Remarkable Andrew*, to support the Pact, bellowed, "This is the beginning of the American concentration camp."

Such performances shocked the studio bosses and the celebrity supporters, who had been expecting an eloquent constitutional defense of freedom of expression. Party membership itself was not illegal, and members could have alluded to the wartime alliance with the Soviets. Many wanted to testify, a phenomenon Norman Mailer dubbed "subpoena envy." As director John Huston (*The Maltese Falcon*), who organized the celebrity support group, later learned to his dismay, CPUSA lawyers had decided on the confrontational strategy, largely to protect enforcer John Howard Lawson and others who had already testified to a California committee that they were not communists.

After another series of hearings in the early 1950s, studios produced a string of now largely forgotten, mostly low-budget anti-communist films, among them *Big Jim McClain* and *My Son John,* in which Helen Hayes informs to the government on her son, Robert Walker. These dealt with communism as a kind of domestic political mafia but left actual conditions under communist regimes largely unexplored. More important was Hollywood's internal reaction.

Studio bosses, fearful of bad publicity, announced that they would indeed fire communists, which they had previously refused to do. This was the beginning of the blacklist, Hollywood's version of the conflict of our time, enshrined in such films as *The Front* (1976), starring Woody Allen and Zero Mostel and written by Walter Bernstein, and the star-studded but bland *Guilty by Suspicion* (1991). Viewers of such fare could easily conclude that communism scarcely existed except as a source of boundless optimism in the hearts of the country's most creative writers. Much the same message emerged from *Julia*, the 1977 Jane Fonda vehicle based on an autohagiographical memoir by Lillian Hellman.

Over the years, a number of book-length accounts have taken up the cause, some written by relatives of the blacklisted, invoking "inquisition" and "red scare" in their titles and bristling with terms such as *witch-hunt* and *McCarthyite*. The senator from Wisconsin, it should be noted, played no role in Hollywood, whose anti-communists, mostly liberal Democrats, found him an impediment to their cause.

As it plays out in the movies, the blacklist story is vintage Hollywood: black hats vs. white hats. The evil government committee rides into town and, for no apparent reason, makes life miserable for a group of noble artists. In one subplot, the victims survive by selling scripts under fake names. The story carries considerable appeal, though it misses the irony that those who thought capitalism evil continued to take advantage of the kind of market that did not exist in the socialist regimes they extolled. Albert Maltz championed East Germany, while fellow Hollywood Ten alumnus Lester Cole favored that bastion of artistic freedom, North Korea.

By the 1960s the blacklist was over; Kirk Douglas and Otto Preminger restored the names of blacklisted writers to the credits of the films they actually wrote. The Hollywood Ten and other communist writers were on their way, as Philip Dunne put it, to being "virtually de-ified." Dunne had been through it all and found the revisionist accounts so distorted that, he said, "I could almost believe that I was reading the chronicle of some mythical kingdom."

The legend of the blacklist, sanitized of all references to Stalin or to the Communist Party's actual record in the studios, became a continuing influence on Hollywood's political life. Hollywood had entered its period of anti-anti-communism, a well-known phenomenon in American cultural and intellectual life. Those motivated by this ideology have vilified such critics of the Soviet Union as Robert Conquest and Sidney Hook, while venerating such paleo-leftists as journalist I.F. Stone, whose 1952 *Hidden History of the Korean War* parroted the party line that South Korea invaded the North. Anti-anti-communism demonizes anti-communists, however truthful their revelations, as paranoid and on the wrong side of history, while praising apologists of totalitarianism as well-meaning idealists, however mendacious and servile their record. Such a vision is not likely to promote a meaningful cinematic treatment of communism.

Witness the longstanding campaign to prevent director Elia Kazan (*On the Waterfront, East of Eden, A Streetcar Named Desire*) from receiving a lifetime achievement award from the Motion Picture Academy. Kazan, a former communist, cooperated with HUAC and defended his position in a *New York Times* advertisement that called on liberals to take a stand against communism. Since Kazan's cinematic achievements are undeniable, his career violates a significant aspect of the Hollywood Ten legend: that those who defied the committee were brilliant artists and noble idealists, while those who cooperated were vile mediocrities who could build their careers only by destroying others.

Kazan finally received his award at last year's Oscars, but amid renewed controversy over whether he should receive any applause at the event. Abraham Polonsky (*I Can Get It for You Wholesale*), a leading Hollywood Communist who led the assault on Albert Maltz, hoped in print that Kazan would be assassinated. But though Kazan finally received his due from Hollywood, Stalin never has.

According to Hollywood, American anti-communism derived not from any deficiencies of socialism or threat from the USSR but from paranoia, xenophobia, and the nefarious influence of Nazis who entered the United States after the war. That was the theme of Walter Bernstein's 1988 *The House on Carroll Street*, which featured a score more appropriate for a 1950s monster movie. Bernstein, incidentally, shows up in the Venona decrypts, which reveal that he was a willing collaborator with the KGB. If nothing else, such a revelation gives new meaning to the Hollywood phrase, "Have your agent call my agent."

On the rare occasion when life under communism is portrayed, its characteristic brutality is virtually never actually represented. Consider, for instance, Warren Beatty's Oscar-winning *Reds* (1981), a psalm to Lenin acolyte John Reed. In that film a character concedes that the Soviet regime "violates human rights" but none of these violations appears on the screen. Likewise, audiences don't see the Khmer Rouge murdering any of their nearly 2 million victims in *The Killing Fields* (1984). Indeed, the real villains in that tragedy, we learn, are Richard Nixon, Henry Kissinger, and U.S. foreign policy.

A similar theme runs through *Missing* (1982), with Jack Lemmon, directed by Constantine Costa-Gavras, a man of the left who, unlike his Hollywood colleagues, is sometimes willing to address communist themes honestly. Costa-Gavras' 1970 film *The Confession* deals with the 1952 anti-Semitic show trials in Czechoslovakia that resulted in 11 executions. After hanging, the victims' bodies were incinerated; the film shows a policeman scattering their ashes on frozen roads around Prague, which was what actually happened. For Yves Montand, who played Czech Foreign Minister Artur London, *The Confession* was "a farewell to the generous sentimentality of the Left, a Left that had been blind to its own crimes and cultivates a messianic pose, proposing to bring happiness to human beings, even if it means slaughtering them."

But Hollywood has yet to show itself capable of portraying what *The Black Book of Communism*, a recent scholarly assessment of communist crimes, calls "politically correct mass slaughter." In *Eleni* (1985), John Malkovich hunts down a Greek communist responsible for the death of his mother, but much of the hostile action takes place off screen. *The Unbearable Lightness of Being* (1988), while generally anti-communist in tone, includes only fleeting glimpses of the Soviet invasion of Czechoslovakia in 1968.

Odd as it may seem, one of the few Hollywood movies that does depict violence in communist countries on screen is a Disney film. The 1983 *Night Crossing* shows a daring escape from East Germany, Albert Maltz's version of the good society. Viewers see German border guards, whom John Hurt calls "pigs," gunning down those who flee. Material abounds for this type of film. Soviet Bloc archives are yielding their revelations about the Katyn Forest murders of Polish officers by Soviet forces, KGB assassination campaigns in the West, and the identity of Stalinist agents in Western governments. Vitaly Shentalinsky's 1996 book, *Arrested Voices,* documented Stalin's campaigns against writers and artists, whose victims included Itzak Feffer and Solomon Mikaels, both of whom had been showcased in Hollywood by Communists as evidence that anti-Semitism did not exist in the Soviet Union.

Films from former communist countries, the 1999 *Thief* among them, show that even the Russians are coming to terms with the communist legacy. But the circus surrounding Kazan's Oscar and other recent events suggest that Hollywood probably will not follow suit. The blacklist mythography casts too long a shadow, one in which a fuller appreciation of the epic battle between communism and democracy remains in the dark. "Hollywood Remembers the Blacklist," staged at the Motion Picture Academy's theater on the 50th anniversary of the 1947 hearings, featured Billy Crystal and Kevin Spacey in dramatic roles. Also appearing were Hollywood Ten veteran Ring Lardner Jr. and fellow party member and *Song of Russia* co-writer Paul Jarrico, who compared the Hollywood Ten's performance with the stand that Jefferson took against the Alien and Sedition Act. Actress Marsha Hunt said that "for over a decade, this was no longer the land of the free, nor the home of the brave."

This event was a colorized, multimedia version of Philip Dunne's "mythical kingdom," but for the anti-anti-communist Hollywood crowd, it proved the feel-good hit of the fall. Such events pass on the myths to younger filmmakers who see themselves not just as entertainers but teachers.

For instance, Tim Robbins' *Cradle Will Rock*, released last fall, takes its title from an agitprop musical written by Marc Blitztein, a doctrinaire Stalinist. The original work was welcomed by the 1930s Federal Theater Project, a group dominated by communists, precisely because of its Soviet-inspired Socialist Realism. The progressive Works Progress Administration (WPA) closed down the show out of budgetary considerations, though Robbins attempts to blame it on an axis of HUAC and capitalists allied with Mussolini and Hitler. The fascist-capitalist bosses, headed by Nelson Rockefeller, raking in the dough selling goods to Hitler, are also out to get muralist Diego Rivera, played by Ruben Blades. Audiences predictably stayed away from this film, but in Hollywood, the mythology of the left remains powerful enough to see such a project through production.

Late last year, the University of Southern California, whose film school is a kind of Hollywood employment agency, unveiled a sculpture garden honoring the Hollywood Ten as victims of the Cold War and champions of the First Amendment. The mythology has become a monument, a kind of museum of anti-anti-communism in a town that welcomed Daniel Ortega of the Sandinista junta but never took up the cause of a single Soviet or Eastern European dissident. The specter that once haunted Europe is gone, yet it still seems to hang over the palms of Southern California, an ideological smog that obscures the view for millions of filmgoers.

2. "I knew my onions on Islam"

"I could hear the muezzin calling the faithful to prayer, but I didn't hear nobody pray, man. No, I didn't. And it's a pretty miserable call too, let me tell you. GWAWAWAWAWAWAKAK. FNHUHUHUHUHUHUH – glottal stop. And I didn't *see* nobody pray, either."

That's how Richard Grenier opened his novel, *The Marrakesh One-Two*, published by Houghton Mifflin of Boston in 1983. Chapter Nine begins like this:

"They're all faggots. I'm not going to argue about it. Fuck you. Scratch an Arab and you find a part-time faggot. Scratch an Arabist and you find a full-time faggot. It just shows how little people know about things. How would you expect to know if your idea of an Arab country is Humphrey Bogart in *Casablanca?*"

Clearly, *The Marrakesh One-Two* is not the sort of book that could be written today. Unlike Salman Rushdie's 1988 *The Satanic Verses*, it did not draw a *fatwa* from Islamic clerics.

Full disclosure: I knew Richard Grenier, who supplied a cover blurb for *Hollywood Party* and even showed up for the Washington book event shown on C-SPAN. He passed away from natural causes in 2002 but *The Marrakesh One-Two* lived on. By the time the book turned 30 it was more relevant than ever.

Murderous Realism Turns Thirty
Frontpage Magazine, October 1, 2012.

NEXT YEAR *THE MARRAKESH ONE-TWO* BY RICHARD GRENIER TURNS 30 but with a video about Islam in the news, Muslim mobs murdering American ambassadors, and Islamic nations calling for international restrictions on freedom of speech, the time to look back is now.

"The Arab world depicted with murderous realism," said a front-cover endorsement from U.S. Senator Daniel Patrick Moynihan of New York, a Democrat who previously served (1975-1976) as United States Permanent Representative to the United Nations.

When Grenier was tapping out his novel, Ronald Reagan was still in his first term. The Ayatollah Khomeini prevailed in Iran, where only a few years earlier Iranian "students" invaded the U.S embassy and took 52 Americans hostage, holding them for 444 days. Col. Gaddafi ruled in Libya, a nerve center of terrorism that Reagan bombed in response to attacks on Americans in Europe.

In the *Marrakesh* story, wealthy Arab oil interests tap filmmaker Burt Nelson to make a movie about Mohammed and Islam the equivalent of Hollywood biblical epics such as Nelson's *Song of Jesus*. Trouble is, Nelson says, "we've got to cut out Mohammed," too holy to be shown or even speak, according to Arab advisors. The model here is *The Message* (1977) by Moustapha Akkad, starring Anthony Quinn and subtitled *The Story of Islam*. Akkad, a Syrian who had worked with Sam Peckinpah, suggested the presence of Mohammed with a shadow. Orthodox Muslims denounced the film and the Nation of Islam took hostages.

Nelson plunges into the Koran for research. He finds reams of "Allah is merciful" along with instructions such as: "You are also forbidden to take in marriage married women, except captives whom you own as slaves." Further, "men have authority over women because Allah has made the one superior to the other."

Also, "Those of you who divorce their wives by declaring them to be their mothers should know that they are not their mothers." To which Nelson says, "Which was a good point to clear up. I mean, I was sure it had led to a lot of misunderstanding until Mohammed cleared it up."

Nelson also researches biographies of Mohammed who, "struck me as kind of a gamey figure for a religious leader" and yet had "a very interesting life." Nelson finds that "Mohammed is marrying a new girl every time you turn around," and "if Mohammed wants something bad enough, you get the impression Allah is going to tell him it's okay."

Nelson brags that "I knew my onions on Islam." He can identify characters such as Mariya, "an Egyptian slave of Mohammed's and mother of his son Ibrahim." He is familiar with Alisha bint Abi Bakr, "the beautiful six year old Mohammed married, but the wedding wasn't celebrated until she was nine."

CIA business and a coup attempt against the king of Morocco disrupt the movie production and send the filmmaker to a series of countries including Libya. Incidents there prompt Nelson to say, "They're all faggots. I'm not going to argue about it."

Nelson fails to get his movie in the can but *The Marrakesh One-Two* did get published by Houghton Mifflin. A major house did not hesitate to publish a comic novel about Islam because some ayatollah, Muslim student group, or politician might not like it. It was Grenier's second novel after *Yes and Back Again* (1967). He was a critically acclaimed writer but not a mega-seller on name alone. So it seems the publisher simply liked the story and went with it.

The book sold well and prompted no hostage takings by the Nation of Islam. Neither did the Ayatollah Khomeini issue a *fatwa* on Grenier, like the one he slapped on Salman Rushdie in 1989, which is still in force. Richard Grenier passed away peacefully in 2002 at only 68. He lived to see the "murderous realism" of 9/11 but as Sen. Moynihan said, he was also a "great ironist," and the ironies continue.

Moustapha Akkad made millions on the "Halloween" horror movies but was killed by a terrorist bomb in Jordan in 2005. Akkad's *The Message* recently ran on Turner Classic Movies and touched off no protests anywhere.

Muslims, meanwhile, have launched violent rampages over mere cartoons of Mohammed. Grenier would have grasped that dynamic. He would have understood *Innocence of Muslims* and the mayhem that followed. In current conditions, such horrific violence night well follow publication of a book like *The Marrakesh One-Two*. Even if Houghton Mifflin were to release a thirtieth-year commemorative version (a good idea) it would not likely bear a cover endorsement from any U.S. Senator from New York.

Daniel Patrick Moynihan died in 2003 and his Senate seat was occupied by Hillary Clinton, who under president Barack Obama duly became U.S. Secretary of State. In that powerful office she apologized publicly for a video few had seen and which terrorists used as an excuse for the murder of a U.S. ambassador and attacks on Americans in many countries. Even the great ironist Richard Grenier might find that one hard to top.

3. "What does it matter?"

Nobody starts for the New England Patriots or Los Angeles Lakers because daddy once played the position or happens to own the team. Not so in entertainment or politics, where family connections are key. Hillary Clinton is hardly alone in leveraging those, and clearly aspires to the Oval Office, where her husband Bill was known to spend some time. Trouble is, the former First Lady behaved rather strangely over the Benghazi terrorist attack in 2012, and that all went down when she was Secretary of State. She explained the whole thing in *Hard Choices*, so I thought I would take a look.

Hillary's Hard Choices an Autobiography for Dummies

Hillary Rodham Clinton, *Hard Choices: A Memoir*, Simon and Schuster, 2014, 635 pages, $35.00.

Carolina Journal, June 27, 2014

THE COVER SHOT EVOKES *VANITY FAIR* AND THE INSIDE PHOTO SHOWS HILLARY Clinton at her desk looking very much in charge. Readers will find it hard to imagine a book like *Hard Choices* if, as Hillary claims on page 595, she has yet to decide whether to run for president in 2016. In that quest the former First Lady faces a big problem, revealed in the book's dedication.

"For America's diplomats and development experts," it reads, "who represent our country and our values so well in places large and small, peaceful and perilous all over the world." One of those perilous places is Benghazi, Libya, where Hillary demonstrated some of the "choices I made as Secretary of State." Readers do not encounter the Benghazi chapter until page 382 but other clues come early.

The death of Osama bin Laden, and the loss of so many of his top lieutenants, she explains, "would certainly degrade the capacity of al Qaeda's core in Afghanistan and Pakistan to stage new attacks against the West." That is the official Obama administration narrative, but the nation's sixty-seventh Secretary of State acknowledges "a more diffuse and complex threat" of terrorist attack. In September 2012, for example, "when extremists whipped up outrage across the Muslim world over an offensive but obscure internet video about the Prophet Muhammad. U.S. embassies and consulates in many countries were targeted as a result."

In *Hard Choices* Hillary Clinton touts a concept known as "smart power" that involves "choosing the right combination of tools – diplomatic, economic, military, political, legal, and cultural – for each situation." She explains, "I felt even more certain that we needed to pursue the smart power approach to counterterrorism." She charts past attacks such as Iran in 1979, Beirut in 1983, along with Kenya, Tanzania and, of course, September 11, 2001 in New York City.

"I knew how essential it would be to lead with strength a reeling Department while remaining focused on ongoing threats," Hillary writes. But in Benghazi in September 2012, the leadership did not seem strong and the Secretary of State showed little evidence that she had learned lessons of past attacks.

"As Secretary of State I was responsible for nearly seventy thousand employees," she says. "When something went wrong, as it did in Benghazi, it was my responsibility."

Hillary Clinton says the events in Benghazi occurred in "fog of war," which is not quite right. The United States had provided military aid, including air support, to forces opposed to longtime dictator Muammar Qaddafi, who was captured and executed. Libya might have been unstable under the new government but strictly speaking the country was not at war.

"There will never be perfect clarity on everything that happened," Hillary says. "It is unlikely that there will ever be anything close to full agreement on exactly what happened. But Hillary's uncertainty disappears when it comes to the infamous video.

"I know there are some who don't want to hear that an internet video played a role in this upheaval," she contends. "But it did." To back it up, she cites the *New York Times* and Susan Rice, U.S. Ambassador to the United Nations. On television Rice said it was "a spontaneous reaction" to what had happened in Cairo, "prompted, of course, by a video." Yet, on page 34, Hillary refers to the "terrorist attack in Benghazi."

On that attack, she says, there has been "a regrettable amount of misinformation, speculation, and flat-out deceit by some in politics and the media." Critics accuse Rice of "trumping up tales of a protest that never happened in order to cover up the fact that this had been a successful terrorist attack on President Obama's watch." She denies that Rice was "intentionally deceitful." And how about the Secretary of State? She includes her famous statement:

"With all due respect, the fact is we had four dead Americans. Was it because of a protest? Or was it because of guys out for a walk one night who decided they would go kill some Americans? What difference at this point does it make?" Then she denies that this was minimizing the tragedy and walks away from the whole thing.

"Those who insist on politicizing the tragedy," she says, "will have to do so without me." Readers will be hard pressed to find a clearer declaration of irresponsibility.

Much of *Hard Choices* is vintage autohagiography, bulked with promotional filler. It took a village to produce this book and the text betrays extensive vetting. The accounts are perfectly predictable and sometimes enlightening.

In North Korea the political oppression is "nearly" total. Fidel Castro rules Cuba with "absolute power" but Chile suffered the "brutal military dictatorship of General Augusto Pinochet." The coup that brought Pinochet to power, says Hillary, is "a dark chapter in our involvement in the region." She does not describe Benghazi attack and the ongoing cover-up as a dark chapter.

Benghazi is evidence that America's enemies are rushing to attack during the Obama administration. After reading Hillary Clinton's book, they may make the hard choice to wait for even better conditions.

Readers might also consult *Hell to Pay: The Unfolding Story of*

Hillary Rodham Clinton, the 1999 book by Barbara Olson, who perished in the terrorist attack of September 11, 2001. For a contrasting account of an influential American woman see Peter Collier's, *Political Woman: The Big Little Life of Jeane Kirkpatrick.*

4. "They always blame America first."

"When our Marines, sent to Lebanon on a multinational peace-keeping mission with the consent of the United States Congress, were murdered in their sleep, the 'blame America first crowd' didn't blame the terrorists who murdered the Marines, they blamed the United States. But then, they always blame America first." That was Jeane Kirkpatrick in 1984. She also said "When Marxist dictators shoot their way into power in Central America, the San Francisco Democrats don't blame the guerrillas and their Soviet allies. They blame United States policies of 100 years ago. But then, they always blame America first."

Comments like that earned Kirkpatrick respect, as Andrei Sakharov told her, "in every cell of the gulag," and also from the totalitarians she challenged at the United Nations. But Kirkpatrick's vocal anti-communism drew unalloyed hatred from the American left and their politically correct allies in academia, entertainment, and the old-line establishment media. That bothered her not at all. Jeane Kirkpatrick played a strategic role in winning the Cold War, and she wound up with a biographer well suited to her gifts and intelligence.

Collier's *Political Woman:* A Larger-Than-Life Story
Peter Collier, *Political Woman: The Big Little Life of Jeane Kirkpatrick*, New York: Encounter Books, 368 pages, 2012, $27.99
Carolina Journal, July 1, 2012.

SHE WAS "THE FIRST WOMAN INDEPENDENTLY TO ACHIEVE REAL POWER IN THE area of international affairs," according to *The New York Times*, one of her primary critics. "No woman had ever been so close to the center of presidential power without actually residing in the White House."

Someone of that stature would surely write a riveting autobiography. Jeane Kirkpatrick tried but did not deliver, so the task fell to veteran biographer Peter Collier, whose elegant *Political Woman*, the first full biography of Kirkpatrick, illuminates the subject and much more.

Jeane hailed not from the Northeast, land of reversible names, but Oklahoma, land of Will Rogers, whose statue she kept on her desk. Her father Frank "Fat" Jordan labored in the oil fields and she did not advance because of family connections. From the academic milieu in New York and Paris, Kirkpatrick easily could have fallen into the Stalinatry of her times, but her intellectual formation would not allow it.

Kirkpatrick "studied totalitarianism all her life and was aware of its tensile strengths and subtle ruses for maintaining power," writes Collier. "She had cut her intellectual eye teeth on documentary evidence revealing the psychological and political consequences of the gulag state." She met Hannah Arendt (*Origins of Totalitarianism*) and Franz Neumann, a Columbia University historian who had fled Germany, and who gave her files about inner workings of the National Socialist regime. These documents, Kirkpatrick said, "changed me forever."

Husband Evron "Kirk" Kirkpatrick, who served with the OSS, forerunner to the CIA, gave Jeane a cache of accounts describing purges, famine, show trials, and such in the pre-war USSR. "How could people do this?" she said. "How could other people let them?" Kirk also served up documentary evidence from Chinese Communist soldiers taken prison in Korea, which described the "systematic violation of the human being."

A three-fold cord is not easily broken. Instead of Sartre's apologies for Soviet tyranny, Jeane preferred the formulation of Camus: Communism = Murder. She believed Alger Hiss was guilty. She wound up "convinced that a diabolical vision of the public good is the greatest horror and the source of the greatest evil in modern times." Further, "It isn't war that's the greatest danger. It's tyranny. Tyranny has killed the most millions of people."

In her famous 1979 "Dictatorships and Double Standards" article in *Commentary*, she observed that traditional autocracies leave the habitual rhythms of life intact and sometimes evolve into democracies.

"Precisely the opposite is true of revolutionary Communist regimes," she wrote. Those ideas had consequences when Ronald Reagan tapped Kirkpatrick as ambassador to the United Nations.

She did not accept the Brezhnev Doctrine that the USSR had a mandate from history to preserve and expand its empire. Rather, she agreed with Reagan that it was an evil empire and that the duty of the United States was to roll it back and expand liberty. Communist bosses were not alone in opposing her.

Collier provides a thorough box score of the conflicts in the American academy, the Democratic Party, the Reagan administration, the State Department, and the United Nations. That body routinely condemned the United States, Britain, Israel, and South Africa while turning a blind eye to Soviet repressions, genocide in Cambodia, and other Communist atrocities. Ultimately, Collier notes, Kirkpatrick achieved her goal of taking the "Kick Me" sign off the back of the United States.

She supported the Nicaraguan Contras and that earned her the sulfuric enmity of the American Left, whose members shouted her down as a "war criminal" as she delivered the 1983 Jefferson Lecture at the University of California at Berkeley. Jeane finished her speech and considered it important to be "rich in terms of the number and kind of enemies I had." As for friends, Andrei Sakharov told her "your name is known in every cell of the gulag." She also befriended George McGovern, a political opponent, after each lost children to alcoholism.

Collier concludes with George Will's observation that Reagan and his sidekick Jeane Kirkpatrick set about deleting the Soviet Union from mankind's future. Neither that, nor her undeniable smashing of the glass ceiling, gained her any points with the feminist movement, then as now the women's auxiliary of the left. Gloria Steinem called Jeane Kirkpatrick a "female impersonator," and Naomi Wolf (*The Beauty Myth*) said she was "a woman without a uterus."

Perhaps because of her husband's intelligence background, Collier speculates, Kirkpatrick seemed to believe that potential readers had "no need to know" about her. At this stage of history, the need to know would seem to be huge. The bulk of this story took place a generation ago, and America has the attention span of a hummingbird. In

Political Woman, readers in the Age of the Tweet can get to know Jeane Kirkpatrick, "prickly eccentricities" and all, and meet or recall the vast cast of characters who jostle in these pages, from Idi Amin to Betty Friedan.

Political Woman may prompt some to study totalitarianism and its current variations for themselves. Since many campuses barred Jeane from speaking, the book should prove particularly useful for students of history and political science, and for aspiring diplomats.

"I've always been passionately in love with my country," Jeane Kirkpatrick said, and it showed. One could not see her abandoning longtime allies or, as currently fashionable in the State Department, blaming the violence of Mexican drug cartels on American guns. As she said in her famous speech, they always blame America first.

5. A Politically Correct Kidnapping

San Diego, California, where I lived for many years, is a Navy town, so as Tom Jones said, it's not unusual that Navy personnel should find themselves in the news. On the other hand, the collateral damage suffered by Navy man James Wade went far beyond the perils he would have faced on surface-ship duty, even in wartime. The story raged for months and at one point I though it worthwhile to get it all in one place. I tapped some contacts, dug up some grand jury reports, and made some telephone calls. "This is Jim Wade," said the voice on the phone. The article below is the result.

PC Kidnappers
Heterodoxy, January 1993

ON THE MORNING OF MAY 9, 1989, EIGHT-YEAR-OLD ALICIA WADE AWOKE complaining of pain deep in her midsection. Her father, 37-year-old Navy enlisted man James Wade, and her mother Denise, took the girl to the NAVCARE facility in San Diego, where initially she either couldn't or wouldn't explain what happened. The doctor found that the child's anal and vaginal regions had been torn in a sexual attack and would need to be surgically repaired. When informed of this, both parents showed great distress and began to weep uncontrollably. The NAVCARE doctor immediately called the local Child Protection Services.

CPS immediately suspected family involvement for two reasons: the rapist, they believed, had not removed the child from her room, and Alicia did not immediately complain of pain. The CPS worker interpreted the hours the Wades had spent at NAVCARE as a delay in reporting the crime, and thus an additional sign of guilt.

Though shaken by what had happened to their daughter and also by the hints of accusation they felt coming from authorities, the Wades cooperated fully in an interview with CPS. They could not hide the fact that they were overweight, which child welfare authorities often take as evidence of general neglect. They did not hide the fact that Denise Wade had been molested as a child and that James was a recovering alcoholic who twice blacked out while drinking in foreign ports. They did not know that they were waving "red flags" that further substantiated suspicions toward family involvement in the crime. They had no idea that authorities were already beginning to build a case against them and were taking particular aim at James Wade, who was a walking bull's-eye because he was a white middle-aged male and a serviceman in addition to his other defects.

The Wades were more interested in the facts. During an evidentiary exam at the Center for Child Protection, their daughter Alicia calmly told the physician that a man came through the window, claimed to be her "uncle," took her out in a green car and "hurt" her. They would have had a better notion of the ordeal ahead of them if they had known that on the space on the medical form for "chief complaint in the child's own words," the examining doctor ignored Alicia's testimony and wrote only that the child showed "total denial."

Alicia provided a detailed description of the attacker's clothing, color of hair and eyes, even a pimple on his face. James Wade, a genial Missourian, cooperated fully with the police, who collected evidence including smeared fingerprints and a partial footprint outside Alicia's window. Wade submitted to a polygraph and a "rape test kit" which included a semen sample. He did not know enough about the murky legal realm he had entered to request that the sample be compared to Alicia's semen-stained panties, which police seized, but did not examine.

After a long interrogation and numerous accusations by the police, James Wade said, "You're so sure I did it, but if I did it, I sure don't remember it." Child-welfare workers, who soon began to direct the examination of the Wades, repeatedly lifted this line from its context and construed it as an admission of guilt, not an expression of frustration, shock or anger. They were not interested in the fact that four of Alicia's friends who lived within a four-block area of the Wade home had also recently been sexually attacked and that, in each case, the attacker had entered through a bedroom window. Five days after the rape of Alicia, in another Navy housing project, five-year-old Nicole S. was abducted through a window and attacked. Some two weeks after the attack on Alicia, police confirmed that someone attempted to break through the bedroom window of the Wades' six-year-old son, Joshua. All these episodes notwithstanding, James Wade was the prime suspect in the rape of his daughter.

While Alicia was being prepared for surgery, guards forcibly removed Denise Wade from the hospital. The surgeon was outraged that the mother was not present. Alicia was crying for her parents, but investigators from the Department of Social Services forbade the parents to speak to her. In spite of a request by the Wades, no one explained what was happening to the girl, whom social workers packed off to a therapist and placed in a foster home. In the argot of the child-abuse industry, what had happened to the Wades is called a "parentectomy."

At this point, the Wades were unaware that their ordeal was part of a national syndrome which began in the 1970s with Walter Mondale's Child Abuse Prevention and Treatment Act and has gained momentum in the last few years with the proliferation of feminist ideologies about the evils of patriarchy and politically correct thinking about the nuclear family as a locus classicus of sexual oppression and violence. Fueled by state monies, the child protection system has grown to immense proportions, like the monster Woody Allen describes in *Sleeper* with "the body of a crab and the head of a social worker."

In *Wounded Innocents: The Real Victims of the War Against Child Abuse*, Richard Wexler examines the national child protection system and documents a number of horror stories. Parents have been charged with child abuse for being late to pick up their children at school, letting them eat breakfast at McDonald's too often, or for not letting them watch television after 7:30. In this Wonderland world, the operant principles have less to do with the Constitution than with the maxim of Lavrenti Beria, Stalin's chief of the NKVD: "You bring me the man, I'll find the crime."

Wexler shows how the statistics which assert the existence of a national epidemic of child abuse are based on reported cases in which some 60 percent are bogus, amounting to one million false accusations every year nationwide. In the police-state atmosphere of child protection, informers remain anonymous, and the accused remains branded with a scarlet A even after they have been cleared of wrongdoing. It is a system rife with abuses and filled with the arrogance of power, yet the child police continue to assure us that child abuse is an "American tradition" for which the only remedy is massive, aggressive intervention by the state.

The case of the Wade family fully magnified all the intrinsic defects of the system. The following account is based on original interviews with the victims, public officials, and some press accounts from an excellent investigative series in the *San Diego Union*. Its primary source, however, is a number of highly detailed reports by the San Diego County Grand Jury, which has been investigating the child protection system since 1988. All told, the jury received testimony from hundreds of witnesses from all areas of the system: the judiciary (Superior Court and Court of Appeal), defense bar, appellate bar, public defenders, Family Court, Center for Child Protection, District Attorney and a number of victims. The jurors also spent many days observing court proceedings, visiting "receiving homes" for children, and attending Juvenile Justice Commission meetings. The jury also received testimony from some social workers who wanted to blow the whistle on corruption. Such workers had to testify without notifying their superiors, lest they suffer retaliation.

One institution in which the Wades found themselves enmeshed was San Diego's Center for Child Protection. The Director is Dr. David Chadwick, who has been described in the local press as a "definitive zealot" for a system ruled by politically correct thinking. Chadwick once told a state legislative committee that his organization performed evidentiary examinations, not in a disinterested search for the facts, but in order to "prove abuse." Reporters at the *Union* found a number of instances where Chadwick's Center "diagnosed molestation when other medical authorities insisted there wasn't any."

Through Chadwick's agency, the Wades learned the concept of

"denial." In denying that James Wade had raped his daughter, the couple was seen not as asserting innocence that could be adjudicated by a review of the facts, but rather, as being "in denial." And "denial," as the Grand Jury noted, is taken by the system as evidence of guilt, a tactic the child police share with the KGB and other professional witch-hunters.

"Denial" is the child protection system's version of perpetual motion, an incantation that makes the presumption of innocence disappear. Richard Wexler records the following classic exchange between a caseworker and a woman named Susan Gabriel, whose husband Clark had been accused of molestation:

CASEWORKER: We know your husband is guilty, you've got to force him into admitting it.
GABRIEL: How do you know he is guilty?
CASEWORKER: We know he's guilty because he says he's innocent. Guilty people always say they're innocent.
GABRIEL: What do innocent people say?
CASEWORKER: We're not in the business of guilt or innocence, we're in the business of putting families back together.
GABRIEL: So why not do that with us?
CASEWORKER: Because Clark won't admit his guilt.

If, as was the case with Denise Wade, the wife should be so stubborn as to support her accused husband, she is adjudged to be co-dependent and "accommodating the denial." And if the child denies the charge, this is considered merely part of the "child-abuse protection syndrome." As the Grand Jury later reported, Alicia Wade's only "denial" was that her father was the attacker. The possibility that Alicia was telling the truth and that James was innocent never entered the minds of the child police.

Once enrolled in the Kafkaesque Center for Child Protection, the Wades soon found themselves in the hands of social workers. Most members of the profession (about 70 percent in San Diego) are female and, according to both victims and longtime observers of the system, many come to the job seeing themselves as liberators, rescuing the innocent from an oppressive, male-dominated dungeon called the family.

Social workers are not required to record their interviews, and their statements, often used in court, frequently include hearsay evidence and are not made under penalty of perjury. After sifting mountains of evidence, the Grand Jury found that social workers "lie routinely, even when under oath." And there were "numerous instances" in which social workers disobeyed court orders. Everything is on the worker's side. They simultaneously acquire evidence for the prosecution and "provide services" to the family of the accused (which the accused end up partially or fully footing the bill for). Families enter the process eager to cooperate, but are soon horrified to find their statements distorted, taken out of context and used against them.

In the Wades' case, for example, a social worker told the couple early on that if they showed any emotion – under the circumstances, a perfectly natural response – they would not be allowed contact with the child. When they complied, the same social worker then accused them of being "unconcerned" about their daughter, using this allegation in court.

Jim Wade found himself "horrified by the absolute power over the lives and freedoms of an individual American that these individuals are allowed to exercise." All of the DSS reports about the Wade family failed to include anything positive. They did not mention that Wade's drinking was not a source of problems, and that he had not been drinking the day of the attack. There was no reference to his Navy record, which, except for his weight problem, was described as "superb." Reports also ignored Denise Wade's day-care business, which ran with no problems, and no one bothered to interview parents of the children she cared for. Reports further failed to mention that Alicia was an A student, who had just been named Student of the Month at her grammar school. There was no mention of family participation in community and church activities.

In a videotaped interview, Alicia was asked with whom she would feel most safe. "My mom, dad, and brother," she answered. The transcript of the tape, however, chopped the reference to the father. A

41

child-protection official later acknowledged that he never bothered to review the video.

Feminist clichés and anti-family zealotry are not the only forces that drive the system. Here, as in political abuses, the Watergate rule applies: follow the money. Therapists who fail to back up the social worker's allegations can quickly find themselves cut out of lucrative court referrals. And referrals applying to military families are particularly lucrative, because they are backed by the fathomless funds of the Civilian Health and Medical Program of the Uniformed Services (CHAMPUS). San Diego County pays court-appointed therapists $40 an hour, but CHAMPUS springs for nearly double: $78.60 for 45 minutes of psychotherapy. The Wades went to therapy twice a week.

Alicia's therapist was Kathleen Goodfriend of the La Mesa Village Counseling Group, who worked on the case entirely without supervision. Like the social workers now pawing through the Wades' lives, Goodfriend ignored the evidence and assumed more or less automatically that Jim Wade had been the attacker, although his daughter continued staunchly to deny this in their sessions. Receiving more than $11,000 in state monies for this case alone, Goodfriend began relentlessly to brainwash Alicia Wade, now totally isolated from her family, pressuring her into naming an "acceptable perpetrator." That is, her father.

The Grand Jury eventually subpoenaed Goodfriend's notes, which contained many comments about how Alicia "liked" her therapist. But Alicia's own testimony makes it clear that the child wanted only to go home. The Grand Jury was also alarmed that Goodfriend taught the child about masturbation "without any parental input or apparent interest by the child."

While Goodfriend worked on Alicia's mind, the Wades' social workers were working on her future. They rejected Alicia's grandparents, aunts and uncles, the pastor of the family church and the father's attorney as possible custodians for Alicia because of their "allegiance with the parents." One social worker told Alicia's grandmother not even to waste her time coming to San Diego because her son James was guilty of raping Alicia, who would not be coming home to anyone in the family. Instead, they were sticking the girl in a foster home and the social worker and Goodfriend would be controlling all access to it.

Children are put into foster homes as quickly as possible because that act opens the floodgates of federal funds. Foster parents receive $484 a month for a child from ages 5 to 18, almost twice the amount a welfare mother receives for her own offspring. Special care cases can bring up to $1,000 a month. And all funds are tax free. Some foster parents are concerned and caring, but others are entrepreneurs in what the Grand Jury called "the baby-brokering business." They depend on the goodwill of social workers to get and keep the little human beings who keep the government checks coming.

Alicia Wade's second foster mother — for unexplained reasons, the girl was traumatically removed from the first foster family where she was placed — believed her story about a man coming through her window. She sought to testify that the child not only had no fear of her father, but desperately wanted to return home. This outraged social workers, who promptly yanked Alicia from that home and reported an "infraction" to the foster care licensing department. The social workers then placed Alicia in a third home. This one had a difference: the foster parents were trying to adopt a child through the "fast track" program. Alicia was offered as an obvious candidate.

By now, the Wades knew they were in a hostage situation. To get their child back, they had to fully cooperate with accusatory bureaucrats who assumed their guilt from the start.

James Wade willingly submitted to polygraph tests. One of these was inconclusive; he passed two others and the examiner found no intent to deceive. Then there were some 700 questions to get through, part of a battery of tests that includes the Thorne Sex Inventory, the Multiphasic Sex Inventory, the Sexual Attitude Scale, the Sexual Opinion Survey and the Contact Comfort Scale. Here are some of the 300 "true and false" questions:

"I have occasionally had sex with an animal."

"I get more excitement and thrill out of hurting a person than I do from the sex itself."

"I have become sexually stimulated while feeling or smelling a woman's underwear."

"I have masturbated while making an obscene phone call."

"Younger women have tighter vaginas than older women."

"Sometimes I have not been able to stop myself from fondling one or more of the children in my family."

And then, near the end, a light touch: "I have fantasized about killing someone during sex."

Virtually all men accused of child abuse in San Diego must then endure a stretch on the "penile plethysmograph." In this procedure, a therapist places the accused in a booth and shows him how to wire his penis to a mercury strain gauge. Then the therapist lowers the lights and starts a procession of erotica that can include child pornography, all the while watching dials that measure erection. During the video portion of the test, the operator stops the pictures, asks the subject how he feels, and waits until his organ "hits baseline" before continuing. (A San Diego social worker who administers the test has composed kiddy-porn audio tracks, with vignettes of fathers performing oral sex on their daughters.) At the conclusion of the test, the machine spits out a "phallometric score."

Operating a penile plethysmograph is also a lucrative business, with some therapists charging $1,000 per session. Those backed by military insurance find themselves booked for more sessions than others. One tester claims to be able to use the device to provide "orgasmic reconditioning" to help the subject "learn to become sexually responsible." He is currently trying to talk the Navy into letting him treat the Tailhook offenders. Specialists are developing a version for women that measures the engorgement of the labia along with a gauge that takes the temperature of the vaginal area.

Penile measurements are part of an inquisition that differs from the Salem witch hunts and the Moscow show trials in that the accused must pay cash upfront for the dubious privilege of being so degraded. The Wades found themselves required to accept all kinds of "services," such as counseling, therapy, parenting classes and "abusers groups."

Though taxpayers shoulder much of the cost, the system bills many of the charges back to the family through a scheme called "Revenue and Recovery." The out-of-pocket costs to the Wades, before being billed for foster care, were $260,000, not the kind of spare change a Navy man keeps around. Some accused have insurance and some don't.

Once stuck in the court system, moreover, the Wades found themselves at a constant disadvantage in trying to establish their innocence. Unlike the prosecution, they had no money to pay for "expert" witnesses. (Jim Wade later pegged his legal fees at $125,000, and his insurance did not cover these costs.) When the Wades realized the deep anti-family animus of the system, they struck a plea bargain by pleading no-contest to a charge of "neglect," part of a deal that would eventually return their daughter home. But after the bargain was struck, the county said that, based on the recommendations of Kathleen Goodfriend, Alicia would not be returning home.

The Wades' attorneys argued that the parents should have moved to have the plea overturned and requested a jurisdictional trial. The DSS countered that if they tried that tactic, the DSS would also seize their son Joshua and put their family "further behind the eight ball." This threat constituted an offer the Wades couldn't refuse.

Later on, as part of its review of the Wade case, the Grand Jury found that the entire juvenile system was characterized by "confidential files, closed courts, gag orders and statutory immunity" and had "isolated itself to a degree unprecedented in our system of jurisprudence and ordered liberties." Said former court referee William Burns: "Any time you have secrecy you have the seeds of corruption…the people who are behind closed doors can do any damn thing they want. And in Juvenile Court, they do." Evidence contrary to the system's position, the Grand Jury found, is "either excluded or ignored" and more than 98% of the system's petitions are granted. (During proceedings in the case at hand, for instance, the prosecution objected to Alicia's own detailed description of her attacker as "hearsay" and the court sustained the objection.)

From October 1989 until June 1990, Alicia had no contact with her parents. While the court proceedings dragged on, devastating the

Wades financially and emotionally, social workers determined that Alicia was "adoptable" and that a parental rights termination hearing was appropriate.

All this time, the eager Kathleen Goodfriend was still interrogating Alicia. One of her therapeutic tactics was to say that that she knew the father was the attacker, and that it was therefore "okay to tell." But the child persisted in her detailed story about the intruder. Alicia continued to speak positively about her father, saying, "I love my parents and I want to see them." As the date for a twelve-month hearing approached, Goodfriend stepped up her efforts, setting up a kind of tag-team system by ordering the foster mother also to pressure the child to "disclose."

Thirteen months of isolation and brainwashing eventually took their toll. In late June of 1990, the nine-year-old girl succumbed. At a hearing later on, she said she couldn't hold out any longer. The record makes it clear that she did this to get the therapist off her back.

After the "disclosure," all questioning of Alicia stopped. Goodfriend's "therapy" had achieved its goal. The foster parents immediately whisked Alicia away on a month-long trip to Disney World, an obvious reward for delivering the goods on her parents, as well as a diversion to keep her from recanting. At this point, Denise Wade, whose social worker had been pressuring her to leave her husband, had to be hospitalized to prevent suicide.

In December, James Wade was finally formally arrested on the charge of raping his daughter and found himself staring down the barrel of a 16-year prison term. The Torquemada in his inquisition would be Deputy County Counsel E. Jane Via, whose legal philosophy was summarized in the comment, made in another court case: "Just because we can't find evidence that this man molested that child doesn't mean that he is not guilty."

Via had perfected one of the child abuse system's key strategies: winning by attrition. Her collaborators in social services farm out the children she is trying to extricate from their families to pet foster parents, and delay "reunification" until the child "bonds" with the new parents. Then they use this testimony, backed by testimony from friendly therapists, to block family reunification and justify adoption. According to one investigator, the child police tell foster parents to take the children on long and frequent vacations. Then they turn around and accuse the natural parents of not seeing their children enough. It was Via who tried to justify removing Alicia's brother Joshua from the Wade home.

Via's zealous pursuit of James Wade involved an irony which soon acquired crushing weight. Before handling the Wade case, Via was the Deputy District Attorney who prosecuted the man authorities now believe was the one who assaulted Alicia. Via was thus fully aware that Albert Raymond Carder had been molesting girls in the Wades' neighborhood, and that his modus operandi involved entering through a window, committing the crime and leaving without a trace. In the case of Nicole S., attacked five days after Alicia, the attacker drove a white truck, which was not consistent with Alicia's testimony about a green car. But it emerged that at the time of the attack, Carder did indeed drive a green car, which he reported stolen not long afterward. The stolen car report was never given to the detectives, who apparently never ran a vehicle check on Carder.

Via ordered blood samples to be taken from Carder, whom she eventually tried and convicted. But later, when Via transferred to the office of the County Counsel and began to prosecute James Wade, she denied that she had ordered these blood samples and that there could be any connection between the cases of Nicole and Alicia Wade. The jury found Via's actions incomprehensible, and recommended that the state investigate her for possible conflict of interest and ethics violations.

In the pretrial maneuvering, police finally examined Alicia's semen-stained panties two years after the attack and determined that they could be tested. It took months for DNA tests to be completed, but they finally confirmed that James Wade could not have been the man who attacked Alicia. It was a clear exoneration, but the D.A.'s office, where Via had previously worked, ordered that the tests be repeated, and the DSS continued to prohibit contact between father and daughter.

Convicted sex offender Albert Raymond Carder, on the other hand, was in the five percent of the population whose genetic profile matched that of the stains. His shoe size matched the print taken outside Alicia's window. But even this powerful evidence was not enough. Once the child police could no longer deny third-party responsibility for the attack, the system marshaled its considerable resources to ensure that, however strong the evidence of Jim Wade's innocence, Alicia still did not return to her family.

The Grand Jury later identified a "race against time to arrange for Alicia's adoption prior to the availability of the DNA results." When the result of the evidence was known, Jane Via strenuously resisted a defense motion to delay a hearing that would terminate the Wades' parental rights. Cooperating with Via, Court referee Yuri Hoffman showed himself willing to have Alicia adopted even when James Wade's innocence had been established.

In November 1991, two and a half years after the ordeal began, the D.A.'s office dropped rape charges against James Wade. Then judge Frederic Link issued a rare "true finding of innocence" for the embattled Navy man, which prosecutor Cathy Stevenson unsuccessfully opposed in court. Wade petitioned the court to have the original neglect charge, which had been part of his desperate plea bargain, set aside to clear his name and free the way for Alicia's return. Wade said that the declaration of innocence was like getting out of jail. But his troubles were not over.

As a result of his ordeal, Wade had become an outcast in the community and so had Alicia's brother Jason, one neighbor having forbidden his children to play with "the son of a pervert." There were what Wade later described as "sleepless night, accusatory stares, the unending tears, the strain on our family, the doubts planted in the minds of our friends." The legal fees, says Wade, "robbed me and my parents of our life savings." And, of course, there was the absence of their daughter during a crucial formative period in her life.

But politically correct Jane Via did not believe that the Wades had suffered enough. Via argued that the finding of innocence for the parents "didn't matter" because the original petition was not sexual molestation but neglect, which still provided sufficient grounds for Alicia's adoption. The Wades appealed to the Grand Jury for help, and it was only through their eleventh-hour intervention that Alicia escaped being adopted away forever.

On November 23, Alicia Wade was reunited with her family. The system that purportedly operated in her best interest returned the girl home using a medicine to which she was allergic, without the glasses she wore when she was taken from her parents and with no record of an ophthalmologist's checkup. Two days later, on Thanksgiving Day, Alicia turned 11.

The Grand Jury found that the Wade case, which they said did not even need to be in the system, was far from unusual. In the San Diego area alone, the jurors found 300 cases with similar elements. No system could be without errors and mistakes, but the Jury was disturbed by the fact that rather than attempting to correct these problems, "the system appears designed to create or foster them, to leave them untested and uncorrected, and ultimately to deny or excuse them, all in the name of child protection." The jurors described the system as out of control, with no checks and balances.

Faced with the overwhelming weight of the evidence, several agencies the Grand Jury criticized, including the DSS, admitted the problems and began to undertake reforms, including an emphasis on family reunification. The D.A.'s office was another matter. San Diego D.A. Edwin Miller is a board member of the Child Abuse Prevention Foundation, and the former head of his child abuse unit, now a local judge, is Harry Elias, married to Kee McFarlane, whose interviews with children were the basis for the McMartin preschool molestation case, the longest and costliest trial in American history. Miller's office justified its handling of the case and defended the vindictive Jane Via, but at least admitted that mistakes had been made. On the other hand, County Counsel Lloyd Harmon, Via's other boss, admitted no misconduct, nor even the possibility of injustice. Harmon's response to the Grand Jury, incredibly enough, maintained that the Wade case "was handled in a thorough and professional manner and with due concern for the rights and interests of all parties."

While the child police circled their wagons, the Wade family languished in debt and tried to deal with the emotional fallout. Yet, except for Court Referee Yuri Hoffman, none of those who had attempted to ruin the Wades' lives stepped forward to apologize. No form of compensation was offered. And as far as can be determined, no one was fired or even severely disciplined over the Wade case. In December of 1992, more sophisticated DNA testing found a 100 percent match between the blood of convicted molester Albert Raymond Carder and genetic markers in the semen evidence in the Wade case. But as of January 1, 1993, the D.A.'s office had still not filed rape charges against Carder, probably because to do so would be to acknowledge the legitimacy of the suit James Wade had filed against the County.

What happened to Jane Via? It was more business as usual, the tragedy of James Wade not having altered her attitude or procedures. In November of 1992, Via represented the DSS in the case of Gavin O'Hara, whose daughter had been seized by a social worker and placed in the care of the social worker's sister. O'Hara had been told that his being a Mormon and presumptive believer in patriarchy made it more likely that he would abuse the child. The social worker and her sister, testimony showed, had discussed taking the girl from him before she was even born. When Yuri Hoffman awarded custody to the natural father, Via went ballistic and petitioned for a new hearing based on the therapist's belief that the child was suffering "separation anxiety." It was the old attrition game that she had played with James Wade, but this time the court was having none of it. Judge Richard Huffman said that a "dumb system" had "brutalized" a child and sarcastically put Via down, to the undisguised delight of people in the courtroom.

And the therapist/masturbation instructor, Kathleen Goodfriend? It would seem that brainwashing a child for more than a year to get her to accuse her father of a crime would at least disqualify someone from getting court referrals. But Juvenile Court is still providing Goodfriend with a steady supply of lucrative clients. When asked if Goodfriend's performance in the Wade case might merit some kind of censure, the official response was that a therapist was "innocent until proven guilty," precisely the presumption that had been denied to the Wades.

Jim Wade retired from the Navy, and moved to his parents' farm in Missouri. There, he hopes to heal the wounds and build a new life among the people he grew up with. He has filed a suit against San Diego County, saying, "I just want to be able to pay my parents back the money they gave me to fight this thing." Slow to anger, Wade nonetheless tells anyone who asks that he believes the child protection system is filled with "pimps and parasites living off the miseries of others."

Wade's ordeal was dramatic, but don't check the listings for a movie of the week. The story was optioned and shopped around Hollywood, but there were no takers. "The reason the networks turned it down," says Wade, "was that they didn't want to show anyone getting off [on a child abuse charge]. They got the wrong message, because that isn't what it was about."

Jim Wade has also undertaken a mission to warn others about the system. He has appeared on the "Larry King Show" and other programs, but he cites the op-ed piece he wrote for the *San Diego Union*, right after his family was reunited, as best representing what he wants to say: "Take heed, citizens of San Diego and all Americans. There is a creature running amok in your midst which can steal your children, your financial future and, very possibly, your personal freedom, as it did mine."

6. "It's my game."

Ray Bradbury's *Fahrenheit 451* is one of those rare books that not only gets better over time but becomes more relevant. The seeds of political correctness had long been in the ground and during the 1960s the toxic crop began to sprout. When the great American writer passed away in 2012, I recalled his thoughts on the subject.

Rest in Peace, Ray Bradbury, Enemy of Political Correctness
Frontpage Magazine, June 8, 2012

RAY BRADBURY, WHO DIED WEDNESDAY AT 91, AUTHORED MORE THAN 27 novels and 600 short stories, plus plays, screenplays (*Moby Dick*) poems and songs, a critically acclaimed body of work that will surely stand the test of time. The masterful writer should also be remembered as a staunch foe of political correctness, which in 1979 compelled him to add an afterword to *Fahrenheit 451*, a novel published in 1953.

During the 1970s a lady at Vassar wrote to express enjoyment of Bradbury's *Martian Chronicles*. The author was glad to hear it but dismayed at the woman's plea for him to rewrite the book "inserting more women's characters and roles." He also received complaints that the blacks in the book were "Uncle Toms," with a hint that he should "do them over." Publishers also got in the act.

They wanted to delete "God-Light" and "in the Presence" from his short story "The Foghorn" in a high-school reader. Another school reader had crammed 400 stories by various authors into one reader by a simple process: "Skin, debone, demarrow, scarify, melt, render down and destroy," Bradbury wrote. "Any simile that would have made a sub-moron's mouth twitch – gone! . . Every word of more than three syllables had been razored. Every image that demanded so much as one instant's attention – shot dead."

Bradbury responded by "firing the whole lot" and "ticketing the assembly of idiots to the far reaches of hell." The point, he wrote, is obvious.

"There is more than one way to burn a book. And the world is full of people running around with lit matches." He invoked fire captain Beatty in *Fahrenheit 451*, describing how books were burned first by minorities, each ripping a page or a paragraph from a book until "the day came when the books were empty and the minds shut and the libraries closed forever."

Bradbury discovered to his horror that editors at Ballantine books had censored 75 sections of that very novel, which deals with book-burning. He took care of that problem but found that political correctness was on a long march. His play *Leviathan 99* had premiered as an opera in Paris but a university theater declined to perform it because the cast had no women. Bradbury wrote back suggesting that they perform his play one week and *The Women* (no men in the cast) the next.

"For it is a mad world," he wrote, "and it will get madder if we allow the minorities, be they dwarf or giant, orangutan or dolphin, nuclear-head or water-conservationist, pro-computerologist or Neo-Luddite, simpleton or sage, to interfere with aesthetics."

Every book, *Fahrenheit 451* showed, represents a person, and for Bradbury it was all very personal.

"If Mormons do not like my plays let them write their own. If the Irish hate my Dublin stories, let them rent typewriters. . . If the Chicano intellectuals wish to re-cut my 'Wonderful Ice Cream Suit' so it shapes 'Zoot,' may the belt unravel and the pants fall." He wasn't done yet.

"All you umpires, back to the bleachers. Referees, hit the showers. It's my game. I pitch, I hit, I catch. I run the bases. At sunset I've won or lost. At sunrise, I'm out again, giving it the old try."

Ray Bradbury tried and succeeded, productive until the end. He has now departed and the world, as he warned in 1979, is a much madder place. More reason to re-read *Fahrenheit 451*, including the afterword, and oppose political correctness with the courage of the master himself.

7. "The big fool says to push on."

At a summer camp in high school we sang "Where Have All the Flowers Gone?" but by way of disclosure I didn't much care for Pete Seeger even when I too was protesting the Vietnam War. I was more into Jimi Hendrix, Otis Redding, Lou Rawls and such. I was never big on banjoists and even in the folk genre I leaned to performers like Bukka White, Tom Rush, Odetta, and of course Bob Dylan. Seeger's fervor seemed affected and it was some time before I learned where he was really coming from, politically speaking. I didn't want to let him leave without telling others about it.

Ballad for the Strummin' Stalinist:
Remembering Pete Seeger, artist in uniform
Carolina Journal, February 14, 2014

FORTY-SIX YEARS AGO, ON FEBRUARY 24, 1968, FOLK SINGER PETE SEEGER appeared on CBS television's "Smothers Brothers Comedy Hour" where he performed "Waist Deep in the Big Muddy," a song with the refrain: "and the big fool says to push on." Pete Seeger was singing about the Vietnam war and President Lyndon Johnson, but the tune sums up Seeger himself better than the tide of hagiography following his recent death at 94.

Peter Seeger was born in 1919 to a musicologist father and concert violinist mother. Beyond the family musical influence, Seeger grew up in an age of evangelical communism. During the 1930s it did seem as though Western capitalism and democracy were failing, and that the future belonged to "scientific" socialism, as practiced in the Soviet Union under the wise leadership of Josef Stalin. Many Americans flocked to the Communist Party USA, a creation of the USSR, and its various front groups.

The eager acolytes included many in the arts but they didn't play by their own rules. The official line was that singers, actors and writers were "artists in uniform" and their work had to advance the Communist cause, otherwise it was just bourgeois decadence. Seeger was an artist in uniform.

In August of 1939 Josef Stalin and Adolf Hitler signed the Nazi-Soviet Pact that divided up Europe and launched World War II by jointly invading Poland. That prompted many Americans to abandon communist causes, and the notion that Stalin was always right.

Pete Seeger was up past his waist in all that, but like the "big fool" in his song, he decided to press on. With the Almanac Singers he recorded "Songs of John Doe," that backed the Communist Party's official positions, and opposed American involvement in the war against Hitler.

In 1942 Seeger formally joined the Communist Party and in 1945 became director of People's Songs, Stalinist evangelism wrapped in populist pieties. At that time, as Bobby Gentry might say, everything was an "Ode to Uncle Joe." Seeger was not the most talented American Stalinist, trailing Paul Robeson, Lillian Hellman and others, but he never flagged in zeal.

After World War II Stalin occupied half of Europe and set up puppet Communist regimes. That prompted many Americans on the left, liberals, and trade unionists in particular, to abandon their support for the USSR. Pete Seeger was up to his waist in that, but like the big fool in his song he pushed on. Stalin's colonization of Eastern Europe drew not the slightest protest from the alleged champion of peace, democracy and human rights.

Seeger supposedly left the Communist Party in 1950 for a milder brand of socialism and pro-labor activism. Stalin died in 1953 and in 1956 Soviet boss Nikita Khrushchev revealed Stalin's crimes. That year the USSR invaded Hungary to crush a revolt, but Seeger did not champion the rebels. Seeger's brand of "peace" turned out to be anything the USSR wanted. Throughout the Cold war, he reserved his criticism for the United States and its allies.

During the Vietnam conflict Seeger became known as an "anti-war" troubadour but that misses the mark. Pete Seeger was not against war itself, just against U.S. military efforts to halt Soviet colonialism. Once a pro-Soviet regime was in place Seeger pushed ahead on other fronts. This did not hurt him because the American ruling class has a soft spot for old Stalinists.

President Bill Clinton awarded Seeger the National Medal of the Arts, and the Library of Congress hailed him as a "Living Legend." And Communist dictators still loved the banjo Bolshevik.

In 1999 the Castro regime gave Seeger its highest cultural honor for his work against racism. As Cuban author Humberto Fontova put it, Seeger proudly visited the Stalinist dictator who brought the world close to nuclear war and "jailed and tortured the most black political prisoners in history."

In 2007 Seeger attempted to make amends by composing "Big Joe Blues," supposedly an acknowledgement that Joe Stalin, not Joe McCarthy, had been the major problem back in the day. But Seeger never released the song.

Barack Obama invited Seeger to play at his inauguration, where he performed Woody Guthrie's "This Land is Your Land" with Bruce Springsteen, a big fan. Springsteen recorded the 2006 album "We Shall Overcome: The Seeger Sessions," and introduced Seeger at Madison Square Garden, on his 90th birthday as "a living archive of America's music and conscience, a testament of the power of song and culture to nudge history along." Others take a different view.

P.J. O'Rourke writes that Pete Seeger is "a good folk singer, if you can stand folk singing. And he's such an excellent banjo player that you almost don't wish you had a pair of wire cutters. His abilities as a composer range from the fairly sublime ("Turn, Turn, Turn") to the fairly awful ("If I Had a Hammer") by way of the fairly ridiculous ("Where Have All the Flowers Gone?")."

Those not on board with Seeger's music can always remember the activism. In recent years Pete Seeger duly joined other leftist celebrities such as Oliver Stone in a campaign to "Free the Cuban Five," all operatives of the repressive Castro regime that gave Seeger a prize. Even in his emeritus years Pete Seeger was above his waist in all that. One might even say he was full of it. But the big fool still pushed on.

8. Come Fly With Me

A major orthodoxy of political correctness is that men and women are "undifferentiated," a formulation Orwell would have deconstructed with his usual flair. Women such as Beryl Markham (*West with the Night*), Amelia Earhart (*Last Flight*) and many others have confirmed women's skill as aviators but in the air and on the ground women had not played a role in front-line combat. By the 1990s some politicians thought they should. The most vocal politician in this cause was Rep. Pat Schroeder, a Colorado Democrat who held forth from 1973 to 1997. Though not herself an aviator or military veteran, she appeared to believe that modern aircraft had made downing a MIG as easy as pushing a button, and therefore an ideal position for women.

Though seldom fond of the military, the politically correct have come to appreciate the reality that it is not a democracy. In a pure command structure, officers must do what they are told, or else. Schroeder and comrades such as Barbara Boxer, Ellen Goodman and others advanced the idea that women should be combat pilots, flying aircraft such as the F-14 Tomcat. It wasn't an explicit order, but the word went out that officers needed to make this happen. And as it happened, I was well positioned to chronicle the ensuing tragedy.

"Dancing with the Elephant."
Heterodoxy, March/April, 1995

LAST OCTOBER, IN WHAT WOULD PROBABLY BECOME THE MOST SIGNIFICANT moment in aviation history since Amelia Earhart dropped from radio contact into the Pacific, Navy Lt. Kara Hultgreen took off from San

Diego's Miramar Naval Air Station in a Gruman F-14A Tomcat. The 29-year-old Hultgreen was the first of only two women to qualify as pilots of the Navy's premier fighter since national policy was changed on the issue of women in combat early in 1993. Everything that Hultgreen did, therefore, had the feeling of symbolism. She was not only a fighter pilot but carried the banner of gender equity, whether she wanted to or not – an airborne equivalent of Jackie Robinson whom fate had appointed to shoulder others' hopes and fears as she climbed into the cockpit.

On this clear fall afternoon Hultgreen climbed to cruising altitude then flew southwest toward the aircraft carrier U.S.S. Abraham Lincoln which awaited her some 50 miles off shore. Setting up her approach, she swung her plane to the "abeam" position 1.1 to 1.2 miles from the ship, at approximately 600 feet in elevation and with 180 degrees of turn remaining before her landing. Her air speed was approximately 155 mph as she prepared to "call the ball," a reference to a visual glide-scope provided by a series of Fresnel lenses on the carrier's deck. Just after 3 o'clock, Lt. Matthew Klemish, the Rader Intercept Officer (RIO) riding behind the pilot, said, "one oh three, Tomcat ball, Hultgreen," as Lt. Hultgreen swung into her final approach. "Roger ball," replied the Landing Signal Officer (LSO) from the deck as Hultgreen made her final turn.

The starboard engine was spewing exhaust but nothing came from the port engine. Whether because of that or some other problem, Hultgreen swung wide of the centerline, critical for an accurate landing. Her F-14A then began to yaw to the pilot's left. "Wave off," the Landing Signal Officer said with relative calm. But then he shouted "Wave off!" twice more with escalating urgency as the plane's air speed dropped dangerously. At that point the LSO used his electronic "pickle" to flash some warning lights on deck. "Power! Raise your gear!" he yelled into the microphone from his platform beside the deck, an area surrounded by a net into which LSOs can dive in dangerous situations. But now Hultgreen's fighter was banking to the left and was *in extremis*, beyond the point of no return. Only one option remained.

"Eject! Eject!" screamed the LSO. Radar officer Klemish initiated the ejection procedure. His chute opened and he got one swing in the air before splashing to the surface with only minor injuries. But by the time Lt. Hultgreen had ejected a fraction of a second later, the F-14 had rolled so far it catapulted the pilot directly into the water. It was not until November 13 that a salvage team discovered her body in 4,000 feet of water, still strapped into the ejection seat that rested some 90 yards away from the sunken aircraft. The first female combat pilot to fly the F-14 had become the first to die.

"A complete understanding of all the facts leading to this most unfortunate incident will never be know," said Admiral R. J. Spane in the Navy's official report on the accident, released on February 28. Yet, despite this apparent agnosticism, the Navy tried to wave off the whole incident by blaming it on engine failure. That caused promoters of women in combat to declare victory and to attack critics of the new policy such as Linda Chavez, who had written about Hultgreen's death weeks earlier in her *USA Today* column. "It's been almost two years since the Department of Defense started it's Brave New World campaign to put women in combat roles, and the casualties are starting to mount. . . morale and military readiness are clearly strained by the Pentagon's attempt to ignore human biology and psychology. [Under such conditions] it is doubtful that any accurate investigation into Hultgreen's tragic death is even possible."

These views infuriated California Senator Barbara Boxer, who said, after the Navy released its report, "I urge Chavez to withdraw the scurrilous and irresponsible charges made about women in the military." In a similar vein liberal columnist Ellen Goodman wrote: "So it was the engine after all, not the pilot. Lt. Kara Hultgreen did not die on the 'alter of political correctness,' or 'preferential treatment' or 'reverse discrimination.' She died because an F-14 Tomcat stalled as it approached the aircraft carrier." Boxer and Goodman may have thought that they had trumped Chavez in the intramural war among feminists over the meaning of the accident, but the basic issues remained unsolved after the Navy's report attempted to affirm the idea of women in combat.

It was not accurate simply to say that the Tomcat had "stalled." Even the Navy report said that only one engine malfunctioned. An

F-14A can fly, and land, quite well with one engine, and Lt. Hultgreen knew all of the procedures for both of these functions before she got in the cockpit. "Single engine emergencies are discussed and trained to daily in flight briefs and simulators," the Navy report on the accident says. Whether she was sufficiently good at handling those procedures is another question.

The fevered statements of Boxer, Goodman and others worried that the accident would set back women's participation in combat confirmed that they knew little about Naval aviation and had not read carefully the Navy report or the anonymous letters of other Navy flyers who saw the accident as avoidable, letters they simply dismissed as "vicious" misogyny.

The communications from Navy that followed the accident were anonymous not because those sent them were cowardly or chauvinistic, or because their authors hated Hultgreen. They were anonymous because, in today's Navy, any public expression critical of gender neutrality, or any complaints about double standards favoring women, can terminate the speaker's career.

Anyone doubtful that this is so should consider the case of Lt. Cmdr. Kenneth Karkhuff, an officer with a superb record – "unlimited potential" and "destined for command and beyond," said his fitness reports – who is being drummed out of the Navy for expressing his belief that women should not be subjected to the violence of combat. At the same time, he told his commanding officer that he was willing to go into combat with women if so ordered. On January 29, the Navy moved to dismiss him for "substandard performance" in the "failure to demonstrate acceptable qualities of leadership of an officer of your grade as evidenced by your refusal to support and execute the policies of the Department of Defense and United States Navy regarding women in combat."

Given this reality, I will guard the identities of my sources for this story, both F-14 pilots who are Top Gun instructors at Miramar, each with thousands of hours in the plane. One of them is a Landing Service Officer qualified to land any aircraft in the fleet. The other is a former safety officer as well. These two officers reviewed with me the official materials, the communications sent by anonymous aviators, and the Navy's video of the crash.

The world of Naval aviation is a small one and both men know key players in the incident, though neither had spoken out before this article. They agree with each other in the conclusions they draw about this mishap. Pilot error was indeed involved, and Lt. Hultgreen was given special treatment in training. These two men believe the record also shows that the Navy has been less than truthful in this incident as well as on women in combat in general. Instead of candidly facing the conclusions that might be drawn from this incident, these pilots believe, the Navy continues to move forward blindly with policies that could mean the needless death of our troops or of civilians and the loss of expensive equipment, not to mention the loss of a combat engagement to our foes.

As the first exhibit in this case, these pilots point to the plane itself. As Saddam Hussein and others have learned by direct experience, when an F-14 Tomcat comes after you, you've definitely got a problem. The all-weather F-14 can hit speeds in excess of Mach 2 and soar to altitudes about 50,000 feet. It can track 24 different targets simultaneously and shoot down six of them at once with it's AIM-54A Phoenix missiles.

Few pilots get to fly this $38 million weapon, which also packs several tons of air-to-ground ordinance and an MK 61A1 Vulcan 20mm cannon. But the Gruman engineers who designed the F-14A, operational since 1973, did so with no consideration that a woman would ever fly it. According to the *Navy Times* there are nine concerns for women with the F-14A and other aircraft: helmets, urine collection devices (there are none for women on most aircraft); torso harnesses; survival vests; anti-exposure coveralls; flyers coveralls; anti-g suits; and cold-weather and summer jackets and boots.

Of these, helmets are particularly important. Standard helmets are generally too big for women because their faces are narrower than men's. A shifting helmet is dangerous and hair worn outside of the helmet is a fire hazard. Navy officials told the *Navy Times* that "politically it isn't acceptable to tell female aviators to have short hair," a confession that politics trump practice, and a possible reference to an incident in which Sen. Barbara Boxer chastised a commander who sent a female pilot home for refusing to keep her hair under her helmet.

Custom-designing equipment for women, which the Navy is doing, is a complicated and expensive process. In addition to the equipment, there is the plane itself. From the beginning of its career, the F-14 has proved a difficult, and particularly with the TF-30 engine, dangerous aircraft. A relatively small percentage of male aviators has the ability to fly the F-14 successfully.

Among the female ranks the Navy had found only two candidates, Kara Hultgreen and Lt. JG Carrie Lohrenz. According to Lt. Cmdr. Tom Pokorski, a Navy investigator and author of a study on muscle strength required for aviators, "pilot strength isn't an issue until something goes wrong. If they lose hydraulics or an engine or two engines, it gets really tough to fly the plane." Having said this, Pokorski is quick to add, "The thing is, we don't want to discriminate against anyone."

The Miramar Top Gun trainer and Landing Service Officer who provided background for this article boats an impressive physique but says that he often required two hands on the stick. Kara Hultgreen herself told the *Navy Times* that flying the F-14 was like "dancing with an elephant – you have to be very careful and stay one step ahead of the airplane."

Despite charges that those critical of Navy waffling on the incident were anti-women, most of the Naval flyers who spoke out the crash were respectful of Hultgreen and felt that her death was a loss to the service. "There is no dishonor or disgrace in making a mistake in the most difficult task in aviation – landing on a carrier deck," editorialized the *Navy Times* on March 13. "[Hultgreen] like her male colleagues, dead or alive, are heroes every time they catapult." The two pilots who spoke to me agreed with that sentiment and it pained them to watch video of the crash.

Kara Hultgreen, who aspired to be an astronaut, held a degree in aerospace engineering from the University of Texas. As the *Navy Times* observed, "Hultgreen has been one of a group of female pilots outspoken and active in pushing the Navy and Congress toward dropping combat exclusion for women." And when the exclusion was lifted, she said, "it was sort of like women being able to vote for the first time. It was historic. I felt super."

The analogy was a stretch. Anybody can vote but not anybody can land a fighter on the heaving deck of an aircraft carrier in the space of a few hundred feet. That's what they do in the Navy, all over the world, day and night, 24 hours a day. The pilot who can't put the aircraft down "on the boat," however smooth his or her landings on dry land, is out of his or her league here. It's dangerous business, as six aviator fatalities in Desert Storm indicate.

"Any landing is a controlled crash," says one of the former Top Gun instructors I interviewed. The massive F-14A NATOPS manual (Naval Aviation Tactical Procedures Standardization) is replete with EXTREME CAUTION warnings. "Every time you see that, it's written in blood," says the other pilot who agreed to speak for this article. "It means that someone has been injured or killed in that procedure."

Kara Hultgreen would have been familiar with all those danger warnings and the procedures for landing with one engine. She would have memorized a number of steps to take in emergency situations. She had flown the EA6B for years, logging what the Navy says was "considerable flight time" before moving on to the F-14, a plane that is far trickier to land. "The F-14 is the most difficult airplane to land aboard," she told the *Navy Times*. "The lineup to land is very difficult. . . It was the challenge they made it out to be." She made that statement just days before crashing as she attempted that very maneuver. At the same time, she also told the *Navy Times* that there had been "incredible pressure to perform" and that was why she and Carrie Lohrenz, the other female pilot, asked the Navy to keep the media away during their training.

Much of that pressure came as a result of the Tailhook scandal of September 1991 in Las Vegas. The wild affair launched a witch hunt and gave anti-military types in Congress, such as Pat Schroeder, a powerful pretext to inflict a PC agenda regarding women in the armed forces. "There was social engineering well before Tailhook," says one of the Top Gun trainers. "That just brought it into the forefront and gave Schroeder something to hook on."

After Clinton's election the restrictions on women flying in combat were soon lifted. The Navy, knowing that a Democratic Congress would be eying the military budget, was desperate to shake the Tailhook stigma by finding and showcasing qualified women pilots, who lobbied Congress in uniform and appeared for the press in flight suits, both breaches of the rules. Hence the pressure to perform for their two prime candidates. And with it the temptation to cut them some slack.

Hultgreen came to San Diego's Fighter Squadron VF-13 in May 1993. She worked out of Miramar, home of the Replacement Air Group or RAG. The RAG commander, interestingly enough, was Tom Sobieck, who had caught considerable flak over Tailhook, even though, as with many other officers, it was far from clear whether he had done anything wrong. But officers under Sobieck's command say he felt he was "under the gun" and that pushing women in combat was part of his atonement. "The man was capable of putting pressure on his junior officers," says one of the F-14 veterans who spoke to me.

Combat pilot training usually takes six to seven months, and there are few rights to privacy. Every landing is filmed and graded, with the grades posted in order of achievement in the "ready room." These grades follow pilots wherever they go. One term used in the Navy's Tactical Shipboard Training Assessment (TSTA) is a "down," which indicates unsatisfactory performance in a critical area. As the term clearly denotes, such a mistake could mean a plane and pilot going down.

On February 28, 1995, when the Navy released its report on the Hultgreen incident, I attended a press conference at North Island Naval Air Station in Coronado, at which I asked Admiral Jay B. Yakeley, commander of Carrier Group Three, if Lt. Hultgreen had any "downs" on her record. Momentarily startled, Yakeley responded that she did indeed have one, but did not elaborate and quickly added that many other pilots also have them. The Navy report released that day does not use the term "down" but does refer to a "mishap" by Hultgreen that was being counted as a "wave-off," adding that the pass "should not be included on [Hultgreen's] landing grade calculations." The Navy calculated these as 3.083 out of a possible 4, a performance "slightly below average compared to the rest of the Air Wing."

Was this "mishap" the "down" to which Admiral Yakeley referred? I have asked the Navy, in writing, to provide the circumstances of Lt. Hultgreen's down, whether there were any injuries, what sort of board reviewed her action, and what kind of remedial training she was require to undertake. The Navy has yet to respond.

The Navy also told the *San Diego Union-Tribune* that last July Hultgreen scored 3.24 on field carrier landing practice, placing third in a class of seven. On her day landings on the carrier she scored 3.22, with a boarding rate of 89 percent, first in a class of seven. Her night grad was 2.82 with a 70 percent boarding rate ranked her sixth in a class of seven. One of the naval flyers who called in to a San Diego radio station in the aftermath of the crash, said he had voted to take away the wings of pilots with grades 3.4 to 3.6. A third F-14 pilot I interviewed said that such a ruling would not be unusual.

The Navy considered Hultgreen a fully qualified and above-average pilot. But both Top Gun pilots, one of whom has landed on carriers out of fuel and with his plane shot up, say there is more to the story.

All combat pilots must be able to land planes on carriers, day or night. But that situation, tricky as it may be, does not approach the physical demands of actual combat, a supersonic slugfest that can easily stretch the human frame and mind beyond the breaking point. Pilots must contend with g-forces that can black them out, hot conditions in the cockpit, and, of course, a well-armed foe trying to kill them. Based on the clear strength differences, it remains dubious if women could compete with men on an equal basis in a shooting situation. And, as George Will has pointed out, sending the second best in a military situation is like having the second-best poker hand. You have two choices: bluff or fold.

One of the Miramar Top Gun trainers has heard reports from other aviators that Hultgreen even failed to get her wheels down during a night landing exercise. Pilots need six of these exercises to qualify. According to this pilot and other, a mistake of that magnitude at this stage of training would be enough to get most pilots cashiered. The *Navy Times* noted that Hultgreen had "disqualified during her first trip to the carrier during F-14 training this April [1994]," adding, however, that such a development was "not uncommon among student pilots."

The Navy says that about 25 percent of the pilots disqualify their first time. But both of the pilots who spoke to me say that, following a "down," the normal procedure is some sort of formal review, such as a Fleet Naval Aviators Review Board, followed by remedial training. Apparently Hultgreen had not been subjected to such a board hearing, something that would have been standard for any male aviator. "Maybe he would not have survived the Fleet Naval Aviators Review Board decision," said one naval aviator in a fax to a local radio station, "but she would be alive."

In April 1994, about the time Hultgreen was failing to qualify, Lt. Ellen B. Hamblet, a Navy reservist and former intelligence officer for early-warning squadron, wrote an article in the Navy journal *Proceedings*, titled "Who's to Blame When Women Don't Measure Up?" Hamblet cited the case of a female pilot who blew a tire and ran off the runway. This pilot was "praised by top leadership for keeping her wits about her but the general consensus among junior officers was that if a male pilot had done the same thing he would have been severely disciplined."

Hamblet also noted the case of "a woman near the bottom of her class being allowed to continue at the training command. . . because the commanding officer needed to keep a female instructor." Hamblet further charged that women were being "allowed to carrier qualify, even though they didn't meet the standards. And while stories of male aviators seem to end with the words "so he lost his wings," stories about women end in, "and can you believe that she is still flying?"

Many female Navy personnel, including some pilots, share Hamblet's views, which correspond to those of the anonymous Navy faxer who wrote a San Diego radio station after the accident that Hultgreen "was an accident waiting to happen. Every one of her squadron mates knew it but could not speak up for fear of reprisal." The F-14 trainers I spoke to agreed and note that special treatment continued after the accident. It is a view corroborated by the *Navy Times*, which wrote "two Navy internal messages sent in the days after the mishap – which outline that Hultgreen had gone too wide on her approach and caused her engine to stall after she tried to correct it – were quietly recalled."

The Navy gave Hultgreen an elaborate funeral at Arlington, with many dignitaries in attendance. It is not normal practice to retrieve downed planes from 4,000 feet. Downed male pilots, says one F-14 veteran, are regularly abandoned "to become part of the food chain" and their planes left in the drink. But the Navy recovered Hultgreen's plane, at an estimated cost of $100,000. In another unusual move, the Navy gave a copy of Hultgreen's flight grades to her mother, Sally Spears, of San Antonio – but not to the press. And two days before the Navy released its February 28 report to the press, Mark Galpin, a commander in Hultgreen's unit, flew to San Antonio to brief Spears on the results of the investigation and to give her a six-inch-thick official report and the Navy video of the accident.

It might be noted that when the Navy released its first report on the Tailhook scandal virtually nobody believed it. The document only confirmed press suspicions that there was more to the story than the Navy was letting on. But the Hultgreen report, since it had a politically correct message, elicited the opposite response. When some reporters asked for the full report, the Navy told them they would have to file a Freedom of Information Act request. Yet what was released for public consumption was enough to raise doubts, if reporters had taken the time to study it.

The report blames the crash on a mid-compression bypass valve but it also states that, "No indication of pre-impact failure was found in the Flight Control System, Hydraulic Power Systems, Electrical Power Systems, Fuel Supply Feed Systems, or Cockpit Throttle Command."

The report concedes that Hultgreen was "relatively inexperienced in the F-14." She had logged 217 hours in the aircraft, compared to 460 hours for her radar officer Matthew Klemish. He did not appear at the North Island press conference and word around Miramar is that Navy is keeping him from reporters. "There existed a very small window of opportunity through which to recognize a deteriorating situation and to make critical flight control inputs," says the report. "If these critical flight control inputs are not performed quickly and correctly, then the aircraft will be place *in extremis*. In this accident, the window of opportunity for a successful recovery was missed. Finally, inexperience prevented the crew from recognizing the point at which recovery was impossible and ejection the only alternative." Note the report's evasive passive-voice construction: "the window of opportunity was missed."

Further, there was "a delay in recognition of the extremis condition, either due to preoccupation with correcting the overshooting start, or the timing of the stall warning system." In addition, "the Landing Service Officer call for wave-off was extremely timely, but subsequent pilot technique permitted Angle of Attack to increase to a point where rudder effectiveness began to be reduced to nil and departure from controlled flight was imminent."

The report further says that in Hultgreen's trend analysis, "her tendency was to make large power on the start due to a lineup of perceived glidescope deviation which caused her to go high in the middle to in close and make adequate corrections on the ramp to catch middle wires." So she had apparently made similar lineup errors before, and the Navy knew it. The *San Diego Union-Tribune*, citing Navy sources, said in early April that the Navy had rigged the tests.

And if, as the report said, the exact cause of the accident will never be known, then attempts by the Navy to duplicate the situation in flight simulators can never be more than speculative. Further, in mid-March, *Newsweek* magazine picked up the Navy's Mishap Investigation Report (MIR). This report, written to exacting standards and for Navy consumption only, is critical of Lt. Hultgreen and even notes that the faulty bypass valve doesn't fully explain the one or more left-engine stalls Hultgreen's plane suffered.

Both pilots contacted by *Heterodoxy*, and many other Navy personnel, say the Navy can salvage something from this tragic accident by using it as an opportunity to review its policy on women in combat. That does not seem to be what they have in mind. At the February 28 press conference, a reporter asked Admiral Yakeley if this accident would cause the Navy to make a change in the training of female pilots. "Absolutely not," Yakeley responded. And in a March 19 interview with the *San Diego Union-Tribune*, Secretary of the Navy John Dalton said he was pleased with current gender policies and argued that all but a few diehards in the Navy were too. But some point the finger elsewhere.

"The fault is not with women," writes Lt. Ellen Hamblet, "but with Navy leaders who allow subordinates to continue doing jobs for which they are not qualified . . . The true fault lies with senior officers who refuse, for whatever reason, to offer honest feedback and criticism and to enforce tough, unpopular decisions. They are perpetuating a disservice to the poorest performers, who are allowed to continue in an atmosphere where they are not allowed to compete safely. At they same time, they also are cheating some of the outstanding personnel – both men and women – who crave and deserve a challenge to perform to their utmost capacity, operating in an atmosphere of excellence."

These tough words from a female officer are backed up by the editorial of the *Navy Times*, which said that "the Navy, still sensitive over Tailhook and gender, has gone out of its way to reach a predetermined conclusion about the cause of Hultgreen's fatal crash" and that "the apparent Navy dishonesty – the shading of truth for fear of making a mistake or saying something politically incorrect – undermines Navy credibility."

The overall record suggest that it is not conservative critics such as Linda Chavez – who was, after all, right about the Navy investigation – who need to apologize. Rather it is the liberal Schroeders, Boxers and Goodmans who promoted the double standards that needlessly took a young woman's life and have made today's Navy a perilous place indeed.

They might have paid heed to another prophecy of the anonymous Navy faxer who write the San Diego radio station two days after the accident. "This death of Lt. Hultgreen was tragic, absolutely could have been avoided, and is waiting to happen again."

They might even pay attention to the testimony of Lt. Kara Hultgreen herself. "Guys like you need to make sure there's one standard," Hultgreen told Admiral Robert Hickey last year. "If people let me slide through on a lower standard, it's my life on the line. I could get killed."

9. Literary Crittercism

Animal Farm is an undeniable work of genius but back in the mid-1940s George Orwell had a hard time getting it published. T.S. Eliot rejected the book on behalf of Faber and Faber, one of the 16 houses that turned it down. *Animal Farm* did gain publication but still sparked opposition. More than 50 years later, in 1986, the overseers of a theatrical event banned a British stage version of the story. With the USSR still throwing its weight around, that came as no surprise. But as it turned out, the man responsible for the banishment of *Animal Farm* won the Nobel Prize for literature that same year. Consider another back story to this piece.

At the time, a Washington think tank was considering me for a book project but the boss wanted the writer to have been published in the *Wall Street Journal*. My work had never appeared there and the think tank's editor said "hell would freeze over" before it did. When my piece duly appeared some six weeks later, I wrote to the friend who had recommended me for the book project: "Hitler and Jim Jones are playing hockey tonight," I said.

Should a Nobel Prize Reward Censorship?
Wall Street Journal, November 3, 1986

THOSE SOMBER SCANDINAVIANS WHO DISH OUT THE WORLD'S MOST PRESTIgious awards set a precedent last month by giving the 1986 Nobel Prize for Literature to an author who has himself participated in censorship.

Wole Soyinka, a Nigerian novelist, poet and playwright, is the president if the International Theater Institute, which sponsored a dramatic festival in June in Baltimore Md. The Soviet Union, a participant, cried foul over the inclusion of the British National Theater's adaptation of George Orwell's classic parable "Animal Farm." The institute, which had originally invited the National Theatre to participate, canceled the performance. A May 24 Associated Press story reported that "according to a memorandum from festival producer Edward Hambleton, the Nigerian dramatist and institute president Wole Soyinka objected to 'Animal Farm.'" Mr. Soyinka later told reporters that an international festival was not the place to discomfit its own members. (The play was performed in Baltimore during the festival but under different auspices.)

Orwell's famous satire portrays Soviet leaders as pigs and savagely satirizes the Communist system, which it calls "Animalism." Though liberal critics have interpreted the story as a general statement against dictatorship, Orwell said flatly that it was anti-Soviet. In fact, "Animal Farm's" open anti-communism and porcine caricatures of Lenin and Stalin led to its rejection by 16 publishers during the heyday of Soviet adulation in the 1940s. One of those who rejected it was T.S. Eliot on behalf of Faber and Faber.

Nearly 40 years after Orwell's death, "Animal Farm" continues to be studied and enjoyed by millions of readers, including children. Its animated and stage versions have drawn wide praise and enthusiastic response. It is no surprise that the Soviet Union would oppose the play since, like all literature not written from a point of view called "Socialist Realism," it is banned in that country.

What should surprise and scandalize everyone is that a group of Western dramatists should conspire to remove it from an international drama festival. After all, for dramatists freedom of expression is the very breath of life and censorship in any form is The Enemy. They not only pride themselves on defying the powerful, but often consider this to be the very flywheel of creativity, which it is not. Apparently, pressure from the Soviet Union is capable of turning their defiance into pliant sycophancy. Perhaps they considered the act of censorship their contribution to detent world peace.

Mr. Soyinka's action is especially surprising since he spent two years in jail in the 1960s for criticizing his own government's conduct in the Biafran conflict, and he is not bashful about talking about it. "I have one abiding religion," he says, "human liberty." He rages against "the propensity of human beings to enslave others." Prof. Henry Louis Gates of Cornell University, who has nominated Mr. Soyinka for the big prize every year since 1981, said that "unlike writers in the West, Wole has put his life on the line fighting tyranny." If all this wonderful self-description and praise are true, then why did Mr. Soyinka capitulate to the whims of a totalitarian regime that tosses freethinking writers and political dissidents into forced labor camps or insane asylums?

That this shameful business detracts from Mr. Soyinka's literary accomplishments goes without saying. It is also robbed the International Theatre Institute of whatever credibility it had. Worst of all, it has tainted the Nobel Prize for Literature and stripped it of moral force. In the past, the award went to those who, like Aleksandr Solzhenitsyn, opposed censorship; now it goes to a man who practices it. Though Mr. Soyinka denies that the award is politicized, he did say of his selection: "I see it more as an historical gesture."

Now that the Nigerian author has won the prize his works will be more readily available. Prof. Gates contends that "long after the issue of Africa today are footnotes in history, people will be studying the works of Wole Soyinka. This may turn out to be true in Ivy League English departments and other isolation wards, but it is not clear so far as the general public is concerned.

A more likely scenario is that long after the works of Wole Soyinka are relegated to the library shelves people will be reading and studying George Orwell. That is, everywhere those works are not banned.

10. Forgotten But Not Gone

I first encountered Anna Louise Strong in *Chronicles of Wasted Time* by Malcolm Muggeridge, once a correspondent in Moscow where he met Strong, then editor of an English-language Soviet publication. "Miss Strong," he wrote, "was an enormous woman with a very red face, a lot of white hair, and an expression of stupidity so overwhelming that it amounted to a kind of strange beauty." Strong was actually quite smart, but wasted her intelligence in willful ignorance and deception. This commentary was one of many for the *San Diego Union*, for which I also wrote book reviews, profiles, and even some editorials. The paper is now the *San Diego Union-Tribune*, having absorbed what used to be the city's afternoon paper. In the Age of the Tweet, those are merely a memory.

"A great deal of intelligence can be invested in ignorance."
San Diego Union, May 5, 1985

PROPAGANDA HAS BEEN AROUND FOR CENTURIES BUT ADVOCACY JOURNALISM – ideology smuggled into the news – is more recent. It began 100 years ago with Anna Louse Strong, a founding sister of the genre.

A minister's daughter, born in 1885, Anna was a precocious child, completing eight years of school in four. She studied in Europe, spent several years at Bryn Mawr and Oberlin College, then became the youngest person to receive a PhD from the University of Chicago, the first woman ever to do so. At this time, she began to write for religious publications. But she soon experienced a different sort of conversion.

In a management role, she was forced to lay off a young man. This proved traumatic. How could this problem be solved? "The only remedy," she wrote, "would be a world quite differently organized. I knew

73

enough to know that such a society was called socialism, and that I must be a socialist."

Modern liberal-left journalists often say they have "grown" beyond their early belief in religion, the family, and a free society, toward which they tend to be hostile. Their new "mature" orthodoxy favors government *uber alles*. Anna, too, had "grown." She moved to a place where her new ideas were already being tried.

In Moscow, her public-relations work began in earnest. Behind a mask of objectivity, she hyped the regime extensively, far surpassing male colleagues like the *New York Times'* Walter Duranty. There was no way of verifying her statistics or anybody else's. Anna's reports amounted to falsifying what was already false.

Similarly, today one reads of great leaps forward in health, education and literacy from such places as Cuba, the USSR, Nicaragua and Vietnam. All the data, of course, come from the ruling juntas. But many journalists who are tough interrogators with Exxon or Ed Meese become eager sycophants with a Marxist dictatorship.

Injustices, they explain, are "problems" or "blunders," due to "old infirm leadership." The latter gem, regarding the cause of Soviet problems, is from Robert Kaiser of the *Washington Post*, a frequent guest on CBS News. It never occurred to him, or Anna, that socialism itself might be the problem.

When the kulaks were liquidated, Anna dutifully reported that these people were "exploiters." Of Stalin, Anna said, "One must not make a god of Stalin. He was too important for that." Like *Time* magazine, which described Yuri Andropov as kind of a Soviet Gary Hart, she gave Uncle Joe the benefit of the doubt.

But Anna, for all her erudition, never read the works of Marx or Lenin, "because these aroused my desire to look on all sides of the question." The modern advocacy journalist must always be vigilant against seeing all sides of the question. In this respect they have remarkably succeeded. "I could admire the Russian communists better when I didn't ready their theories," Anna said. This advice, too, has been well heeded.

Charles Krause, chronicler of the Jonestown suicides, was utterly blind to the reality of Jim Jones and very nearly perished in the massacre. "The truth was," he explains, "that I rather admired Jim Jones goals." Anna admired Stalin's goals. Many today admire the Sandinistas goals, or even speak well of the late Albanian Enver Hoxha, who gave new meaning to the word "dictator." Harry Trimborn of the *Los Angeles Times* wrote that under Hoxha, "women have made remarkable strides."

Strong wrote in her biography, "it amused me to see how much I could put over" on editors of prestigious publications like *Harper's* and *The Atlantic*. She managed to put over a lot, including the report that Soviet prisons were so humane that criminals applied for admittance. This is a tough act to follow, but one can see many valiant efforts in progress, in print and on television. Marxist ventriloquists find ready squads of coiffed, blow-dried dummies in Western media.

This is not so say that Strong's contemporary clones are stupid people. Like her, many have PhDs. In general, they do not falsify deliberately, as she did, though this does happen. Why, then, do they so often employ their tough "investigative" posture to downgrade the open societies of the West and embellish dictatorial regimes? Perhaps Saul Bellow said it best: "A great deal of intelligence can be invested in ignorance when the need for illusion is deep."

So it continues. Anna Louise Strong, born 100 years ago, is forgotten, but not gone.

11. "Be fraternal, promote democracy, off the commies, power to the people."

During the 1960s I was more into the counterculture than militant radical movements. Even so, New Left founder David Horowitz invited me to the Second Thoughts Conference in 1987. I was slated to speak but gave up my spot to Stanley Crouch. I did contribute "A Balance Sheet for the Left" to the proceedings, during which Christopher Hitchens asked speaker Stephen Schwartz, "are you as stupid as you look?" Peter Collier responded, "Shut-up Christopher. Manners are the only thing you Brits have that's worth a shit anymore." That exchange failed to make the news and, as I noted, the event failed to draw the coverage it deserved.

The Vocal Ex-left: A Potential Political Force
San Diego Union, November 1, 1987

A GENERATION AGO, ARTHUR KOESTLER, ANDRE GIDE, IGNAZIO SILONE AND other luminaries contributed to a book called *The God That Failed*. Though a diverse group, they all rejected revolutionary socialism and repudiated their part in its advancement.

In the 1960s, American leftists, radicals and anti-war activists marched in the streets against United States involvement in Vietnam. Twenty years later, many of them want to tell they world that they, too, have changed their minds.

The October 16-18 "Second Thoughts Conference" in Washington D.C. was sponsored by the National Forum Foundation and organized by Peter Collier and David Horowitz, former editors of the leftist *Ramparts* magazine. Now defunct, *Ramparts* ran articles with such carefully nuanced titles as "Better Red Than Dead." It was something of a public relations organ for the Black Panthers and even provided gas masks for street protesters.

Horowitz was a "red diaper baby" born to Communist parents in New York. Raised in strict adherence to the faith, he authored three books on Marxist themes and became a leading anti-war activist in the Berkeley area.

The former radical told the gathering that the so-called New Left was really a continuation of the Old Left. He lashed out at utopianism, the "world's oldest heresy," and its destructive legacy. He contended that anti-communism is "the beginning of political morality" in our time.

Horowitz and Collier burned their bridges to the left in a 1985 article titled "Lefties for Reagan." As Horowitz put it in a *Commentary* magazine piece, they said goodbye to the "self-aggrandizing romance with corrupt third Worldism; to the casual indulgence of Soviet totalitarianism; and to the hypocritical and self-dramatizing anti-Americanism that is the New Left's bequest to mainstream politics." A more complete turnaround could hardly be imagined.

Also in attendance were Jeff Herf, former member of Students for a Democratic Society, now teaching at the Naval War College; Stephen Schwartz, a poet and founder of the Young Communist League; Joshua Muravchik, former chairman of the Young People's Socialist League; Richard John Neuhaus, one of the founders of Clergy and Laity Concerned; Michael Medved, former anti-war crusader and now how of PBS television's "Sneak Previews;" Doan Van Toai, vice president of the Saigon Students Association in the 1960s and many other ex-leftists. These included former Sandinistas such as Arturo Cruz Jr., Xavier Arguello and Fausto Amador, brother of FSLN founder Carlos Fonseca.

While not all participants were "conservatives" or "neo-conservatives," there was agreement on Vietnam. They had said that the National Liberation Front (NLF) was more nationalist than communist, basically peaceful and not repressive. They also contended that an American withdrawal would promote peace, justice and human rights, and that there would be no bloodbath.

As it turned out, the NLF vanguard were in fact orthodox Stalinists who have turned their country into a Soviet base. They were brutal and not peaceful, herding untold thousands into "re-education" camps. Millions preferred to become "boat people" rather than live under such a regime. Without doubt, many thousands were slaughtered.

Moreover, the American withdrawal did not promoted international peace because the North Vietnamese were imperialists, not nationalists, and have since occupied Laos and Cambodia, where two million perished under Pol Pot's Khmer Rouge. There was a bloodbath after all. Marxist practice was different from Marxist ideals.

Worse still, emboldened by this American retreat, the Soviets have made sweeping moves in Africa, Asia, and Central America.

One of the Washington conference's more moving testimonies was that of Doan Van Toai, who, having worked much of his life for "liberation," soon found himself tossed into prison by the new regime. He has since written *The Vietnamese Gulag* but has not become a regular on the American talk show circuit.

Richard John Neuhaus, former colleague of Dr. Martin Luther King Jr., noted that it was a mistake to form coalitions with those who disagreed on fundamental principles. It was also wrong, he added to say that nothing could be worse than the war.

Some of the Scoop Jackson-type Democrats had praise for their early idealism and said they found the sixties a learning experience. Though they disassociated themselves from supply-side economics, it seemed clear that they were promoters of a bipartisan anti-Soviet foreign policy similar to that of the 1950s. It might surprise the current Democratic presidential candidates that Herf and Barry Rubin both support American nuclear deployments in Europe.

The former Sandinista Nicaraguans, now leaders of the resistance forces, described their "pathological" anti-Americanism, their long fight against Somoza, and their adventures in the FSLN government. Arturo Cruz Jr. explained how he finessed money out of American government representatives.

Like Horowitz, participant Ron Radosh had roots in the Old Left but gradually became disillusioned. He set out to prove the Rosenbergs were innocent but wound up convinced of their guilt. The left saw this a betrayal and attacked him. One writer accused him of having "succumbed to the facts." A specialist on Central America, Radosh outlines how the Sandinistas deal with the American press.

The conference was not all breast-beating recantation. Michael Medved confessed to having attended marches to meet girls. P.J. O'Rourke of *Rolling Stone* saw the 1960s as a big party, and said he believed everything except what his parents told him. For instance, he believed that growing his hair long would bring justice and peace, and that stones had souls. His commune in Baltimore had been terrorized by a group of Maoists called the Balto Cong.

Prominent neo-conservative Irving Kristol spoke fondly of his radical days in the 1940s. Norman Podhoretz of *Commentary* owned up to having rejected at least 50 political conversion articles of the type found in *The God That Failed*. Hilton Kramer of the *New Criterion* contended that things were actually worse now than in the 1960s. At that time, he said, the counterculture and radical types were on the outside, whereas now, in effect, the Balto Cong is safely within the gates. Counterculture ideas are now mainstream ideas.

That the media practically ignored the event might be considered evidence of that observation. When these people were denouncing the United States and all it stood for, they were regarded as oracles. When they said they had been wrong, and pointed out the awful consequences of their actions, no one was interested. The media missed the biggest follow-up story in some time.

It might be pointed out that many other '60s refugees have had no second thoughts whatsoever. When Vietnam did not turn out as expected, they plugged their ears to the cries of the suffering, put on their cardboard helmets, mounted Rosinante, and charged off to the next battle on behalf or the oppressed. As Koestler wrote, "they repeat every single error of the past, draw the same faulty conclusions a second time, re-life the same situations, perform the same suicidal gestures."

Prominent among this group are Peter, Paul and Mary, court crooners for the Sandinistas. In the government ranks there is Tom Hayden, once hailed as the "next Lenin," along with Ron Dellums and George Crockett.

Will anything come of this gathering? Or was it just preaching to the converted?

In France, the ex-left is a powerful political force and something of a movement. That has not happened in the United States and may never take place. Jeff Herf said that whenever he hears the word "movement' he reaches for his word processor.

In the session "Where do we go from here?" Joshua Muravchik outlined a strategy for unity. He urged the resurrection of the word "communist," not as a tool for government committees or police raids but simply for the sake of accuracy. He pointed out that the *Washington Post* described the Soviet-installed government of Afghanistan not as communists but "agrarian reformers."

Muravchik cited the struggle between communism and democracy as the major conflict in the world. Democracy is the only system, he said, that puts people's destiny in their own hands. He reminded the participants that their differences on the welfare budget, taxes, social issues and so on were of minor importance compared to the struggle against totalitarianism. He said in summation: "Be fraternal, promote democracy, off the commies, power to the people."

This may well prove a rallying cry not only for ex-leftists who have had second thoughts but for all who love freedom and believe that American needs to be preserved rather than transformed.

12. Gender Junkthought

The all-volunteer military, contrary to what some predicted, did not make for a shortage of volunteers. Some eager recruits wound up in "gender integrated training." In that regime they learned that political correctness is inherently imperialistic and expansionist, sparing nothing. Gender integrated training would confirm that, despite politically correct orthodoxy, male and female soldiers are differentiated indeed, and that to pretend otherwise is dangerous folly.

Feminist Forced March
Heterodoxy, June 1995

THE ARMY RECRUITMENT VIDEO SHOWS THE YOUNG MEN COMING TO FT. Leonard Wood in Missouri looking like a bunch of low-lifes about to be arrested for loitering. Then the hair gets sheared as the first step in a change of identity from private citizens to GIs. Recruits find their own will replaced by that of a drill sergeant with the temperament of a junkyard Doberman. Then comes boot camp – a grueling marathon of pushups, rope climbs, tear gas, marches and weapons training. The recruits smash each other with pugil sticks and charge through a bayonet course yelling, "Kill! Kill!"

By the end of their training one assumes that Army instructors will have molded this bunch into what recruiting posters used to call "the fighting man." But some versions of the video append a section showing women in basic combat training. The effect is akin to clicking from *The Battle of the Bulge* with Henry Fonda to *Private Benjamin* with Goldie Hawn. When the women run through the bayonet course shrieking "Kill!" and jabbing ineptly at rubber dummies, the effect is unintentionally comic. Some women have trouble with the pins on the grenades, and one doubts that their clumsiness in covering up would have protected them or their fellow soldiers from the blast. Some handle their standard-issue M-16 rifle as though it were a broom.

The army tapes leaves little doubt that any regular troops or guerilla forces anywhere in the world would quickly slaughter these women. That reality, evident to most veterans of actual combat, has not prevented the return of the "gender integrated" combat training that is now the keystone of a campaign to move women into front-line combat. Of course, that reality has not deterred liberal-left politicians such as Pat Schroeder, for whom current policies are the end of a Long March.

For Schroeder and her feminist comrades in arms – most of whom are, on issues not having to do with women, hardcore anti-military – the issue remains entirely ideological. They believe that if women cannot be gassed, shot, blown up, or tortured just like men, they remain incomplete human beings bereft of their constitutional rights. As in other arenas, these feminists confuse equality with sameness in their view of the military and ignore basic realities about the differences between men and women.

Ignoring basic realities, in fact, is probably what accounts for the death of Kara Hultgreen, the first woman to fly the a carrier-based F-14 fighter jet. Hultgreen was killed in an abortive landing six months ago, and at first, Schroeder and her allies were able to mislead the press and the public into believing that the problem was mechanical malfunction. But recent evidence, suppressed by the Navy, shows that Hultgreen had recorded several "downs" – potential crashes in combat conditions – during training maneuvers. These failures, which would have long since grounded a male flyer, had been ignored in Hultgreen's case to pacify those like Schroeder, who had made Tailhook a national scandal and women in combat at civil-rights issue. So the death of Kara Hultgreen, in some sense, was Pat Schroeder's first kill.

It is true that, according to Army data, that female recruits are usually better qualified academically than males, have more work experience, and are almost always better behaved, losing less time for disciplinary reasons and not being as inclined as their brethren to abuse drugs and alcohol. But it is also true that soldiering is a strenuous business, and women's upper-body strength is roughly half that of a man. They miss more than twice as much duty time on medical grounds and are four times more likely to complain of spurious physical ailments. Women suffer higher rates of attrition and lower rates of retention. The injury rates of woman can be as high as 14 times that of men.

At the outset of World War II, the only women in the U.S. Armed Forces were nurses. As sociologist Charles Moskos points out, by the end of 1945, some 350,000 had served in various female auxiliary corps, doing everything from refueling aircraft across the Atlantic to breaking enemy secret codes. Most served with distinction, some with heroism. But women did not serve in direct combat, and based on the horrors they had seen in World War II, nobody was arguing that they should.

Following the war, the military imposed a 2 percent ceiling on the number of women, who served for the most part in administrative, clerical and health care until the advent of the all-volunteer force in 1973, a year after some were permitted to enter the Reserve Officer Training Corps (ROTC) and just when military feminism was hitting stride.

In their push for the Equal Rights Amendment, the National Organization for Women and the Center for Women's Policy Studies challenged the Defense Advisory Committee on Women in the Service (DACOWITS) to integrate women. In open hearings during 1974, representatives of the Center for Women's Policy Studies and the Women's Lobby unified in favor of such integration. Among the members of Congress expressing support were such well known types as Don Edwards and, of course, Patricia Schroeder, who argued that immanent ratification of the ERA made integration inevitable. Gender integration of the service academies was the immediate cause but women in combat was the long-range goal.

Pointing to Israel and the Soviet Union, New York Democrat Charles Rangel contended that "women should join the men" in fighting. Rangel was unaware that at the time, the USSR did not deploy women in front-line positions, and based on severe losses in early conflicts, Israel immediately moves female soldiers to the rear in event of hostilities.

In 1976, the service academies began accepting female cadets. Most military men objected but they were outflanked by Schroeder and her feminist troops. The new policy marched under the banner of "equality," but as Brian Mitchell pointed out in his 1989 *Weak Link: The Feminization of the Military*, it also meant that some recruits were more equal than others.

The data that piled up as a result of the forced entry to the service academies actually helped Schroeder's opponents. The Air Force Academy's physical fitness standards required, among other things, pushups, pull-ups and a 500-yard run. But very few of the women, it turned out, could perform even one pull-up. So the academy gave them credit for the among of time they were able to hang on the bar. And the women who could manage one pull-up could thereby earn extra credit.

While male cadets averaged only 2.5 visits to the medical clinic, the women averaged eight. In Basic Cadet Training, the women suffered nine times as many shin splints as the men, five times as many stress fractures, and more than five times as many cases of tendinitis. The efforts of some men to help the women often dragged down their own performance and created further resentments over special treatment. Rather than put up with such blatant unfairness, more than a few of the men simply bailed for non-military careers. The Academy's class of 1980, the first to be sexually integrated, lost 22.5 percent of its male cadets in the first year alone and only 44.4 percent of those who started in 1980 finished, compared to 37.4 percent of the women.

West Point experienced similar difficulties with female cadets. The injury rate in field training proved a staggering three times that of the men. And the women reported for sick call an average of 6.3 times per female cadet, as opposed to the male average of 1.7 times. A similar system of "dual standards" evolved but the more accurate "double standards" designation is forbidden. On the five mile run, 85 percent of the women scored D or less and 61 percent failed to complete the physical test. When women had difficulty scaling an eight-foot wall, trainers added a two-foot stand to help them over. On drill, the women carried light M-16 rifles while the men packed heavier M-14s. Trainers found that the gripping strength of a woman is 65 percent of a man's. After eight weeks of intensive training, the men showed 32 percent more power in the lower body and far outstripped the women in the bench press. Compared to the men, female cadets also fared poorly in a 2.5 mile endurance run in full gear.

Unlike the men female West Point cadets did not box or wrestle. In map reading and military heritage and related subjects, 60-70 percent of women scored below the mean. The dual standards, however, meant that a woman could pass with a lower score than a male. This created widespread resentment and many cadets departed for other lines of work.

By the late 1970s, the Department of Defense found itself allied with the ACLU in its quest to integrate women. By 1978, Congress opened up nearly all military assignments to women by abolishing the separate women's auxiliary corps. That year, the Army began an experiment in "gender integrated training" at Fort Jackson, South Carolina, the largest basic-training facility in the Army. It ran until 1982, when the military suddenly and somewhat mysteriously dropped it.

Typically, the U.S. Army keeps meticulous records of everything, and a four-year departure from 200 years of standard military practice would likely receive massive scrutiny and documentation. Yet, anyone attempting to obtain papers on those four years finds themself staring into a black hole.

"There is no report about 1978 to 1982," Jacqueline Mottern, a social psychologist with the Army Research Institute told me. "We can find no written documentation why the army cancelled that project in 1982. There is nothing in the archives to explain what happened, and why it happened." Mottern, who said she was unable to refer me to a single person involved with that project, concedes that the absence of a record is "unusual." It also happens to be false.

"It's impossible that there are no records. They have been lost on purpose," says Korean War veteran Col. Robert Maginnis, now retired and working with the Family Research Council in Washington D.C. Working outside official channels, I finally located a senior military official who was one of the first to supervise the training of women, as well as a captain and a colonel who had taken part in the first gender-integrated project. All seemed certain that taking the wrong position on gender correctness can wreck a career, or even a retirement, so they requested anonymity.

"It was a disaster, plain and simple," says the captain, "absolute abject failure, beyond stupid." While the Army concedes that there may have been "a perception that the men were not being physically challenged enough," the captain responds, "it was not a perception, even the troops said it. They would run a while, stop, then sit and wait for the women. It was "keep up with the slowest." He describes women breaking down in tears during the basic training, especially on the rifle range, as commonplace. Or, in his own words, "they would come unglued."

On the grenade course, the soldier stands five feet away from a wall seven feet high, over which he or she must toss a grenade. "I've watched women bounce hand grenades off the wall," the captain says. "They broke into tears in a flash," says the senior military official, one of the first to supervise the training of female soldiers. He adds that their very presence, segregated or integrated, affected the men." The men want to believe that very few can do what they are doing, that they are being challenged to a point where only a few succeed. They are told that the women have to be allowed to do it too. That's just shattering to them."

After the Army stopped the gender integration without explanation in 1982, it went back to separate training for men and women. But the debate continued, along with the search for accurate data. A study by Dr. David Robertson at the Navy Personnel Research and Development Center in San Diego tested 350 male recruits and 195 female recruits in such damage-control tasks as carrying litters on level surfaces and up and down ladders, moving and starting emergency pumps, turning engine bolts and directing fire-hose streams. Virtually all of the male recruits were able to perform all of the tasks to standard, even before training, but the only task most female recruits could perform to standard was directing a fire house and even after significant training 99 percent of the women could still not carry a pump down a ladder.

"The Navy's recent enthusiasm for putting more and amore women aboard ship makes little sense," says Paul O. Davis, "unless the Navy doesn't mind sacrificing survivability and possibly the lives of sailors for the sake of enhancing opportunities for women." Davis was the principal investigator of the multi-year study to validate the Marine Corps Physical Fitness test and also served as the lead instructor of the Navy's training and certification program for Command Fitness Coordinators.

The invasion of Panama gave new impetus for lifting combat restrictions for women, but the Gulf War proved the real watershed in this movement within the military. The Pentagon and media praised the performance of the 35,000 women who served in that conflict. But sociologist Charles Moskos points out, surveys of soldiers yield a murkier picture. "Over half rated women's performance as fair or poor." This was not merely a subjective assessment.

In September, 1992, Col. William Gregor, professor of advanced military studies at Fort Leavenworth, testified to the Presidential Commission on the Assignment of Women in the Military that the Army Physical Fitness Test (APFT) showed that the women who pass standards are at the upper end of the female population's potential. "Additional training and herculean efforts," said Gregor, "will not significantly change the results." These results showed that, with a few week's additional training, the most marginal male recruit can surpass the performance of the best-trained women. Gregor also noted that adopting a male standard of fitness would mean that 70 percent of women would fail and no one would receive an Army Fitness Badge because not a single women achieved a score equal to what the men must meet to get the badge.

In 1993, the Marine Corps conducted a three-month study with 50 women to determine whether they cold be conditioned to meet male fitness standards. Details of the study are sketchy, but an *Army Times* article notes that "officials found they could not be." While some women can reach the lower ranges of male ability, they are operating at the peak of their performance and therefore under maximum stress. Col. Gregor testified that finding one woman of 100 who could meet the standards as opposed to 60 percent of the men who can means that the Army has in effect "just traded off 60 soldiers for the prospect of

getting one." But these "cost considerations," along with the physical
date acquired over the last 15 years, have proved no obstacle to zealots
like Pat Schroeder, who were anti-military during the 1970s and 1980s,
but by the time of the Clinton administration, had changed their tune on
the military from a dirge to an anthem.

Pat Schroeder "does not like the military at all," Rear Adm. Martin
Carmody told the *Navy Times*. "She's always negative on military pro-
curement." James Bush, a retired Navy captain who twice serve as
Schroeder's staff defense expert, says that Schroeder refuses to meet
with those who disagree with her. Catheryn Schultz of the liberal Center
for Defense Information says that those men are merely threatened by
Schroeder because her position in Congress makes her "a woman in a
position to control the fate of boys' toys."

During the Cold War, Schroeder opposed virtually every effort to
bolster our defenses, especially the construction of new aircraft carriers, to support our allies, and to roll back totalitarianism, attributing all
East-West tensions to our own machismo and xenophobia. But then in
the late 1980s, she and other McGovernite liberals in Congress were
interested in using the U.S. military as the ideal institution to imple-
ment their race/gender/sexual orientation/class dogmas. As onetime
Secretary of the Navy James Webb puts it, "the military had become
a test tube for social experimentation." The incoming Clinton administration gave the PC forces a long awaited window of opportunity to
turn their agenda into a forced march.

Partly due to the efforts of Pat Schroeder, the Marine Corps now
spends more on family housing than on ammunition, $156 million ver-
sus $132 million, and more on child development and family centers
than on repair parts, $32 million versus about $30 million. But when
Marine General Carl Mundy restricted the number of married enlistees,
Schroeder, appearing on The *MacNeil Lehrer News Hour*, dismissed
him as a cultural Neanderthal who had "taken leave of his senses," adding, "even the Pope allows his Swiss guards to be married." As is often
the case, the congresswoman was misinformed. Unlike U.S. Marines,
who recently rescued a downed U.S. pilot in Bosnia, the Swiss guards
never deploy on dangerous missions thousands of miles from home.

They must serve for seven years before they are allowed to marry, and the Vatican does not accept married Swiss recruits.

When James Webb demanded that Schroeder apologize for insulting Gen. Mundy, she said he had no sense of humor. Webb shot back that a number of aviators had lost their careers because Pat Schroeder had no sense of humor about the risqué skits Navy fliers had staged about her in San Diego. Nor does she have a sense of humor about Tailhook, which she parlayed into a political windfall.

Schroeder used the scandal to leverage the military into opening all occupations, including combat, to women. She led the charge to put women on combat ships and in fighter planes, a policy now in place and, despite glowing reviews in *Time* magazine, showing decidedly mixed results. (The press, which was uniformly critical of initial Navy reports on Tailhook, was uniformly supportive of initial Navy reports holding that the death of F-14 aviator Kara Hultgreen, was due to mechanical malfunction.) Schroeder introduced the legislation to overturn the ban on homosexuals in the military. She proposed an amendment to cut the number of troops in Europe to 100,000 from 150,000, which the Department of Defense wanted. She pushed through a measure that entitles divorced spouses to the retirement pay of their former mates.

In 1989, Schroeder told the *Washington Post* that she wanted job assignments in the military to be determined by individual qualifications rather than by definitions of combat that have become "obsolete in modern warfare." But Schroeder's advocacy of equal opportunity for women did not include the requirement that women meet the same standards as men. This is not to say that the Colorado Democrat is insensitive to disparities between the sexes, however, or that she has given up on remaking the physical nature which stubbornly stands between women and their male counterparts in the military.

One of Schroeder's pet projects is the Defense Women's Health Research Project. Her office somewhat disingenuously describes this project, funded at $40 million last year, as catch-up work to "keep the force healthy." But one of its current studies suggest that this project is trying to trump nature and create the female cyborg soldier. The Army Research Institute of Environmental Medicine in Natick,

Massachusetts, is spending $140,000 in an attempt to being women into the strength and fitness range of men. Project director Everett Harman selected 40 civilian women aged 18-32 and paid them $500 each to undergo weightlifting and aerobics five times a week for 24 weeks, under the guidance of professional strength coaches. The women also carried a 70-pound pack for two miles as fast as possible, repeatedly lifted a 40-pound box, and performed other demanding exercises.

Harman acknowledges that right now the women are "almost completely out of the male range" and that "the strongest female is generally weaker than the weakest male." While women typically have 55-60 percent of the upper-body strength of men, his goal is to bring it up to 75 percent.

"The public perception persists that the experiment will finally answer the question of whether training will make women as strong as men," writes military expert William Gregor. "The fact that that answer is already known, but ignored, is not an issue of data, it is a matter of politics." The subjects of Schroeder's attempts to create a super-female, says Gregor, "will be working under Olympic trials decathletes to achieve what male contemporaries achieve through routine training." In response to one subject who told the press that "a muscle is a muscle and it should do the same regardless of gender," Gregor says, "in the world of politics it appears some muscles are special and worth additional expense. . . You can't thwart biology." Yet, this is what Schroeder and others are spending millions to do.

Secretary of the Army Togo West, an engineer and lawyer with only four years of military experience, and that in a bureaucratic role, has revived interest in the gender integrated training which was such a disaster in the 1978-1982 period. Press reports say that last year West visited soldiers at Fort Jackson who had participated in tests, which the Army has kept secret and which laid the groundwork for men and women recruits to train side by side. An Army press release says that "all training will be without favoritism and accomplished to Army standards." But in light of what is going on at Forts Jackson and Leonard Wood, that can only be a reference to "dual standards."

For example, men are required to do 32 pushups in two minutes, the women 13. The obstacle course for women is different, and the required time for the two-mile run is slower. And the present experiment in finding some of the same realities about female psychology as the previous attempt in 1978-1982.

"You find the women are more emotional," Lt. Col. Ron Perry of Fort Leonard told the *Washington Post*. "For instance, when they stand on the rifle range and are told they've failed, many of the women will break down, while the guys will kick a stone and curse."

Military brass staunchly deny it, but there is abundant evidence that gender-integrated training has lowered standards across the board. As the *Detroit News* recently pointed out, at Fort Knox, recruits have traded combat boots for running shoes and are now allowed to go around a six-foot wall they were previously required to scale. Formerly mandatory overnight bivouacs may now be canceled because of bad weather. And one training march avoids Heartbreak Hill, which some deemed too tough.

At Fort Leonard Wood, Pvt. Vanessa Overhaus, a 19-year-old from Buffalo, broke down and cried on the first day of training. Then she fell five times on the bayonet course, forcing several officers to walk her through the maneuver. A full seven tries later, she scaled the wall. Like most of the women, she now feels better about herself, but the physical limitations remain. And there are social factors as well as physical ones.

Even the most generous press reports acknowledge continual complaints from the women over bathroom and shower facilities. Sgt. Steven Buie of Fort Leonard Wood said that higher rates of injuries and sick call with female trainees have handicapped training, as they did in the 1978-1982 experiment. The male recruits know that the drill sergeants would be much tougher on them without women around.

Army spokesperson Jacqueline Mottern echoes the Army claim that all is well, that everybody in the military loves the policy, and that women are performing as well as the men. But according to Col. Robert Maginnis and other critics of the feminization of the military, performance can only be rated equal by changing definitions of cohesion and "soldicrization." Maginnis says "they change the whole *modus operandi* as to how measure performance. Before it was physical, now they measure non-physical, map reading, first aid. When you gender-norm these things, the women will come out at or above the level of men."

Women make up about 12 percent of America's 1.5 million troops on active duty, a greater proportion than any other nation. According to Col. William Gregor, however, there is no real need for current policies. "We arbitrarily exclude 40 percent of our men from military service," he says. "Having blocked suitable males from enlistment, does it the make sense to adopt special training methods to make women more like men?" given declining training budgets, why should the Army embark on a specialized training effort to achieve what normal training efforts to achieve what normal training methods would otherwise do?"

The former Army trainers hold no doubt that the PC contingent in Congress and its allies in the Defense Advisory Council on Women in the Service will be satisfied with nothing less than women in front-line combat. Yet unlike the PC forces, these men have actually engaged in combat and understand what the new policy will mean. They estimate that gender-integrated training has reduced our readiness by 5 percent and that women in combat would reduce it by 30 percent.

"This is social engineering at its worst," says former Navy Secretary Webb, a Vietnam veteran whose article, "Women Can't Fight," got him banned from the Naval Academy for four years. Possession of the article, members of a presidential commission were told, can constitute sexual harassment at the academies. "The problem in purely objective terms is that it doesn't stress the men. Females fall behind in the aggregate and you basically water down the training." Webb adds that "the greatest damage of this issue is the way the political process has perverted the sense of integrity of the officer corps. When the commander of a ship stands up in front of the world and says none of these pregnancies occurred on board ship, every sailor in the Navy knows they are lying. When you see your leaders as hypocrites, integrity goes out the window."

In his early days as a comic, Bill Cosby had routine about a referee who handed out the rules of engagement before every war. But real warfare is no laughing matter, and there are no referees. In a real war,

Vanessa Overhaus will have only one chance, not seven, to get over the obstacle, and when she fails she will be shot dead along with those males lending her a hand. Their blood will cry out from the ground, all the way to the Capitol Hill offices of Pat Schroeder and her comrades who have been engaging in their own war against nature on this issue.

"Unfortunately, we are going to have to get a lot of people killed before what these people have done is clear," says the captain who participated in the ill-fated 1978 gender integration experiment "If seeing women come home in body bags is their idea of equality, then we're in deep trouble, in this society and in the military which protects it."

13. Post Script

Political correctness is not something confined to faculty loung-es at UC Santa Cruz, Berkeley, and Harvard. As I learned, it had even permeated the vaunted Smithsonian Institution and in *The Washington Post* I duly took notice.

Institution With an Attitude
The Washington Post, October 13, 1996

"THE SMITHSONIAN IS A NATIONAL TREASURE," THE INSTITUTION'S Undersecretary Constance Newman told a cheering crowd gathered on the Mall in August to celebrate the 150th anniversary of the institution. But the Smithsonian's leadership is tarnishing that treasure.

In 1846, British scientist James Smithson left a $500,000 estate "to found at Washington, under the name of the Smithsonian Institution, an establishment for the increase and diffusion of knowledge among men."

Smithson could never have imagined the "Etiquette of the Underclass," a temporary exhibit in 1992 in which visitors would lie down in a morgue drawer and hear the voices of transients nar-rate scenes of criminals preying on crack teens, a simulated rape and a transaction between a prostitute and her customer as a woman's voice intones, "Who is smarter? The girl who gets paid for it or the one who gives it away?"

Or take the "After the Revolution" exhibit, which is now on dis-play. An introductory film describes marriage in early 19th century America as a "dark leap" for women, who "had more legal rights as a widow than wife." Exhibit labels scorn the "free market," sneering that sailors of the day were "free to be unemployed" – the sort of thing Soviet economists used to say about Western societies.

Then, in 1991, the American Chemical Society put up $5.3 million for an exhibit called "Science in American Life." According to *Lingua Franca* magazine, it "looked to some chemists like it had been scripted by the Unabomber." Guides told visitors that scientists are "the source of some of our biggest problems," and scientists were portrayed developing IQ tests and birth control in order to "rationalize racism."

No blatantly political exhibitions appeared at the Smithsonian until the advent of Secretary Robert McCormick Adams, dubbed an "establishment radical" by *The Post*. Adams said that as head of the Smithsonian he intended to promote "confrontation, experimentation and debate." How Adams would pursue these goals became clear during the 1986 bicentennial of the U.S. Constitution.

The exhibit was called "Toward a More Perfect Union." One section, titled "Concentration Camps USA," led the visitor into Japanese American internment camps of World War II, instructing that the relocation centers were not exactly like Dachau and the other German camps but for "the imprisonment of a people."

The text added: "Although we may not be confortable with the term, the fact remains that these were, by definition, American concentration camps."

One year later, the Smithsonian unveiled "The West as America: Reinterpreting Images of the Frontier, 1820-1920." The exhibit interpreted portraits of cavalrymen making a last stand as "an allegory of the plight of capitalism" in an era of labor-management conflict and equated manifest destiny with the U.S. war in Vietnam. According to *The Post's* Style section, the exhibit "reduced the saga of American's Western pioneers to little more than victimization, disillusion and environmental rape."

This guilt-steeped world view recently led to perhaps the Smithsonian's most highly publicized case of revisionist history: the proposed Enola Gay exhibit at the Air and Space Museum. It intended to portray fascist Japan as a victim of Western imperialism and the United States as a kind of racist, Dr. Strangelove villain.

Among the veterans rightfully outraged were Smithsonian regents Barber Conable and Sen. Daniel Patrick Moynihan, who, like thousand of others, believed that the atomic bomb had saved their lives and brought the war in the Pacific to a swift close. The curator subsequently dropped much of the editorializing from the exhibit. An investigation revealed that "a number of [Smithsonian] staff objected to the nature of the Enola Gay exhibit as early as 1987, but their comments were ignored by the director." The investigation found that Smithsonian curators were "frequently out of touch with the public."

The Smithsonian receives $376.1 million from the federal government, about three-quarters of its annual budget. But the infusion of political correctness has led politicians to take a hard look at the institution's budget. With its federal appropriation under fire, the Smithsonian is now looking for more corporate sponsorship. But it may learn that biting the hand that feeds it is bad policy. The American Chemical Society, for instance, now actively discourages other companies from donating to the Smithsonian.

The Smithsonian is a national treasure for all Americans, but if it is to continue in this role it needs to rededicate itself to James Smithson's vision of truth and knowledge rather than spouting propaganda that relies on political correctness and revisionist history.

14. Desexegrated Follies

Pat Schroeder's call for a "desexegrated" military certainly had a politically correct ring to it. But as this piece showed, in the real world it also had consequences. I should make it clear that I favor women in the military, but not in front-line combat. And just so readers know, I have nothing in principle against poontang. Like most everything in life, poontang has its place, but that place is not military duty, for reasons this piece should make clear.

Booty Camp: On maneuvers with the coed military
Heterodoxy, April-May, 1997

ON A CLEAR DESERT NIGHT THE SWEAT BEGAN TO POUR DOWN MAHMOUD'S face as he guided the truck toward the perimeter of the American encampment. Here he expected to find resistance and was ready to return fire with his H&K G-5 submachine gun. But to his surprise, the headlights revealed no sentries blocking his path. He thought it might be a trap, but when no guards appeared he thanked Allah for blessing his mission and sent the truck hurtling toward the tents. Now he could hear the American soldiers yelling, amidst the pop of rifle fire, but it was too late. "Allah is great!" Mahmoud screamed as he detonated the thousand pounds of explosive, perishing in the fireball but turning the infidel encampment into an inferno of blood, with body parts raining down amidst twisted metal.

Nothing of this sort actually happened during the Gulf War, but not because, those who want to blow hundreds of sleeping American troops to chunks, in the style of the Lebanon truck bomb of 1983 or last year's attack in Saudi Arabia, didn't have their chances. Back in 1992, in testimony that received no national press coverage, Sgt. Mary Rader of the

213th Supply and Service Battalion told the Presidential Commission on the Assignment of Women in the Armed Forces: "We had females and males that would go to guard duty together and be caught necking and they're supposed to be out there protecting us and pulling guard duty at 2, 3, and 4 o'clock in the morning. And they had no idea what was going on there."

The reality that, in the middle of a Middle East war, co-ed American sentries were slipping off to a sand dune to kick up a little dust did not manage to penetrate the consciousness of feminists led by former Congresswoman Pat Schroeder who for years have been telling anyone who would listen that the "masculinist military" needed to "desexegrate," and that problems of Tailhook machismo and sexual harassment would eventually vanish under a regime of gender equity that centered on allowing women in combat. While Pat Schroeder and her sisters have had their way with the Armed Forces, the evidence of what actually happens in the co-ed regime has become apparent.

In co-ed theory, women are interchangeable with men, but on the other hand they are held to lower, gender-normed standards. Being equals, women should pull combat duty, but because we live in a world of rampant sexism, women also need special protection from predatory males. This leads to the contradictions which have come to govern, and to some degree, deform contemporary military life. Most striking among these contradictions is the notion that the sexual drive, which in other contexts radical feminists see as determining what people are and do, will supposedly fade away in the sexually integrated military, like the state in Marx's utopia.

The tragic tangle at the Aberdeen Proving Grounds, which ended in late April with Sgt. Delmar Simpson being judged guilty of committing 18 rapes, shoots down that theory. The day the judgment was announced, a female spokesman with the Army rushed to CNN to assure viewers that "this was not about sex." The implication, following feminist clichés, was that it was about power. But sex was exactly what it was about. In some cases, drill sergeants had converted their units into a kind of bordello, using their rank to dominate females and leverage favors from them. But as testimony revealed, it is also true that women have been willing sex partners in the new military.

The high-profile Simpson case will no doubt be used by feminists in and especially out of the military to prove the predatory inequities that rule the military and thus launch another Tailhook-style inquisition. One of the subsidiary tragedies of this event will be muffled-that the present chaos in the military is the result of an impossible desire to reconfigure human nature, to keep boys from being boys and girls from being girls. The metaphor for the new military is less *Courage Under Fire* than a zany co-ed version of Bill Murray's *Stripes*, a G.I. spring break where everybody enjoys a good shot at becoming a liaison officer of sorts.

Co-ed tents are the latest trend with U.S. forces in Bosnia, as the *Washington Post*, the voice of the beltway establishment, recently noted in a highly promotional article titled "Engendering a Warrior Spirit: Women Easily Assimilate in U.S. Army Forces in Bosnia." Author Dana Priest writes that "it is often impossible to tell the women from the men." Priest has evidently never seen a female soldier drop her camos and squat to relieve herself in open terrain, (To resolve this physical inequality, the Army has studied the "Freshette Complete System II" device supposedly allowing women to pee standing up) A photo shows a pair of male and, female sergeants at Camp McGovern trading back massages before going to sleep, "What's the big deal?" protests Sgt. Steven Davis. "We're not sleeping together, we're just sleeping together."

Here advocacy journalism meets high concept: all is perfectly platonic camaraderie, with snapshots of women smoking cigars, explaining how cool it is to fire the M-19 grenade launcher and blast away with Serb AK-47s, and generally acting like one of the guys. At Camp Demi, PFC Kristi Dowds crouches with her M-16 as though posing for a recruiting poster, or maybe a still for *Platoon*. But, later in the *Post* piece, the happy picture of androgynous harmony in Bosnia begins to fade.

It turns out there were seven allegations of sexual misconduct and three of improper consensual relationships among the troops of the 1st Infantry Division, Out of 4,970 women in the Bosnia operation since last

November, including those who worked in logistics bases in Hungary and Croatia, 174 were sent home early because they were pregnant, a pregnancy rate of 3.5 percent. However much these coed forces might enjoy cigars, grenade launchers, and bunkhouse back massages, they were not deployable, and therefore useless to the Army.

During the American deployment in Haiti, male and female personnel, both officers and enlisted, lived in co-ed tents and barracks with no barriers for privacy. Explained Major Cindy Sito: "In my opinion, it's easier to run a unit if you're able to reach out and touch everybody," Plenty of such touching was going on in Haiti and certainly during Desert Storm, where 40,000 females were deployed and where the stakes were higher.

"It may have taken five of us females to three males, but we did the same physical labor as they [the guys] did," Sgt. Mary Rader proudly told the Presidential Commission. But if she was confused on the issue of women pulling their weight in the new military, she was explicit on the subject of fraternization, In fact, for many of the women, the military is not just a job, it's an adventure.

"We had one female that we could not keep out of one of the male bunks, She was caught sleeping in the male tent more than once." Commissioner Elaine Donnelly asked if such events involved a large or small number of people.

"It was very heavy," said Rader, "Our company only has 69 people and it was very heavy in our E-4s and below. It didn't just stop there, We had a captain and an E-4 having an affair, I had a female officer who had an affair with an E-5 male she worked with. It was very heavy."

"When you say 'very heavy,' would you say more than a majority, a heavy majority?" asked Donnelly.

"Yes."

"When these things happened, what kind of discipline was there?"

"There wasn't any."

"There was none?"

Rader shook her head, "No."

The commissioners asked if other witnesses would comment on that.

"Okay, the situation was the same," said Sgt. Lori Mertz of the 39th Ordinance Battalion. "First of all, there is no discipline required. Well, the guard duty and that, there, of course, but the relationships that developed were, some of them were wrong, the captain and the E-4. You know, I don't know you know, in the military that's fraternization and that's wrong, and I'll give you that. But the fact is friendships were made that helped us get by. . .

"When I would go – we went for one of our R and Rs on what was called the 'Love Boat.' And you would get on and these men who were in all-male units had not seen a female for this many months, and they just – you know, they're raping and attacking and it's just – the friendships helped us get by, and I don't think there's anything wrong with that."

"When you say friendship you mean a sexual relationship?" said Donnelly.

"There were some that were sexual, there were some that were, you know, if you kissed him or whatever. And that happened, and there were friendships."

"You mentioned rape," said Donnelly. "That's not friendship. Was that a serious problem?"

"We went on the Love Boat or you went into the cities and stuff like that, the men who were without women. I mean, these men would come up to you, and you know the ratio with men and women in the Army in the first place. 'You know, I haven't seen a woman in this long. I've been out in the field. I've been living in a tank.' You know, it might not have gone as far as rape." However far it went, there were consequences.

Overall 9.1 percent of women assigned to the Gulf War were "non-deployable" vs. 2.4 percent of men. Nearly half the non-deployable women were pregnant, with the number of pregnancies soaring after orders for deployment. The number of military careers ended by parenthood jumped from 97 in 1989 and 85 in 1990 to 610 in 1991.

Sex in the military goes on without distinction of rank. An officer who served in Desert Storm says a general ordered one of his subordinates to dragoon a group of nurses into their private compound, where they all consented to get up close and personal. Another general lodged a young female medic in his tent on the pretext he was "protecting" her. Both incidents were well known and created resentment among the troops.

"The presumed code of behavior is so Victorian, completely out of touch with what goes on among kids," says David Wood of Newhouse News Service, who has covered the U.S. military around the world. "They are having sexual relations in high school, and by the time they get to the military they are experienced, but expected not to do it. Well, guess what?"

In addition to past sexual experience, many new soldiers are away from home for the first time and put in close proximity with members of the opposite sex in situations of sudden stress interrupted with long periods of boredom. That Victorian anti-fraternization rules have little effect on the troops will come as no surprise to all but the willfully blind.

"It's going on all over the place," said Capt. Chris School. "Where there is a will, there is way." Favorite sites include Humvees, a vehicle providing concealment if not comfort, as well as tents, closets, barracks, underground bunkers and even latrines. "Any time they can, get alone there are going to be liaisons," says retired Lt. Col. Robert Maginnis. While the grunts do it in the road, the Navy provides other opportunities for fulfilling the adage perhaps best articulated during the 1960s by Wayne Fontana and the Mindbenders: "The purpose of a man is to love a woman and the purpose of a woman is to love a man."

Aboard one supply ship, scantily clad off-duty female sailors sunned themselves in full view of the men, as though posing for a Club Med brochure on the deck of some giant Chris-Craft. As for the men, they need no such encouragement. When the Navy limited females to non-combat ships the pregnancy rate was as high as one in three. Since 1994, when women began serving on combat ships there have been five babies born at sea. On the aircraft carrier Eisenhower, 39 out of 400 women on the first co-ed cruise became pregnant. The Navy lamely explained that the couplings had taken place in port. One Navy pair went so far as to prop up a minicam and tape their below-deck maneuvers and were caught only when they screened the performance for others. On another ship, an officer opened a boiler room closet and a half-naked couple, suddenly disengaged, tumbled out onto the floor.

The *Abraham Lincoln*, one of the combat ships refitted at great expense to accommodate women, was formerly the "Abe" but is now known as "the Babe." The *USS The Sullivans*, an Aegis-class destroyer commissioned April 19 in New York, is the first ship specifically designed to accommodate male (314) and female (6) crew members. Dating shipmates is not permitted but based on past experience, that rule might be tough to enforce. During the Gulf tour of the *USS Acadia*, dubbed "The Love Boat," 36 out of 360 sailors had to be evacuated for pregnancy: The *USS Samuel Gompers*, was described by sailor Elizabeth Rugh as "a big high school" And according to another officer, the Navy's only two female JAGs (Judges Advocate General) who have served aboard ship both had to be shipped ashore, one for pregnancy the other for fraternization. As in the Army, everybody's doing it.

The co-ed regime is imposed from the top down and to defy or criticize it is to risk ending one's career. That is why military personnel clam up tighter than a bathysphere when asked to speak on the subject, even off the record. Little has emerged from the Marines, the branch of the service with the fewest women, but the problems likely differ little from those of the Army. And the lack of sexual news from the Air Force does not mean that nothing is going on. An officer who has often flown in the C-5 notes that the giant aircraft is honeycombed with all sorts of cabin areas providing ideal places to hide. Many C-5s have mixed crews and "it would be easy" he says, to form a military mile-high club.

Lt. Kelly Flinn, the nation's first female B-52 pilot, of the 23rd Bomb Squadron in Minot, North Dakota, was pulling G-forces with both an enlisted airman and the civilian husband of a junior enlisted woman. Flinn disobeyed an order to stay at least 100 feet away from one of the men she was seeing. While Flinn's flagrante is nothing out of the ordinary, not even chaplains can escape the desexegrated regime.

In April and May 1996, an Arm reserve chaplain and former infantry officer who served in Desert Storm wen on a two-week training exercise with 50 male and 3 female chaplains at Fort Monmouth, New

Jersey. These broke down into three groups of 18 men, each with a woman in the tent. The former infantry officer objected, verbally and in writing, but the brass ignored his complaint. As some observers see it. This co-ed chaplains retreat had a strategic purpose. Those who object to the soldiers co-ed arrangements can now be told that even the chaplains are sharing tents.

While promoters of the PC regime see these policies as a groundbreaking experiment, the military has previous signs of what happens when males and females serve together. Signal battalions have had women for some time, many of them drivers. A former high-ranking officer recalls that in Europe, a commanding officer was using military vehicles to, as Big Daddy put it in *Cat On A Hot Tin Roof*, cut himself a piece of poontang. "It was often the scenario," the veteran says. "You are always on the move and basically live in the vehicle." During the early 1970s at Fort Riley, Kansas, soldiers who were supposed to be on the firing line were found in the back of the ambulance (regulations require that one be kept on hand) getting horizontal with members of the medical crew. A Vietnam veteran says that troops in the Mekong Delta would crawl through mines and concertina wire to bring prostitutes into camp.

Gender-integrated training was tried in the early 1980s and abandoned, with most of the records of it mysteriously missing. Those involved say it was a complete disaster. For a wartime comparison, one could consider the Women's Army Corps of World War II.

In *Creating GI Jane: Sexuality and Power in the Women's Army Corps during World War II*, Leisa D. Meyer notes that in May 1943 there were approximately 61,000 women on duty, 70 percent single, 15 percent married and 15 percent widowed, separated, or divorced. Though barred from combat, WAC officers were given weapons training and some WACs also served with the Army in Italy in 1944, as part of an experimental unit to determine if it was possible to employ women in Army ground forces tactical units, They lived in tents, wore shirts and trousers, and were generally 12-35 miles behind the front lines, But Meyer, a feminist, concedes that their very presence caused tensions.

The presence of a few women among many men created a lack of sexual restraint with many WACs suffering "burn out" from the barrage of requests for dates. Sometimes things weren't so delicate. So many soldiers tried to enter the WAC barrack that high wire fences had to be put up to keep them out. After men invaded their compound at Fort Benning, WACs were issued nightsticks and told to "use their judgment" on interlopers. But many WACs' welcomed the attention.

One of their songs was the self-explanatory "I Want a Man," and another favorite, "Real Camp Girl," went like this:

She's got a private in the Service Company
She's got a T/5 in the Motor Pool
She dates a corporal in Demolitions
And her sergeant, he's a jewel
And from Company B of the 52nd
He's the one who has her in a whirl
though she swears that she loves them all the same
For she's a typical Camp Abbot Girl.

In one WAC unit, "sex crazed females" would pick up men and a patrol stumbled on a sergeant and his WAC lover frolicking naked in the woods. Meanwhile, lesbian WACs couple in hallways, barracks, and latrines. Integration of the sexes into combat units has expanded the opportunities for nature to take its course.

"Guys are saying it's just not working, that it's okay to have a few women in office jobs but we can't keep shoehorning women into these places," says David Wood. Two years ago, Wood went to Fort Jackson, South Carolina, for a story on black female drill sergeants. Without prompting, he was told how female recruits hitting on female drill sergeants had become a huge problem.

A former high ranking officer tells *Heterodoxy* he gets calls from contacts in the Israeli military telling him how "stupid" the co-ed policy is. (After one experience, Israel has kept women away from frontline combat.) But the U.S. military, alone in the world, keeps to the PC course. And things appear to be getting worse.

Secretary of the Army Togo West has taken as his adviser Madeleine

Morris, a feminist Duke University law professor with no military background who authored "By Force of Arms: Rape, War and Military Culture." In this piece, she recommends that the military eliminate the "masculinist" tendencies and adopt an "ungendered vision" in which units look to Alcoholics Anonymous, religious orders and other groups as models. The Army, she says, must combine its "aggressivity" with compassion, and cultivate idealism and moral conviction instead of manly "posturing."

"Surely," Morris writes, "if armed force is ever to be deployed, then idealism and moral conviction are preferable motives to macho posturing." Her examples of cohesive groups centered on ideological rather than "gendered bases" for bonding include Communist Party cells and the French resistance underground. Masculinist military culture, she says, promotes violence against women and Morris urges and end to the land-combat exclusion which, she says "may tend, in both concrete and symbolic ways to reinforce the traditional military gender and sexual norms that may be contributing to the military rape differential."

Elaine Donnelly counters that if anything promotes violence against women, it is the real policy of training women for combat, where they will certainly get equality in death. When Peruvian commandos recently broke into the Japanese ambassador's compound in Lima to free the hostages, two teenage female guerrillas of the Tupac Amaru rebels shouted "We surrender." Displaying no gender bias of any kind, the commandos shot them dead.

U.S. Air Force Lt. Laura Boussy says that the claim that soldiers can be trained to conduct themselves properly in an asexual, professional manner in brutal ground combat is "a utopian fantasy." Boussy says that sexual tensions and misconduct would be sure to increase and unit morale and cohesion would suffer.

Morris was hired by Secretary West to look into the Aberdeen incidents of rape and sexual harassment. But whatever specific recommendations she makes, the truth is, as Stephanie Guttman says in a recent issue of the *New Republic*, that the Aberdeen incidents "are bound to recur. In a military that is dedicated to the full integration of women, and to papering over the implications of that integration as best they can. .

106

. sex and sexual differences will continue to be a disruptive force." She adds, "We will not really know [the full costs] until the forces are called on to do what they are assembled to do: fight."

UCLA anthropology professor Ana Simons, who spent a year and a half living among Special Forces soldiers for her new book *The Company They Keep: Life Inside the U.S. Army Special Forces*, does not hold high hopes for the result if and when it comes to fighting. "Allowing women into ground combat units could hurt the morale and cohesion of the armed forces," she recently wrote in the *New York Times*. "A combat unit's very success depends on something that is hard to measure, but too easy to discount: male bonding." One way they bonded was to talk about sex, which "allowed men to define themselves separately, which not challenging the group's unity." Adding women to combat units, she says, "would obviously alter, if not completely stop these discussions."

Like Elaine Donnelly, Simons believes that women are capable of filling many jobs in the military – but not in combat units. "Men who volunteer for combat, men who are willing to put their lives on the line," she says, "have their own way of communicating, and all the political pressure in the world can't change that."

Simons told *Heterodoxy* that she is "not sure that women are capable of the same kind of teamwork" and said that the presence of two women with a Special Forces unit in Arkansas cause "significant behavior changes" among the men. She was sure that the female presence "will just eat up cohesion." A male professor told Simons that maybe men and women can fight together, but added, smiling, that if the combat slacks off, then aha! we'll all have some fun. "Most guys will admit it if they are honest," says Simons. "But too many of the PC crowd can't be honest about this."

The gender warriors have already begun to attack Simons, who doubts she will get tenure. Meanwhile, free at last to speak out, former fighter pilot and retired Marine colonel Jerry Cadick recently unleashed a salvo in *Newsweek* titled "On Being a Warrior." He writes, "We gotta get down to basics, like where we evolved from and some real hard natural selection rules Mother Nature wrote in the Standard Operating

Procedures manual." Cadick has heard the argument that technology has mad the military more female-friendly but doesn't buy it.

"The only test of who can function in combat is combat," he says, and those currently in the "stampede toward correctness" have embarked on a mission impossible.

15. "More cultural revolutions"

Some American Protestants had long espoused a theology that believed the end was near, and so best not to get too involved in politics. These groups came to realize this self-exclusion was a mistake, and began to participate in politics with some degree of fervor. That sparked alarm in the fever swamps of the old-line establishment press, which held the "religious right" to be a violation of the First Amendment, if not a threat to the American way of life. At the same time, the old-line press disregarded the religious left, whose new players seemed bent on making the same mistakes as the old religious left, people such as Anna Louise Strong and the Rev. Hewlett Johnson. As I learned in writing *From Mainline to Sideline: The Social Witness of the National Council of Churches*, the religious left can be worshipful of Communist regimes and indulge some curious descriptions of actual human beings.

Mutant Social Growths
First Things, January 1995

ON AUGUST 12, 1994, RUSSIAN WORKERS WERE DIGGING THE FOUNDATION for a new bear cage at the Moscow Zoo when they made an unexpected discovery: a mass grave of skeletons and skulls, some marked with a single bullet hole, the calling card of Stalin's executioners. The cache was one of dozens found in recent years all over the former USSR.

At about the same time, the *Washington Post* carried an article by Daniel Southerland titled "The Staggering Cost of Mao's Vision." Southerland estimates that the Great Leap Forward, the Cultural Revolution, and various man-made calamities such as famine claimed a total of eighty million lives, roughly the population of Mexico. Like

Stalin, Mao knew that one death is a tragedy but a million deaths a statistic.

In the summer 1994 issue of *Dissent*, Marxist historian Eugene Genovese acknowledged that Marxism-Leninism "broke all records for mass slaughter, piling up millions of corpses in less than three-quarters of a century," and charged that the left knew it from the beginning but remained silent and was therefore guilty of abetting mass murder. Until the left owns up to its mistakes, Genovese argued, it will lack credibility in addressing current social ills.

One province of the left stands in particular need of repentance: the religious left. When the Chinese regime was at the nadir of its brutality, the religious left was hailing it as a bastion of social progress, if not the very kingdom of God on earth.

"While Liberation turned the whole society towards socialism, the Cultural Revolution deepened and continued that process. Mutant social growths were identified and unceremoniously uprooted. And, the Chinese conclude, there will be more cultural revolutions in the future as their society moves along in a socialist direction." A quote from a Party publication or a line from one of the regime's tour guides? Actually, it comes from *China: People-Questions*, published by the National Council of Churches (NCC) in 1975, while the Great Helmsman was still in power. The book was widely used among member communions during the 1970s and 1980s. The editor was Michael Chinoy, currently the China correspondent of the Cable News Network (CNN).

"China's Communist revolution has propelled a backward, poverty-stricken, virtually medieval society into the modern world," wrote Mr. Chinoy in his introduction, adding that starvation had been eliminated and that "serving the people is the dominant social value."

Moreover, Chinoy added, "A violent revolution and bitter civil war were necessary to sweep away the decay, exploitation, and backwardness of old China." Further, "With the Communist victory, the revolutionary process did not stop. Indeed, it was accelerated." But, the editor conceded, problems remained. "The recent Great Proletarian Cultural Revolution and the present campaign against Confucius indicate that traditional values and attitudes still exist in China, even as the Chinese attempt to eliminate them."

The Reverend Donald MacInnis, former director of the NCC's China program, wrote the chapter on religion. He denied that communism had become the nation's official creed, but a photo of the Great Leader is captioned, "Chairman Mao – his photo and sayings – replace Confucius in this altar setting." In short, he writes, "Most Chinese today appear to believe that the new China can move forward very well without religion and the new values, stressing 'serve the people,' are adequate substitutes for religious disciplines." One gets the feeling that the Reverend MacInnis believed it, too.

The bit about "mutant social growths" being "unceremoniously uprooted" comes from Stuart Dowty, an American automobile worker who had visited China in 1972. "Layoffs and unemployment were no problem," Dowty writes, "because China's planned economy could handle such changes rationally." He refers to Mao's writings, cites various Happy Workers, and concludes: "There is no doubt that socialist motivations, as opposed to individualist perspectives, have produced an impressive record of social and economic growth during the past two decades."

Rhea Whitehead, formerly a member of the NCC's China research staff, opines that "the Chinese believe that the study and application of 'Marxism-Leninism-Mao Tse-Tung thought' will provide the basis for change." And so it did, as the death of eighty million attests.

Most of the mass atrocities committed by the Chinese Communist regime were already known when the NCC published its worshipful tract. But the Council has never issued an apology and the religious left in general has never been called to account for its spiritual lend-lease to totalitarian regimes.

But, the reader may protest, 1975 was a long time ago, and a lot of people were saying stupid things then. Yes, but the blindness to the evils of communism on the religious left was persistent, systematic, and unaltered by the massive available evidence about the horrors being perpetrated. Does anyone suggest that we impose a moratorium on criticizing those who persisted in praising Hitler?

A little history seems pertinent in view of the fact that the church bureaucracies of the NCC's member communions are again becoming politically active in the form of the Interfaith Alliance, formed to counteract what they perceive as the extremism of the "religious right." Before anyone takes them seriously on the subject of political moderation, they might ask about those happy workers and mutant social growths in China.

16. Politically Correct Presidential Pastor

The Reverend Jim Wallis, a frequent visitor to the White House, is spiritual advisor to Barack Obama. The president's mentors include Frank Marshall Davis, an old-line Stalinist, and the Rev. Jeremiah Wright, a preacher who has spent his career stoking a fire-and-brimstone hatred of the United States. In such company the Reverend Wallis is a perfect fit.

PC Agit-Prophet
Heterodoxy, January 1995

THE COVER OF A RECENT *LOS ANGELES TIMES MAGAZINE* SHOWS A MAN SErenely posed and staring mystically into the light streaming in from the window. A collection of crucifixes on the wall gives the room the air of a shrine. Inside the issue there are three other pictures of the subject, all giving him the heft of a modern-day John the Baptist. Apparently, the author of the article doesn't feel the photos do full justice to Jim Wallis. So there is this description of the 46-year-old political activist cum spiritual guru: "A man of middle height with a bodybuilder's physique, Wallis has a soft face. His burly arms are hairy, his sandy hair is combed in an early rock and roll style, his complexion is reddish." It gets even better.

Wallis is a "progressive evangelical," a "man with a mission to seize the moral issue from the Right, social conscience from the Left and take politics-as-usual to a higher ground." He sounds "like a righteous voice crying in the wilderness" and wants the rest of us to follow him, which may make him "a saint." And while the knock on most saints is that they are insufferable, this one is way cool, a baby-boomer and veteran of the anti-war movement who at the end of a hard day cranks up rock music on his stereo. The prophet of a new politics of meaning, this saint attends prayer breakfasts with none other than Bill Clinton.

The *Wall Street Journal, Newsweek,* and *U.S. News and World Report* have also given rave reviews to Wallis, who has hit the radio and TV talk-show circuit promoting his new book *The Soul of Politics.* From his current cult of personality, one would never guess that Pastor Wallis has a past. But he does, and it is one that tells a good deal about how activists of secular ideologies have jumped into the mainstream of the spiritual quickening and religious revival that are becoming increasingly important factors in America's social life.

Even though he has recently repackaged, if not quite invented, himself, Wallis has been on the scene since the 60s, when the scene began. He likes to tell the reporters who write such flattering things about him that he grew up in Detroit and at the age of 14 was kicked out of his local church for opposing racism. More accurately, Wallis grew up in Southfield, Michigan, an upscale Detroit suburb. His father Jim was an executive with Detroit Edison and the leading figure in Dunning Park Chapel, an assembly of the Plymouth Brethren, an evangelical group that does not maintain formal clergy. Art Pearce, a church elder, says that Wallis was never "kicked out" of the church and that it was not until he went off to college that "his political activism took off."

At Michigan State, Wallis made a name for himself as an anti-war activist. Wallis explains that while his anti-war colleagues drifted back into the mainstream, he experienced a "deeper conversion" that resolved the "split between personal faith and social action." But his own writings suggest that Karl Marx was part of the deal and that the new evangelical mission was to liberate the church from the evils of capitalism. Wallis explained a few years ago: "As more Christians become influenced by liberation theology, finding themselves increasingly rejecting the values and institutions of capitalism, they will also be drawn to the Marxist analysis and praxis that is so central to the movement. That more Christians will come to view the world through Marxist eyes is therefore predictable. It will even be predictable among the so-called 'young evangelicals' who, for the most part, have a zeal for social change that is not yet matched by a developed socio-economic analysis that will cause them to see the impossibility of making capitalism work for justice and peace."

At Trinity Evangelical Divinity School in Deerfield, Illinois, where he enrolled in 1970, Wallis and some disciples in a Chicago commune started putting out the *Post-American*. The magazine, at first little more than a mimeographed sheet, claimed to be anti-war, but when the tanks of North Vietnam finally rolled into Saigon in April 1975, two years after the U.S. withdrawal, the editors offered no objection to the invaders' military conquest and treaty violations. Nor did they urge them to hold democratic elections at the earliest convenience. Pastor Wallis was too busy oraculating: "It's over, thank God it's over. I don't know how else to express the quiet emotion that rushed through me when the news reports showed that the United States had finally been defeated in Vietnam. There was an overwhelming sense of relief and thankfulness that he American intruders had finally been thrown out and that the desire of the U.S. government to control the destiny of Indochina had been thwarted."

In 1976, Wallis changed the name of his publication to *Sojourners*. The theology was Anabaptist, a sectarian vision of a "called-out" pacifist community shared by Quakers and Mennonites. But unlike these groups, which are content to let Caesar be Caesar, the Sojourners community wanted Caesar to act like them. Wallis and his flock interpreted the "principalities and powers" of the New Testament as political, not cosmic, and took a highly selective, adversarial stance. Nominally evangelical, the interpretation of their Great Commission was to give religion, at that time foundering in America, a broadly anti-American tone. In fact, the United States and its capitalist economy was the likely candidate for the beast of St. John's Apocalypse, since it was a place where "the rich worked within the law and followed accepted business practices" in a way that "God calls violence and oppression."

When the Sojourners, as Wallis and his followers were known, attacked the American beast, they were "speaking prophetically," engaging in a radical Christian version of hellfire rhetoric and a fact-free zone that answers statistics with homilies. Wallis had seen that evangelicalism was the one real growth industry in American religion and he sought to be part of that movement, although his creed was evangelistic only in the sense that it sought to convert mainstream evangelicals to a hostile political ideology tricked out in religious language. Wallis summed up his vision in a May 1978 article: "A whole new generation of radical Christians may turn America's traditional affirmation of the biblical heritage on its head. That biblical heritage can then be used to attack the system rather than to defend it. . . An American radicalism that is biblically based and conceived in the churches could be a far more serious challenge to the established order in America than political responses that are based merely on secular ideology."

Once Wallis set out on his Commission, key allies stepped in and helped make him a national figure. One of these was Richard Barnet, a left-wing anti-capitalist intellectual and co-founder of the radical think tank, the Institute for Policy Studies. As Steven Powell showed in *Covert Cadre*, IPS is an interlocking directorate of the American Left as well as a longtime hangout for Eastern Bloc diplomats, KGB agents, pro-Castro propagandists like Sol Landau, and misunderstood liberals like Alger Hiss. Although not known as a particularly religious individual, Barnet introduced Wallis into the IPS network and began to write for *Sojourners*.

Barnet and churchman Gordon Crosby encouraged Wallis to move his commune and his magazine to Washington, D.C. Soon the "Sojourners community" consisted of 40-50 people living in six houses. "They were mostly young people who shared their income," says Denise Giardina, a novelist and former seminarian who lived in the commune in the late '70s and early '80s. "They were people with a gift for frugality." Giardina denies that a personality cult grew up around Wallis but concedes that others looked up to him. "It was tedious," says another individual who spent six years in the community but asks not to be identified. "Decision making was 'consensual' as opposed to democratic. I don't remember votes being taken. Jim's a very strong person, and a lot of the decision making was with him."

Though wearisome to some inmates, the St. Francis-like posture of a "simple lifestyle and deeper commitment" enabled the Sojourners to seize the moral and theological high ground in debates with other religious movements and to attract key evangelicals, particularly seminarians eager to distance themselves from a fundamentalist upbringing. Reading *Sojourners* was an easy way for a young evangelical to prove he had "grown" both spiritually and politically. Though satirized as "So Boring," the magazine always wielded an influence far out of proportion to its 45,000 subscriptions. One of Wallis' big coups was an interview with Billy Graham in which the evangelist confessed his doubts about U.S. nuclear policy. Circulation grew, and by 1985, according to the *Wall Street Journal*, the magazine boasted 170,000 readers.

Wallis denies ever receiving any money from the Institute for Policy Studies. But a former official at a foundation where Wallis sought a grant in the late 1980s asked in the application questionnaire what other supporters *Sojourners* could name. Wallis' list of bankrollers included the Pillsbury Corporation and McDonald's heiress Joan Kroc. (Kroc gave $1 million to the Democratic Party and sent copies of Helen Caldicott's hysterical *Missile Envy* to thousands of elected officials and, in what may have been a quid pro quo, *Sojourners* in turn also published Helen Caldicott.) But the most intriguing contributor Wallis listed was Cora Weiss, the daughter of Samuel Rubin, a Communist Party member who used his Faberge cosmetics fortune to establish the Institute for Policy Studies. Weiss, who administers the Rubin Foundation and the Fund for Tomorrow, once worked for Church World Service, a branch of the National Council of Churches, where she channeled aid to the Communist government of Vietnam.

While religious magazines such as *Eternity, Reformed Journal, Christianity and Crisis,* and others went under, the radical *Sojourners* made the move to full-color and glossy paper. Whether or not he took Institute for Policy Studies money (or whether, given the largesse of Cora Weiss, he had to), Wallis was not reluctant to make his magazine a pulpit for IPS officials who also wanted to deploy the church in radical causes. In the March, 1978, *Sojourners*, Richard Barnet, who was then campaigning against the Carter administration's first tenuous moves to confront the Soviet challenge, wrote: "Is it possible for the Christian church to play a prophetic role at this critical moment in human history by launching a massive public education campaign to help the American people confront the moral bankruptcy of the policies and institutions that are providing them with the illusion of security at the cost of sacrificing their most precious beliefs?"

The new Vietnamese leaders applauded by Wallis, Barnet, and other Sojourners were Stalinists to a man and more repressive than their Kremlin sponsors. This proved unsettling to a number of former clergymen involved in the anti-war movement. For instance, Richard John Neuhaus, one-time liaison of Clergy and Laity Concerned to the Reverend Martin Luther King and a staunch opponent of the war, joined with other religious leaders to draw up a petition protesting massive and systematic violations of human rights by Hanoi. Neuhaus recalls that Jim Wallis was one of those who attacked him and other critics of the Hanoi regime. In 1976, when that regime's oppression was hitting full stride, Wallis ratcheted up his stridency: "The antiwar movement, though no longer with us, had been thoroughly vindicated in its dogged opposition to the American war in Vietnam. What antiwar activists said about the nature and purposes of American war policy have been shown to be true. . . In Vietnam, the U.S. government exposed itself as an essentially lawless and predatory regime. The criminal destruction of a whole people and their way of life was a deliberate policy choice made to secure American economic and military objectives in Southeast Asia. It is not a rhetorical ploy, but a statement of fact, to charge that the American government and the American people are guilty of war crimes comparable in substance, if not in scope, to the offenses of German leaders in the 1930s and 40s."

"Look at what happened," says Neuhaus, pointing to the time these remarks were made. "There were hundreds of thousands of boat people, hundreds of thousands who perished at sea." In September 1979, at the height of this exodus, Wallis wrote in a chilling editorial: "Many of today's refugees were inoculated with a taste for a Western lifestyle during the war years and are fleeing to support their consumer habit in other lands. . . The burden of responsibility for the refugees falls heavily on the United States. . . We must not support the boat people as a way of vindicating ourselves and showing Vietnam to be a bad country after all. . . Ours must be an informed response that does not play into the hands of our government's desire to further discredit and isolate Vietnam."

It was a hard act to follow, but the ever-zealous pastor was more than up to the task. By 1980, the story of the Cambodian genocide had been fully told, but that same year Wallis wrote that "the bloodbath we so confidently predicted did not occur. . .The sin of Vietnam is still with us. Our foreign policy continues to be based on the desire to control the political economies of other nations."

In the *Sojourners* style book, only America and the West commit "sins" and are judged by their record. On the other hand, leftist regimes are judged by their rhetoric and intentions, not by the disasters they create. They make only the occasional "blunders."

Spurred on by the victory of their proxies in Vietnam, the Soviets and their Cuban foreign legion were on a roll in Angola, Mozambique, Ethiopia, and other hotspots in the early '80s. Pro-Soviet guerrillas were gaining strength in Latin America. The same month Soviet tanks rolled into Afghanistan, Wallis wrote that "the political consensus the Right is seeking to forge is the idea that the greatest threat to peace today comes from the Soviet Union." For him and his followers, Amerika was still the biggest threat to world peace. A major tenet of the Sojourners' creed was that the USSR and the USA were moral equivalents, that there was no practical difference between dictatorship and democracy, between freedom and unfreedom. When Poles formed the first independent trade union in the Eastern Bloc and the pro-Soviet regime responded with martial law, Pastor Wallis wrote that "the pain of Poland's agony was only worsened by the self-righteous pronouncements of our own government." In an "analysis" mirroring that of Richard Barnet and other IPS intellectuals, he cited El Salvador, Guatemala, Chile, South Korea, and every other place where military rule has been imposed, human rights trampled, people imprisoned, tortured, and killed, all with the support of the United States government—first cousin to the Soviet Union."

So what should a *Sojourners* reader do? "We must refuse to take sides in this horrible and deadly hypocrisy," wrote Wallis. Yet under the guise of being above the Cold War fray, his magazine provided plenty of spiritual lend-lease to the USSR. The late Leonid Brezhnev was a tyrant, imperialist, and persecutor of unusual ferocity even by Soviet standards, but his passing caused Wallis to play a dirge for this man who was "a moderate man, a man open to reason" and one who "genuinely desired peace."

And while not taking sides against the USSR, Wallis and his followers, like the Eastern Bloc's puppet clergy, didn't hesitate to run to the barricades against Western missile deployments meant to stop communist imperialism. "While the U.S. government has remained intransigent in the face of the growing opposition to the missiles," Wallis wrote, "the European peace movement has grown more steadfast in its commitment to block the missile deployment."

In August 1983, when the USSR deliberately shot down a Korean airliner, killing all 269 passengers, Wallis called the act a "tragic blunder" but reserved his moral wrath for "the vicious and frenzied name-calling that came from the United States." One expected such responses, along with the obligatory descriptions of Soviet bosses as "men of peace," from paid propagandists such as Vladimir Pozner or Georgy Arbatov, or the alibi armory of paleo-left apologists such as Corliss Lamont and Herbert Aptheker. One did not expect pro-Soviet pillow talk, however, from someone who proclaims himself a pacifist and a politically neutral pastor.

During the 1980s, while Wallis continued to denounce U.S. sins in stern-as-death hellfire style, his magazine also maintained a jihad against figures in the culture of religion like Michael Novak, who showed that democratic capitalism had allowed religious beliefs and philanthropy to flourish and had done more to help the poor better themselves than any system in history. For Wallis, Novak and his friends were traitors, apostates, corporate sellouts, or worse, just like the millions of ordinary Americans whose consumer lifestyle caused Vietnam. But while the radical pastor could dish it out all right, he couldn't take it.

In a 1985 interview, Richard John Neuhaus described Sojourners as "an echo of every predictable kind of far left, mainly pacifist far left, mishmash of conventional leftisms, presumptuously entertaining—and indeed proclaiming—the conceit that they are prophetic, and I find that pathetic. But it is worse than pathetic because it contains an element of blasphemy." Neuhaus also questioned whether *Sojourners* could be accurately described as evangelical. (As many have pointed out, Wallis' theological heroes, after all, are not evangelicals like Dwight Moody and Billy Graham, but Catholic activists such as Dorothy Day and Daniel Berrigan and liberal Protestants such as William Stringfellow.) Wallis knew his job description was to radicalize the evangelicals and promptly went ballistic. "The job of people like Richard Neuhaus," Wallis concluded, "is to try and discredit genuine religious dissent by always screaming 'left-wing' or 'communist.' Neuhaus does his job well as a paid intellectual assassin on behalf of wealth and power." But Wallis' record makes it clear that he was not opposed to all forms of power.

When the Soviets tried to extend their power into Central America in the mid-'80s, Wallis was on board. Under his leadership, *Sojourners* had supported Fidel Castro's dictatorship for years. In 1977, when the regime was at the zenith of its brutality and spreading its toxins in Africa, and long after Jean-Paul Sartre and other former supporters had denounced Castro for persecuting dissidents and failing to hold elections, *Sojourners* described Fidel as a man "serious about basic reform." So it was no surprise when Wallis got behind Nicaragua's revolution. The Maryknoll litany of a "preferential option for the poor," so often repeated by *Sojourners* in other contexts, became a preferential option for the Sandinista junta.

"The new Nicaraguan government has a clear bias," wrote Wallis. "Its policies are designed to benefit the poor majority of the country more than the middle and upper classes." While the regime had made some errors – such as persecuting the Miskito Indians – "they have thus far evidenced a sincerity and integrity that is quite unique among political leaders and generates trust among the people. Most importantly, they have brought a measure of justice to Nicaragua that has never been known before."

Through the 1980s, Wallis railed like some script Savonarola against U.S. policy. But then, in 1990, when the people of Nicaragua were finally given a chance for a free, supervised election and immediately tossed out the Sandinistas, Wallis wrote that "the gift of democracy to the Nicaraguan people came from the Sandinistas." The article was accompanied by a photo not of democrat Violeta Chamorro, a landslide winner, but Marxist-Leninist pin-up boy Daniel Ortega. It was Wallis' Vietnam strategy; just say you won and pull out.

About the same time, the Berlin Wall came tumbling down. Wallis saw only tunnel at the end of this light: "Most U.S. political leaders are drawing all the wrong lessons from the tumultuous happenings in the Eastern Block. They see it as vindication rather than prophecy. Communism has failed and we won. . . That perspective is as short-sighted as it is self-serving. History will overtake the West as well. It is only a matter of time. Here too the system is failing while we struggle to keep up the illusions."

Since the end of the Cold War, *Sojourners*, like its radical brethren in the universities, has taken to peddling political correctness, particularly the gender/race/class brand. The magazine now promotes gay rights and feminist theology as articulated by some of its most extreme proponents, such as contributing editor Rosemary Ruether, author of *Women-Church*. And here is the supposedly pacifist Wallis on the "rebellion" in Los Angeles in 1993: "The next time someone says violence doesn't work, tell them they're wrong. It doesn't solve any problems, but it surely gets attention. In America, violence is about the only thing that makes us see the poor or even remember that they exist. . . This violence is not only rooted in crushing poverty, but also in our painful separation from one another. . . Looting is a crude shopping spree reflecting a system that pillages and pollutes the rest of the world."

In spite of all that has happened since the '60s, the Rev. Jim Wallis still nurtures his cherished hatreds for the United States and its people. He apparently believes that the United States, not Saddam Hussein, invaded Kuwait, and claims to have fasted for 47 days over the Gulf War, writing that "the peace of America, like the peace of Rome, is no peace at all."

And so it goes, in the wilderness, a voice crying through a bull-horn. This 25-year record of intellectual fecklessness and truckling to tyrannies around the globe should disqualify Jim Wallis from wearing the saint's mantle. But the America for which he has such scorn has a short memory. The media remains determined to crown Jim Wallis the national prophet.

From the beginning, Wallis has received endless favorable publicity, much from high-profile evangelicals who appear not to know the roads he has traveled. For example, in its article on last November's elections, *Christianity Today*, flagship publication of American evangelicalism, featured six quotes from Wallis. Though he represents no denomination, the World Council of Churches welcomed him to its recent convention, where his dominance prompted complaints from theological liberals. Pastor Wallis has repeatedly recycled his own story in autohagiographical volumes such as *Revive Us Again: A Sojourner's Story* and *The Call to Conversion*. And he has pulled all this off while claiming that people of his persuasion are "excluded from dialogue."

"The press knows, but basically admires the positions he took," says Richard John Neuhaus, who now edits the monthly *First Things*. "They believe that his head may be wrong but his heart is on the right side, which is to say the left side. This covers a multitude of sins."

Rather than being trodden down by the conservative turn of events in America, Jim Wallis is still in the middle of things. The Clintons, he says, "have contributed to the start of a much needed discussion on the 'politics of meaning,'" a phrase borrowed from former '60s radical Michael Lerner, the editor of *Tikkun* magazine whom Hillary briefly adopted as a guru before getting a whiff of his hypocrisy. The politics of meaning, in fact, is the theme of Wallis' new book, *The Soul of Politics*, which recycles much material from *Sojourners* and has been praised by liberals as diverse as Garry Wills, a *Sojourners* contributing editor, and Desmond Tutu.

"It's perfectly predictable," says Richard Neuhaus. "Where can somebody like Jim Wallis go?" Neuhaus, like Irving Kristol, cites the increasing hunger for spirituality in American life, and names Wallis as one of those "trying to use it for their own purposes." Even in this effort Wallis walks in lockstep with other '60s radicals. Michael Lerner is one. Even Tom Hayden is jumping on the bandwagon for which Jim Wallis is wagon master. Hayden is working on a book about resurgent spiritual values, which he says "represent nothing less than the maturing of the awkward formulations of the Port Huron Statement into the cultural vocabulary of the mainstream of American life."

And so the Long March through the institutions continues, in its latest incarnation, with no rear-view mirror. The people cry for the bread of true spirituality and the self-ordained chaplains of the Left offer the stone soup of their destructive and discredited politics. But something has changed since Jim Wallis got started in the Sixties. The vanguard is now the rear guard. They are still marching, but they are way out of step.

17. Crackpot Conspiracy

To fund the Contras in Nicaragua, the CIA was targeting the black inner cities of America for destruction through crack cocaine. That was the biggest story of 1996 and the politically correct in high places bellowed it through a bullhorn. Trouble was, the story wasn't true, and as I outlined in this piece, it wasn't even news.

Déjà Voo-Doo: The *Mercury News* Dredges Up the Christics
Heterodoxy, December 1996

"GOD PUT ME DOWN TO BE THE COCAINE MAN," RICKY ROSS, HEAVYWEIGHT champ of the southern California drug trade, liked to brag. But on November 19 in San Diego, "Freeway" Ricky, as he was known in cocaine circles, the 36-year-old coke kingpin with two prior drug convictions, was sentenced to life in prison. This should have been the beginning of the end for the man who had been such a plague to public safety that the Los Angeles police had set up a Freeway Rick Task Force in 1987. But it was actually only the end of the beginning, for even as Ross headed toward his life sentence, he was becoming part of a story that was far bigger than even his lucrative drug career. He had become a "patsy" in a conspiracy theory which holds that the U.S. government, working through the shadowy efforts of the CIA, had spread crack cocaine, the drug world's equivalent of fast food, throughout America's black community as part of an effort to fund Contra rebels in Nicaragua during the 1980s.

The notion that government officials are responsible for the drug plague in the inner cities has previously been a murmur, but now it has become a roar. Rep. Maxine Waters, head of the Congressional Black Caucus, is one leading partisan. Another is her running mate,

Rep. Juanita Millender-McDonald, who criticized Ross's sentence as
too severe and dragged CIA boss John Deutch to a raucous inquisition in Watts, where enraged activists bombarded the embattled official
with abuse, a preview of a similar episode which was played out during
a November 26 Senate Intelligence Committee hearing, when activists
interrupted testimony with screams of "Cover-up!"

What had prompted these bizarre scenarios was "Dark Alliance:
The Story Behind the Crack, Explosion," a series of articles by Gary
Webb that appeared in the *San Jose Mercury News* last August, in
which Ricky Ross was portrayed as a pawn in a larger scheme by the
CIA to fund the Nicaraguan Contras by targeting the black inner cities
for destruction through drugs. This was no subtle investigative report
but rather a full-court propaganda press. The *Mercury News* promoted
the series on its Web page with graphics of a figure smoking crack su-
perimposed on the CIA seal.

Rather than an occasion for reflection, Webb's story was the catalyst
for a harmonic convergence of rage and paranoia. Louis Farrakhan's
Final Call turned the series into a cover story. Before the *Mercury
News'* ink had dried, the Rev. Jesse Jackson rushed to the barricades,
and Maxine Waters called for congressional investigations. The question of whether or not the story was true got lost in the shuffle. In fact,
the *New York Times, Washington Post* and *Los Angeles Times* launched
careful investigations of their own and found that the *Mercury News*
had failed to make the case. But for many the story was true despite
what the facts said. The *Mercury News* had offered a no-fault "explanation" for the disturbing phenomenon of self-destructiveness expressed
in drug use. Webb's story allowed black leaders to say, in effect, we
have seen the enemy and he is not us. As in the old Flip Wilson routine,
"The devil made us do it."

Not since Janet Cooke's sham journalism at the *Washington Post*
won her a sham Pulitzer has there been a hoax of this proportion perpetrated by an American daily. Yet, in the face of criticism, *Mercury News*
editor Jerry Ceppos would continue to insist that "not for once second"
did he have any regrets about going with the story. A more intriguing
question, one that the press investigations which discredited Webb's

findings failed even to explore, was whether the story even qualified as news. Here Ceppos conceded a point when he blurted out something approaching a Freudian slip. "We have advanced a *10-year-old story* that is clearly of great interest to the American people." (emphasis added)

To understand the provenance of this decade-old paranoid fantasy, it is necessary to remember the glory days of the Christic Institute, a self-described "nonprofit, interfaith center for law and national policy in the public interest" which began in the early 1980s under the auspices of the Quixote Center, a left-wing Catholic group in Brentwood, Maryland.

The Christics soon slipped the bonds of their religious origins and struck out on their own under prime mover and president Daniel Sheehan, a Harvard-trained lawyer who made his name defending nuclear martyr Karen Silkwood. Sheen and Christic executive director Sara Nelson believed that Marxist dictatorships could liberate their peoples and establish social justice. As the Cold War turned hot in the western hemisphere, they turned their attention to helping Nicaragua's Marxist Sandinista junta, primarily by attacking those who supported the resistance forces, dubbed "Contras." Said Nelson, "These guys behind the friendly face of Ronald Reagan are fascists. There isn't any other word for them, and they are murderers just like the Nazis were."

One of those so accused was U.S. Gen. John Singlaub, who actually fought Nazis by parachuting into Nazi-occupied France to supply the Resistance. But that decorated hero of three wars, a supporter of the Nicaraguan anti-communist resistance, found himself under attack in the legal system by the Christics in what his lawyer Thomas Spencer called "courthouse terrorism," adding, "the Weathermen just went to law school."

In May, 1986, the combative Sheehan filed a lawsuit under the RICO (Racketeer Influenced and Corrupt Organizations) statute, a 1970 anti-Mafia law allowing citizens to go to court to prove patterns of criminal conspiracy. The Christic's suit charged that a "secret team" of former military and CIA officers, Singlaub among them, were running U.S. foreign policy. The idea was not a new one. In 1973, former Air Force officer L. Fletcher Prouty authored *The Secret Team: The*

127

CIA and its Allies in Control of the United States and the World, which charged that the Jews held excessive control over U.S. policies. Prouty was an adviser for Oliver Stone's *JFK*, in which he is named "Col. X" and played by Donald Sutherland, whose monologue in the film practically recites the Christic philosophy.

In the Christic vision, U.S. policy from the late 1950s was a massive anti-communist plot, funded by profits from drug dealing. CIA man Ted Shackley and Gen. Richard Secord were alleged to be part of a "shooter team" assigned to kill Fidel Castro. In the plan, Shackley also ran a mercenary army in Southeast Asia that teamed up with Secord and Gen. Singlaub to work with opium-growing tribesmen in Laos, where Singlaub, the Christics charged, personally killed 100,000 people. As the suit had it, a Marine named Oliver North joined in the Laos drug operation, which was only the beginning. It was Shackley, the suit said, who mounted the 1973 military coup against Allende in Chile before helping the Shah's Savak in mid-70s Iran, as well as other dirty work in Libya, South Korea, and now Central America.

The same omnipresent secret team, the Christics charged, was helping the Nicaraguan Contras and financing its dirty work by trafficking in cocaine. The suit further charged that the secret team hired a terrorist known as Amac Galil, masquerading as a Danish journalist named Per Anker Hansen, to bomb a 1984 press conference along the Costa Rican border. The bomb killed eight journalists, including one American, and wounded resistance leader Eden Pastora, *Comandante Zero*, and 27 others, including Tony Avirgan, an American cameraman. Avirgan and his wife Martha Honey were among the plaintiffs seeking $23 million in compensation and punitive damages.

In the mid-80s, as the Contra war escalated, Danny Sheehan hit the talk-show circuit and quickly became a national figure courted by liberal Democrats such as Sen. John Kerry. Besides their Washington headquarters, the Christics boasted regional offices in Los Angeles, Portland, San Francisco, and North Carolina. On July 9, 1987, Christic supporters got into the Senate Caucuses room and disrupted the testimony of Oliver North by unfurling a banner reading: ASK ABOUT COCAINE.

Both the lawsuit and the conspiracy theory played well in Hollywood. There Sheehan hung out with Ed Asner, Mike Farrell, Martin Sheen, Darryl Hannah, Jane Fonda and others, who helped him stuff his war chest with an estimated $3 million – much of it raised at a $100-a-plate fundraisers and benefit concerts with Kris Kristofferson, David Crosby, Graham Nash, Bonnie Raitt, Bruce Springsteen, and Jackson Browne. The Harvard lawyer even packaged some deals. The Christic conspiracy provided the story for episodes of *Miami Vice* and *Wiseguy*, and was also discussed on an episode of *Cagney and Lacey*. Taxpayer-funded Pacifica radio stations broadcast a weekly Christic report, and public broadcasting icon and former presidential aide Bill Moyers championed the Christic cause in *The Secret Government*, a PBS special later turned into a book that the Christics peddled for $9.95 as a resource in their "Tools for Truth" catalogue.

While Sheehan was becoming a political celebrity, the pre-trial maneuverings of the Christic lawsuit were bankrupting the defendants, one of their intended effects. But ultimately the law-school Weathermen would also have to go to court, where their charges would be weighed in the balances.

On June 23, 1988, U.S. District Court Judge James King dismissed the suit and all charges, even against the defendants who had not moved for dismissal. Citing "deceptive" affidavits and "fabricated testimony," King ordered the Christics to disclose the names of 79 anonymous individuals, many of whom recanted statements, denied ever having made them, or said that words had been put in their mouths. Besides this legal fraud, wrote the judge, the Christics had advanced no direct evidence nor made a good showing of a genuine issue of material facts with respect to their allegations.

King's judgment provided cover for critics in the liberal press which had previously held their fire about the Christics. The liberal *Boston Globe* described the Christic Institute as a "far-left, celebrity fueled conspiracy boutique" and even in the *Nation* magazine, Jonathan Kwitny wrote "For a year, I have repeatedly asked Sheehan to provide sources for documents to corroborate his contentions . . . he has always backed out." In *Mother Jones*, James Traub wrote that the Christic lawsuit was a "gorgeous tapestry. . . woven of rumor and half-truth and wish fulfillment" and that Sheehan was a man "in whom passion has overcome reason."

Even the congressional Democrats sympathetic to both the Christics and the Sandinistas had to conclude that the vision of a "secret team" of intelligence operatives using drug trafficking and other violent measures to further their anti-communist ends was a fantasy. Congressional investigator Robert Bermingham noted that hundreds of interviews, reams of documents, including files of the Departments of State, Defense, and Justice, FBI, CIA, DEA, NSA, and Customs had uncovered no evidence of Contra drug trafficking, nor evidence indicating that any U.S. government agency condoning drug trafficking by Contras or anyone else. Michael Messick, an investigator during the 1980s for the Senate Foreign Relations Committee, says "We were unable to find any credible source" for the allegations. In July 1987, the House Select "Committee on Narcotics held closed-door hearings in which Sheehan was one of the witnesses. Reporters eagerly waited for the scoop of the secret team but Rep. Charles Rangel, one of the staunchest critics of the Contras, told the press that "None of the witnesses gave any evidence that would show that the Contra leadership was involved in the traffic of drugs."

The Christics used Sen. John Kerry's name in their fundraising appeals, but the congressional subcommittee headed by Kerry revealed a 1989 report concluding that there was no evidence that the CIA participated in the cocaine trade, nor any evidence that Adolfo Calero's FDN Contra group made money from drugs. Jack Blum, chief investigator for the panel, supports that conclusion today. Kerry eventually distanced himself from the Christics, writing two letters asking that his name be removed from their materials.

On January 13, 1992, the U.S. Supreme Court ruled that the Christic Institute had to pay $1,218,000 in compensation to the victims of their bogus lawsuit. The Christics went out of business and Denny Sheehan blew town. He is currently holed up near Santa Barbara, where he doesn't return phone calls even though his weird theories gained life after death in the *Mercury News*.

"Cocaine – a drug that was virtually unobtainable in black neighborhoods before members of the CIA's army started bringing it into South Central in the 1980s at bargain basement prices," reads the lead piece of Gary Webb's "Dark Alliance" series. The purple-hued articles purport to expose "one of the most bizarre alliances in modern history: the union of a U.S.-backed army attempting to overthrow a revolutionary socialist government and the Uzi-toting 'gangstas' of Compton and South Central." While this war is now barely a memory, "black America is still dealing with its poisonous side effects."

The Christics charged that the drugs came in through Mena airport in Arkansas, then governed by Bill Clinton. In Webb's version, the stuff was flown from El Salvador to a U.S. Air Force base in Texas, a charge that Nicaraguan anti-Somoza revolutionary Ternot MacRenato, a former U.S. Marine, says is "right out of the X-Files." MacRenato is one of many who see no empirical evidence for Webb's writing. But as in the '80s, activists raised the decibel level, politicians demanded investigation, and radical Pacifica stations turned the story in to a marathon.

It is not clear that Gary Webb is on the same wavelength as the radicals who have exploited his pieces. According to former colleagues at the *Cleveland Plain Dealer*, Webb is not a doctrinaire leftist but a dogged journalist. His former partner there, Walt Bogdanich, won a Pulitzer and now works for *60 Minutes* as a producer. Webb himself wanted to bag an award, but his efforts sometimes backfired. Promoters for the Cleveland Grand Prix auto race sued the *Plain Dealer* for libel over articles Webb had written from 1984-86 accusing them of cutting sweetheart deals and profiteering over their efforts. A jury awarded the plaintiffs $13.6 million. While the award was ultimately overturned, Webb cost the paper a lot of money.

Webb's bulldog style played better at the *Mercury News*, a liberal-left Bay Area daily with a growing reputation for recklessness. (On April 27, for instance, the *Mercury News* ran a story that the rival *San Francisco Examiner* would fold "in about a week," touching off wild rumors and prompting Willie Brown to call the Justice Department. The story was wrong and the paper is still in business.) Webb told me that he came across the Contra-CIA conspiracy while working on an article dealing with asset forfeiture. He doubtless saw this tale as his ticket to the big-time, asked for room to run, and got it. Webb says he interviewed "dozens and dozens" of people for his story but declined to reveal who they were. One of them, however, was Martha Honey, who was present at the 1984 press conference bombing on the Costa Rican border. Now working in the "peace and security" program at the Institute for Policy Studies, the Pentagon of the American left, Honey tells anyone who will listen about "Guatemalan hit teams" operating stateside.

Webb studied Honey's book, *Hostile Acts: U.S. Policy in Costa Rica in the 1980s*, now listed as a resource on the paper's web page. "Thank goodness there are still papers where they let you dig for information," says Honey, who applauds Webb's series and credits him for showing what the CIA-Contra axis did with the cocaine, making it into crack for the ghetto.

Webb says he knew about the Christic case during the 1980s but had never been associated with the group. What did he make of their charges? He told me that for a "reportedly false" case, it sure had stirred things up in government. When pressed as to which parts of the case were true, he failed to respond but in recent public statements he left no doubt where he was coming from.

"The cocaine that was used to make the crack that flooded into L.A. in the early 80s came from the CIA's army," Webb said on a radio talk show. "Now we know what the CIA really stands for, Crack in America." Thousands of African Americans were in jail, Webb said, "for selling a drug that was never even available in black America before the CIA's army stated bring this stuff in." To those who said he had not provided proof, Webb scoffed, "that's like saying there's no proof of General Motors involvement in making Chevrolets."

Investigative writers at the *Washington Post, New York Times* and *Los Angeles Times* dug deep to examine Webb's charge that "millions" in drug profits went to the "CIA's army." But after scouring reams of documents and conducting hundreds of interviews and investigations – not just in this country but in Central America, reaching even into Nicaraguan prisons – the press investigations found that a couple of convicted drug dealers might have funneled no more than $50,000 plus maybe a pickup truck or two back to the Contras. That was chump change compared to the total of $195 million in aid the U.S. government provided the resistance in Nicaragua from 1981 to 1988, not to speak of $43 million from foreign governments.

Further, the press investigations noted that Nicaraguans were bit players in the drug trade, dominated by Colombians, Mexicans, Jamaicans and Americans. The *Washington Post* found that Ricky Ross had been selling crack long before he met Danilo Blandon, the Nicaraguan Webb described as the "Johnny Appleseed of crack."

The investigations by other newspapers not only torpedo Webb's conclusions but shed light on his techniques and his relationship with Alan Fenster, attorney for Rickey Ross. Web fed Foster leading questions for Blandon, a man not known for truthfulness, at the Ross trial and then used the very Blandon testimony Fenster had elicited to support his thesis of CIA involvement. And then Fenster, in what became a legal-journalistic circle-jerk, cited the *Mercury News* articles as a basis to over turn Ross' conviction on grounds of government misconduct. This was ventriloquism, not journalism.

Webb's charges also fail the test of reason and common sense. Other cities, such as New York, had crack problems with no hint of CIA-Contra involvement. Moreover Los Angeles' drug problems had started long before the Nicaraguan conflict began and the crack problem has long outlasted it, growing worse with each passing year. But the test of reason was not one Webb wanted to take.

On a recent television show in Los Angeles, he said the *Washington Post* and *New York Times* had only "allegedly disproved" his story. He was, among other things, protecting what could become a high-concept entertainment product and indeed what might well have been this from the beginning. In a book proposal circulating among New York publishers, Webb said that the CIA dumped tons of cheap cocaine into the black neighborhoods of Los Angeles, "sparking the worst drug plague in the nation's history and financing the rise of the Crips and Bloods." So now even gangs were the work of the CIA. Further, Webb says he will prove that "the Contra war was not a real war at all. It was a charade, a smoke screen . . . to provide cover for a massive drug operation" by criminal CIA agents. So, the entire history of Central America in the mid-80s, an epic of revolution and counterrevolution, was only the pretext for a drug deal.

Amidst the smoke of sensationalism, one conclusion stands clear: Gary Webb and the *Mercury News* took a ten-year-old piece of left-wing disinformation to regions where no Christic crackpot had gone before. Professional ethnics and the congressional left picked up the story, shrieked it through a megaphone, and Washington caved in typical craven style, creating the spectacle of then-CIA head John Deutch's absurd performance in Los Angeles. Arlen Spector even allowed Maxine Walters, probably the most left-wing member of Congress and not even a member of his Senate Intelligence Committee, to question Nicaraguan resistance leaders Eden Pastora and Adolfo Calero. Spector also refuse to eject demonstrators crying "cover-up!"

Los Angeles County Sheriff Sherman Block did a little better, assigning seven full-time investigators to the CIA-Contra rumors. On December 10, Block released results of a 3,500-page investigation which found no evidence of government involvement in activities of Blandon and Ross. But the investigators did uncover some fascinating information about Gary Webb.

A New York literary agent offered Ricky Ross a deal for "dramatic rights to his story." The agent sent his letters to Ross in care of Gary Webb and the deal it described proved identical to one Webb has accepted. As the *Los Angeles Times* reported, deputies concluded that Webb had grown too close to the defendant to be considered reliable. Said a federal prosecutor in San Diego: "It is now clear that the pretense of Gary Webb being a detached journalistic observer has been dropped and that there is now no doubt that he was an active participant in the Ross defense team."

The *Mercury News* is still hyping the series and peddling reprints while its star scribe is being rewarded for his efforts. Webb boasts that he has briefed members of Congress and says he expects to assist the congressional investigators." The Bay Area's Society of Professional Journalists named him "Reporter of the Year" and bigger prizes are doubtless in store. Following the footsteps of Joe Eszterhas, another former *Plain Dealer* reporter known for wild stories, he has already sold a film project to Disney's Touchstone Pictures. But while the newly minted celebrity counts his money, other observers are calculating the fallout from the story.

"It has caused a lot of people pain," says black author Shelby Steele. "To come forward with something like that in the racial atmosphere of our times seems irresponsible. The function of conspiracy theories is that they remove blame and create the shroud of victimization. It's not our fault if our kids are shooting each other. Someone brought in the guns. They put crack here. It's dusting over culpability." Steele, a former professor at San Jose State, says the story "calls for a mea culpa, like in 'Jimmy's World,'" a reference to Janet Cooke's bogus *Washington Post* story.

"In the black community today, a small and embattled but growing number of religious leaders are saying that victimization is dead-ended and that takes courage," says Richard John Neuhaus, now a Catholic priest, who served as a Lutheran pastor in a black neighborhood of Brooklyn and worked with the Rev. Martin Luther King in the Civil Rights Movement. "Then for them to be undercut by people outside the community, to simply indulge their Oliver Stone-like fantasies at the expense of poor people, is unconscionable."

Besides reinforcing the CIA demonology, Webb's tale serves as a kind of fog, obscuring the real and largely untold story of the drug epidemic that continues to devastate the black community. It serves also to cloud the international routs that bring drugs into the United States.

While it is politically correct to blame the Contras, the press looks the other way when left-wing movements and regimes are implicated. Yet Roger Miranda, former chief of the Sandinista Defense Ministry, confirms that during the mid-1980s the Sandinistas trafficked in cocaine, collaborating with both the Medellin cartel and the Cuban Communist regime of Fidel Castro. Peru's Sendero Luminoso controlled key areas of coca production and used the profits to finance their terrorism. And, like the FSLN, the Sendero and rival Tupac Amaru movement supported the flooding of America with drugs as a way to fund their revolution and weaken the *"yanqui* enemy of mankind."

How many tons of cocaine from the Sandinistas, Fidel Castro, the Sendero and Mexico made its way to South Central Los Angeles? What happened to the profits? What are the "poisonous side effects" today? Will Gary Webb hop on this story as his next big exposé?

Note: Gary Webb resigned from the *Mercury News* in late 1997 and the next year the California Assembly hired him as an investigator. When that well-paid gig ended he free-lanced for publications such as the *Sacramento News & Review*, writing articles on themes such as red-light cameras. In 2004, Gary Webb put a gun to his head and killed himself.

18. Memoirs Are Made of This

I lived in Detroit, Michigan, as a child but never imagined I would some day write for the *Detroit News*. That came about in 1988, when Tom Hayden, who grew up in nearby Royal Oak, wrote a massive memoir. The year before I met some of Hayden's former New Left colleagues at the Second Thoughts Conference. I had also visited the Vietnam memorial and befriended some veterans of that conflict. So I had good background for this piece, which ran, like most of my work, pretty much exactly as I wrote it. Detroit, meanwhile, has fallen a long way from its heyday in the 1950s. But that, as they say, is another story.

A Memoir: Tom Hayden's Workout Book
Detroit News, August 24, 1988

TOM HAYDEN, ONCE HAILED BY A COMMUNIST PARTY ACTIVIST AS THE "NEXT Lenin," often complains of being unappreciated. Indeed, a group of Vietnam veterans recently greeted him with signs that said: "Hayden, You Still Stink!" While there is considerable evidence for that judgment, an examination of *Reunion: A Memoir* confirms that the author is at least misunderstood.

On the populist level, this is a radical to riches story in which a Big Star rescues the Angry Young Man and gives him $300,000 toward the purchase of a political office. There, as Mr. Tom Fonda, he can be an American Celebrity. It is a political Iacocca story, a nostalgic "feel good" tale for the MTV generation.

True to form, Hayden, who grew up in Royal Oak and co-founded the militant Students for a Democratic Society, drops names on every page. Samples of his prose: "Ralph Nader would burst on the scene,"

"Rennie was the spark plug on campus," "I enjoyed expressing myself in words," "its dreams napalmed," and, a favorite, "It was winter in America. The sixties were over."

But on a deeper level, the book also provides the key to understanding Hayden and the movement of which he was part.

The dominant belief of this age is that politics is the cure for human ills. *Reunion* makes it clear that Tom Hayden is a true believer, an evangelist of this secular faith. Like many of his generation who rejected their traditionally religious upbringing, he turned to leftist politics for salvation.

"When we first used the term *revolution*," Hayden writes, "it was not about overthrowing power but overcoming hypocrisy." As SDA veteran Paul Berman notes, revolutionary action in the 1960s was as way to "save one's soul." Of course, if you could seize political power, that was fun too.

This leftist political religion has produced a new literary genre of which *Reunion* is part: the auto-hagiography. Here the author carries self-righteousness to new depths. Hayden was part of a "new vanguard" with a "messianic sense." He and his colleagues were "too good" to fall into the errors of the past. He was one of the "children of light," possessed of "acute moral sensitivity." Protesters were "angelic" and riots full of "magic" moments.

The opposition, of course, was the incarnation of evil, "militant" anti-communists, hawks, fascists, conservatives, sexists, racists, sellouts. In a word "pigs." It was a starkly Manichean vision, The People vs. Them. If you weren't part of the solution, you were part of the problem, etc.

Hayden says his goal is to tell the truth "as I *felt it* [emphasis added] then and as I view it now." It is difficult to take seriously someone who "feels" the truth. One is clearly not dealing with a deep thinker here, and, as it might be imagined, he often gets it wrong.

Consider the riots at Columbia: "Since I kept no notes," Hayden writes, "I can only rely on the images of memory, but none are negative." Libraries being burned, students attacking professors and other vignettes of random violence might qualify as negative images. For a thoroughly documented view of how destructive that and similar epi-sodes were, one should read Sidney Hook's *Out of Step.*

Hayden neglects to mention that Harrison Salisbury's award-win-ning articles in the *New York Times* were largely verbatim repetitions of North Vietnamese propaganda. Other distortions and lacunae will be of interest to historians. For the real story, the reader might consult Guenter Lewy's *America in Vietnam.*

The auto-hagiographer, unlike other religious writers, is not strong on confession. Hayden admits to being "wrong in certain of my judg-ments," but his chapter on Vietnam is pitifully brief – nine pages out of 507 – full of trap doors and escape hatches, and freighted with unctuous filler. Hayden was "overly romantic" about the Vietnamese revolution. Worshipful would be a better word. He traveled there at the behest of Herbert Aptheker of the Communist Party USA and acted as though he were in Disneyland.

Hayden owns up to a "numbed sensitivity" to the pain he caused U.S. soldiers and their families. Actually, he hated these people. Hayden allows that he displayed a "minimal concern" over North Vietnamese atrocities at Hue during the Tet offensive. In reality, his only concern was to deny or defend those atrocities, or any others committed by His Team. He omits any reference to the "tears of joy" he shed when Saigon fell to the Communists on April 30, 1975.

And what about his famous comment that American prisoners of war were liars and hypocrites? It was "inaccurate and insensitive," he says, but "temper had carried me away." He adds, "I was as capable of 'Vietnam flashbacks' as any veteran." Of that there can be little doubt.

The North Vietnamese were "heroic" and comparable to Sitting Bull. And it is a "revisionist" and "Rambo" idea that domestic oppo-sition such as that fomented by himself played any role in the U.S. pullout and subsequent enslavement of Vietnam, which it certainly did. In a more hysterical vein, the American government "bears responsibil-ity for continuing to bleed and besiege Vietnam today." Why, as Tom Hayden "feels" the truth, things have greatly improved in that land. In reality they are much worse, particularly the economy.

Whenever his conscience begins to bother him, Hayden trots out statistics about U.S. bombing. He portrays himself as one trying to "heal the wounds" of war. But not even Pol Pot's genocide convinces him "that Nixon and Kissinger were right." All in all, quite a performance in terms of his basic vision.

For the Old Left, paradise was the Soviet Union. For the New Left it is always someplace or something yet to be attained: the "new society," "economic democracy," or the newest Third World "social experiment." The farther away and more obscure the better. The main certainty of the contemporary left, as represented by Hayden, is that the United States is an evil place, oppressive at home, aggressive abroad and automatically at fault in every conflict. It is a fundamentally destructive vision that, as Hayden acknowledges, has "taken hold throughout society."

Hayden berates what he perceives as current "obsession" with a "mythic past," but is himself obsessed with a mythic future. His vision is utopian, forever beyond verification and responsibility. When one version fails, he puts on his blinders and cardboard helmet, mounts Rosinante, and charges off to the next front.

"I believe violent revolution is inevitable where peaceful reform is blocked," Hayden writes. And he makes it clear that he means Central America, not Poland. "No more Vietnams" is not a slogan for Tom Hayden.

19. "We made the right move."

"Vietnam," reads the T-shirt, "If you weren't there, shut the fuck up." I knew a few people who were there, such as San Diego City College history professor Ternot MacRenato. He was in Vietnam with the Marines in the 1960s, and there learned a thing or two. The professor was born in Nicaragua, and during the 1970s, when Nicaraguans set about toppling dictator Anastasio Somoza, he decided to pick up a rifle and lend a hand. The rebels managed to pull it off and back in 1991 he was eager to talk about it. Readers might compare his account with the politically correct version from those who weren't there or didn't fight at all.

Riffraff Revolution: One Part Graham Greene to Two Parts George Orwell, and Presto! It's the Sandinistas in Nicaragua
San Diego Reader, September 5, 1991

"I WAS WALKING ACROSS THIS OPEN FIELD, ALL BY MYSELF, KIND OF DAY-dreaming, when the dirt started erupting all around me. I couldn't figure out what it was, then I looked up and saw this plane swooping down, machine guns blazing. It was one of Somoza's T-33 jet trainers. I threw myself on the ground when I finally heard the reports, but by that time he had passed me. I got the hell out of there. Oddly enough, that day I was in charge of security."

We are sitting in the coffee shop on C Street across from City College. Professor Ternot MacRenato is remembering the Nicaraguan revolution. He has just returned from comparing notes with his former comrades in arms. MacRenato was born in Diriamba, Nicaragua, in 1942 and moved to the United States at age 14. He earned degrees from the University of San Francisco and UC Berkeley and has taught history at City College since 1971. But he didn't spend all his time in the classroom.

MacRenato served with the Third Force Reconnaissance Company in Vietnam. Several times he saw action, and this experience was later to serve him well in his homeland. His direct role in the Nicaraguan revolution ended in 1980, but it's all coming back to him now.

During the 1970s, Anastasio Somoza was the prevailing heavy of a dynasty that had run Nicaragua as a private fiefdom for decades. The National Guard, or La Guardia, served as Somoza's personal army and police force. The corrupt dictator had become unpopular with virtually every segment of Nicaraguan society and had taken to hiding in a concrete bunker.

"I met Somoza once when I was a little kid in Diriamba," says MacRenato. "He had given me an award as a member of our soccer team.

"The next time, I met him as an adult when I interviewed him for my master's thesis. He was a pretty impressive person when you saw him close up. Of course, he had deep flaws in his personality. He used to put thugs and criminals in his inner circle and give them a lot of power, sometimes more power than the generals."

In the late 1970s, discontent erupted into outright revolution, with a number of factions trying to topple Somoza. Chief among them was the FSLN, the Sandinista Front for the Liberation of Nicaragua.

MacRenato became part of an anti-Somoza support network in the United States. In 1978, a group of commandos led by *Comandante Zero* Eden Pastora seized the national palace and captured the government. Though not then a combatant, MacRenato was in the Nicaraguan capital of Managua at the time.

"We got within two blocks of the place and saw the firefight. Then an army patrol came and told us to get out. We could see the helicopters firing into the palace. That was an historic moment, when the whole government was captured. Eden Pastora masterminded the whole thing." MacRenato stresses that the Ortega brothers, Daniel and Humberto, future Sandinista president and minister of defense, were absent that day.

"The founder of the Sandinista front, Carlos Fonseca, once expelled the Ortegas because they were not in the country enough," says MacRenato. "They spent too much time in Havana. All during the *ofensiva final*, they were playing politics in Costa Rica. They never came near the front line."

MacRenato returned to the United States in 1978 and kept working with the support network. Then, in May 1979 he took a leave of absence from teaching and joined the armed struggle against Somoza. Before he left, he got word that his cousin, Eduardo Sanchez, had been killed in action.

"My cousin was the commander of a camp in Costa Rica that officially didn't exist. I was in a tent when I heard all these people talking, including a voice I recognized. So I went into the next tent and there was my cousin, alive. They didn't have enough eating utensils, so you had to wait in the dark until somebody was done with their dirty plate and fork. Then you took those and got some food for yourself. I remember thinking that I was going to die right there."

What MacRenato found in camp was not exactly the Delta Force. It was more like the United Nations. "There were so many people from all over Latin America, with different accents. Sometimes the soldiers would ask where I was from. I would tell them 'Nicaragua' and they would look at me in disbelief. I had been away for 20 years and my speech had changed. They thought I was an *internacionalista*."

MacRenato's immediate superior was Hugo Spadafora, whom General Omar Torrijos, Panama's strongman, was grooming for the presidency. Torrijos was backing those trying to get rid of Somoza and Spadafora was one of his liaisons.

"Hugo had become a legendary figure throughout the area," says MacRenato. "We hit it off and became friends One day these two Venezuelans showed up. One was a colonel in the Venezuelan army and the other was this rich guy. They called for Hugo and wanted to offer help, give us weapons, special equipment. But they didn't want to deal with the Sandinistas about the trip and they said no, we don't want you to go. Afterward he regretted having asked them. They were jealous of him." Other foreigners were not so popular as Spadafora.

"The Cubans didn't say much and a lot of the Chileans were elite upper and middle-class Marxists and very arrogant. They didn't get along with the Nicaraguans, who were mostly poor farmers. The Chileans were often in charge because they had been trained in Cuba in artillery, and that's not something you learn on the job. At one point Hugo and a Costa Rican fighter named Bernal went and complained bitterly about the attitude of the Chileans. You would talk to those guys and they wouldn't even answer you back. A lot of them got key posts in the government after the war. One of them was Humberto Ortega's right hand man."

In spite of the dissidence in the ranks and poor equipment, Nicaraguan recruits flowed into camp. "Many were young teenagers running away from conscription," says MacRenato. "If you weren't in the army, the Guardia assumed you were the enemy. They would come into a neighborhood and grab all the teenagers and ask to see their elbows and knees. If they had scratches, they would accuse them of attacking the army and they would shoot them sometimes right on the spot, sometimes in front of their family.

"You could tell that a lot of the young people had been indoctrinated," says MacRenato. "I heard one guy saying that as soon as the war was over, he was going to get even with the other factions. Everybody was saying that after the war, don't give up your gun to anybody, because nobody trusted anybody.

"Training lasted between three and five days. A lot of our people would shoot each other. They didn't know how to handle weapons and broke every rule I had learned in the Marine Corps. They were always pointing guns at people, putting their hand over the end of the barrel. There was no discipline. The only time I was really scared was when I was surrounded by my own troops."

Women handled all the radio communications for the rebel forces on the southern front. A number of women also served in combat. "One of them was nicknamed Monimbo, this squat little Indian girl. She would be in charge of a radio station that broadcast Sandinista propaganda. One day we were under artillery bombardment, and everybody ran into the trenches. "She stayed and continued fixing meals all the time we were under attack, shells falling all around. She had balls." Another problem was the lack of equipment.

"Many fighters didn't have any knapsacks, so they got this plastic bag and tied it with string. Some didn't have belts to hold up their pants. This young guy asked me to help put on his knapsack, and I wondered why since it wasn't a very hard job. Then I noticed that he had a plastic hand. He had been making bombs in Managua and one went off in his hand. His father had a little money, so he sent him to Mexico where he got a plastic hand. He could move his fingers if he had a battery but the battery was dead so he was out of luck."

MacRenato's luck served him well. "When I was in charge of a column, there was this young kid we called Transito, who said he pulled out of the front line because of migraine headaches. He was sort of a training sergeant. I gave him some of my Marine belts and dark T-shirts, the kind we wore in Vietnam. We were ready to go inside when they called me to headquarters. So this young guy took my place. They went with this group of about 15 men and crossed a river. As they walked down this road, the Guardia ambushed them. The guy with my shirt and belt was the first to fall dead. That's the column I was supposed to lead."

MacRenato and his troops were eager to engage the enemy and would soon get their chance. "When we were fighting the National Guard we felt we were on a mission from God. We felt good about what we were doing. Sometimes we would send combat patrols into certain areas, and our guys would go out raising hell. They were singing and slugging, like they were going to a football game. The guys on the other side were quiet. I think they were intimidated by this. The morale on the other side was shot to hell. They didn't have much to fight for except to defend Somoza.

"The Guardia were disciplined and they didn't run away. They held tight until the end and didn't collapse until Somoza left. Militarily it was a standoff, though we had no air power and only limited artillery.

"One of my first memories was when I came across this National Guard truck that had been ambushed. It was in the middle of the highway in no-man's land. Everybody was killed. I climbed in the back and found that the soldiers had been dead for several days. The rain and the sun had kind of melted the bodies into each other. There were several soldiers on the road covered by vegetation. One of them couldn't have been more than 15 years old, a tiny little thing. His boots looked like children's boots. I remember thinking that Somoza was a criminal for sending those kids out here, so I felt bad for him. I didn't feel hatred for the National Guard. I felt pity. The average soldier was just a peon who had no place to go and joined for economic reasons or was conscripted."

MacRenato's men operated on the southern front in an area around Sapoa, near Lake Nicaragua. The distance between the front lines was between 100 and 300 yards.

"One day Hugo wanted me to go on a special mission. We need to know how much ammunition was left, that kind of thing. So I went out with my rifle and notebook. That's when I got out on the front line and they ordered us to move from one hill to another.

"The guy who led this particular group was from Spain. We called him Pedro el español, and everybody went by one name only. He was dumb as hell and lost the whole column, 300 men. That night it rained, a real monsoon. We were walking around in circles, with the National Guard a few hundred yards away. People were beginning to panic, and you could feel it. A lot of the young guys were saying we should get out of there and everybody take off on their own. A rout was beginning.

"I stood up in the dark and said if any motherfucker leaves his place I'll stay here because I came here to die for my country, not to fuck around and be a coward. Nobody is going to fucking move out of here because if he does I will shoot him. That's one thing they teach in the Marine Corps. To prevent a rout, you shoot the first guy who runs. That's what they teach you.

"Finally in the morning, we came up to this dirt road that went through a kind of tunnel made of trees. We could see the legs of people standing there but we didn't know if they were our guys or the National Guard. We didn't know what to do. Finally somebody decided to shout, and it turned out they were Sandinistas. They didn't even know we were around.

"Then somebody said 'is Pablo here?' and that was me. Hugo wanted to talk to me. So I went to ranch house where they had a radio. I walked down this trail and called Hugo, who said to report back to headquarters. About an hour or two later, this guy from Panama walked down the same trail and a sniper picked him off."

As it turned out, even revolutionary leaders could have been picked off with relative ease. "One time at night I came to report some strange lights out on Lake Nicaragua. I had to drive about five miles to where Eden Pastora was. We had an anti-tank weapon that I could use to take out a patrol boat. There were a lot of cows in the area and they were restless, so I thought there might be an enemy patrol around. When I got to headquarters, there were no sentries. If the Guardia had been smart, they could have sent a combat patrol and pulled a fast one on us. We weren't very well organized as a military.

"This one young guy fell asleep on guard duty and got me very upset. So I tied him to a tree. He spent several hours there and it rained. Then there was an artillery barrage and he was still tied to the tree, all through the attack. Then I let him go but the point was that you had to take all this seriously. This is war."

The revolutionary zeal they had shown in camp was not enough to keep others in the fight, particularly the *internacionalistas*.

"This guy from Venezuela asked me for permission to go out and have his eyes checked, and I sensed that it was a bullshit story," MacRenato recalls. "He never came back. Another guy was in his 40s and had been in the field for a long time. He left and never returned. There was no relief for the troops, and that was one of the problems. It was mostly stress, and they didn't know how to deal with it.

"The Guardia had helicopters that would circle like vultures and drop 500-pound bombs. This Costa Rican guy, Tico, was in charge of his own column. He was talking to us when this helicopter came and dropped a bomb that dug a huge crater. A big piece of shrapnel ripped through his shoulder. I couldn't find his arm but his hand was in perfect shape. You could see his lung and his eyes were still open.

"Another day there were about eight of us in a truck. The windshield had been blown away, so the driver had put up a burlap sack to keep out bugs and dirt. He cut a little hole so he could see. Then this enemy plane fired some rockets at us and they exploded above the truck. All I remember is that the driver's eyes got real big. I couldn't stop laughing, but it was a close call."

On other occasions the rebels captured key figures from the other side. "We had a guerrilla band operating behind their lines. We wanted to take Rivas, the major city in the south. This young school teacher named Ezequiel led the operation. They captured a man who used to be president of the Liberal party and president of the legislative chamber. His name was Cornelio Hueck, a very famous and totally corrupt politician. A couple of years earlier, Somoza had a heart attack and was afraid this guy was going to make a move to take over the presidency. Somoza came back and fired him.

"During the war, Hueck found himself on this farm in the middle of this area controlled by guerrilla bands, a no-man's land. I was in headquarters when Ezequiel called in. Eden was out and *comandante* Marvin was in charge. 'What should I do with this guy?' Ezequiel asked. Marvin told him to apply revolutionary justice. Later I asked Ezequiel what happened. Hueck offered him one million pesos to let him go. Ezequiel turned him down and they executed the guy."

President Carter, toward the end of his term, cut off military aid to Somoza. Without U.S. support, the regime's days were numbered Somoza eventually abandoned his bunker and fled to Paraguay.

"When Somoza left, the Guardia blasted us with everything they had. They rained shells on us the whole night. In the morning we saw that they had left their positions and ran to the nearest port, San Juan del Sur, and there commandeered every boat they could find and sailed up to El Salvador."

On July 19, 1979, the victorious revolutionaries poured into Managua, a jubilant MacRenato among them. "We came to the main square of Managua in the back of a truck. We were really high with excitement, and all these people surrounding us. We were grubby and they thought we were starving. Someone chopped up a pineapple and gave it to us. We had a megaphone and started shouting slogans like '*El pueblo unido, jamas sera vencido!*' and '*Viva el pueblo heroico de*

Managua!' There were thousands of people, and they all responded. We used to call each other *compañero* and *compita* and now the people called us that. It was a real good feeling." But as the victorious revolutionary explains, the celebrations quickly got out of hand.

"After the war everybody was confiscating cars and crashing them left and right. They couldn't drive worth shit and would just abandon the cars when they stopped running. There was no control. The country almost ran out of cars.

"I knew a guy named Baltazar, from Esteli, who used to drive around in a pickup truck. If you were a *comandante*, you would just go to the station and fill up. He would burn a tank every day just driving around Managua taking furniture from abandoned houses. I started asking what he did before the revolution and found out he ran a cantina and house of ill repute. He was just doing what came naturally."

MacRenato also found hangers-on who didn't fight but tried to pass themselves off as revolutionaries.

"Everybody was there after the *triunfo*, the PLO, East Germans, the Russians. It was a circus. Torrijos was there. Trotskyites were there, but they were expelled for trying to organize the people in the factories. Che Guevara's sister was there. Fidel Castro made several secret trips."

The Cuban leader proved an inspiration to Tomas Borge, head of the Sandinistas secret police. "Tomas Borge immediately began talking like a Cuban and acting like Fidel Castro," says MacRenato. "He even tried to dress like Fidel but couldn't figure out which hat to wear. He looked like a clone. Before you never saw the guy. He never came to the front lines.

"There was a story that Somoza's men had tortured Borge and crushed his balls. In Nicaragua the slang word for currency is *bola*. At the time, *La Prensa* was selling for two pesos or *dos bolas*. The joke was, 'Why doesn't Tomas Borge read *La Prensa*?' Because he doesn't have *dos bolas*.' Borge knew about the jokes and it infuriated him. He told one of my friends that he was going to drop his pants in front of a crowd to prove that he had *dos bolas*."

With two months of the triumph, says MacRenato, new conflicts were starting. Without a common enemy, the revolutionary factions turned on each other, and often on the populace.

"It was chaos. There was no organized authority. The revolutionary leadership, the Nine, were too busy in front of the news cameras and giving bullshit speeches to attend to the real business, to establish some kind of order. The Sandinistas needed another 20 years of maturity before they knew how to rule. They appointed this guy from Chinandega, about 21, to be ambassador to Cuba, which they considered the most important country. You had teenagers exercising authority. They had no notion of how to organize anything. A lot of people got shot by teenagers brandishing weapons and firing into the air.

"There was a lot of getting even, terrorizing neighbors by informing on them. The person being arrested had no idea of the charges, who made them, or how long he would be in jail. There was no access to lawyers. The families had no idea where these people were. One guy I went to school with was terrorized by interrogations. The only one who was safe was a guy with a gun, a uniform, and a beard. I kept my gun until the end."

The first post-Somoza government was a coalition of Marxists and non-Marxists, but the hardline faction of the Sandinistas, headed by the nine *comandantes*, quickly tilted the country toward the Cubans and Soviets. Like Baltazar the furniture thief, the Sandinistas also helped themselves to property.

"It was the worst looting in the history of our country," says MacRenato, "worse than Somoza because now nine people were doing it instead of just one. They did it at the beginning when they first came in, and they did it on the way out. Tomas Borge had three houses and spent thousands on air conditioning."

MacRenato worked for Bernardino Larios, the minister of defense appointed by the coalition, and one of his tasks was serving as a liaison with the immigration department. "Borge had jurisdiction over immigration and a few times I went to his building to get him to stamp passports. He had this young woman there who controlled the flow of people, a real bitch. I was in civilian clothes that day, and she gave me a lot of shit. I went back to the office and wrote a letter on official stationery and sent it to Borge with my title, assistant to the defense and *jefe de protocolos* – chief of protocols. He immediately removed her from the post.

"The next time I went in there I was wearing my uniform and packing a .357 magnum. I came up to the elevator, the door opened and there she was. She started staring at me, and her eyeballs got real big. She thought I was going to shoot her." But as MacRenato tells it, the lady in question wasn't the only one causing problems.

"When Somoza was in power, he had a mistress and everybody had to cater to her. Now, with the Sandinistas, there were about six of those women." One was Gioconda Belli, the sister of Humberto Belli, the current minister of education.

"Gioconda comes from a very wealthy family, and the Sandinistas came to power foaming at the mouth about the *burgesia*. Anybody who had a good pair of shoes and a clean shirt, they called him a *burgues*. But the Sandinistas still grabbed mistresses from the wealthiest families, and Gioconda was one of these.

"Gioconda had made a name for herself writing revolutionary poetry published by *Casa de las Americas* in Havana. She worked for Henry Ruiz, one of the nine *comandantes*, who was from a poor family. They were as opposite as you could imagine. Gioconda became the person who was running the ministry of economic planning. They used to joke that her best revolutionary credential was her pussy. Everybody was mad at her because she had a very abrasive personality. Even Ruiz eventually broke up with her.

"The Sandinistas moved quickly to squeeze out anyone who was not a Marxist. They made their working conditions unbearable. They would take you out of your office and make you listen to some idiot Marxist for three hours. Henry Lewites, minister of tourism, would drag everyone to these Marxist seminars. Lewites is now worth over $20 million, and he made all that during the Contra War. The people were starved for consumer goods and anyone who wanted them had to buy them from this guy. The country was the mercy of the government monopoly."

MacRenato also encountered the political tourists who became known as Sandalistas. "They were thoroughly despised by the people," he explains. "Many were dogmatic Marxists and more anti-American than the Sandinistas. One of them was Margaret Randall. She gave up her U.S. citizenship in the '60s and moved to Cuba, where she married a carpenter. I was at dinner with her once. She had only been in Nicaragua two weeks and took the side that the government was right no matter what. It was a perfect example of someone coming to a country and telling the natives what was good for them. That was paternalism – maternalism in this case. She wrote some book about Nicaraguan women and then decided she wanted to be an American citizen again and left."

MacRenato stayed but became increasingly disturbed about the direction the revolution was taking.

"Obviously there were people with hidden agendas, a Marxist blueprint for Nicaragua, but that's not what people were fighting for. People never wanted to impose a more controlled society than before, with censorship worse than any Latin American nation except Cuba. People used to throw rocks at photographers from *Barricada*, the official Sandinista paper, because they regarded them as spies for the secret police.

"In late December of 1979, they removed Larios from defense and put in Humberto Ortega. It was a coup d'état and nobody protested, not even Violeta Chamorro or Alfonso Robelo, who were in the government. Now, eleven years later that is the only post the Sandinistas refuse to give up, even with an overwhelming electoral defeat. This tells you how significant the move was at the time."

MacRenato found some of his best efforts rejected. "I was there to fight a revolution and use my military knowledge, but I also had a Peace Corps mentality. I even tried to get the Peace Corps to come back, but the *comandantes* were not interested. The Sandinistas wanted the Cubans. I also brought an offer of $9 million, and all they had to do was ask for it. They wouldn't have anything to do with that either.

"Some Sandinistas didn't trust me because I was not a Marxist and had a mind of my own. 'This guy thinks too much and asks too many questions,' they would say. Others knew what I did in the war and liked me. But I refused to become a political Moonie for them."

MacRenato stayed until March of 1980, a year before the Contra War began, and left on good terms. He emerged unscathed, unlike Somoza, who was assassinated in Paraguay. MacRenato believes the Montoneros, a group of Argentine revolutionaries, killed the dictator as an act of solidarity.

Another victim was Ezequiel, the teacher who led the guerrilla band behind enemy lines. "The Sandinistas killed him after the war," MacRenato says. "He was not a Marxist."

Eden Pastora survived an assassination attempt and is back doing what he did before the war, fishing for sharks. MacRenato's comrade Hugo Spadafora was not so lucky. His mentor Omar Torrijos died and Manuel Noriega took over.

"I heard that Noriega said, 'bring me the head of Hugo Spadafora,' who had exposed his drug dealing. Noriega's men took him literally," says MacRenato. "They pulled off Hugo's head by tying a rope around his neck and dragging him behind a vehicle. Now Kevin Buckley claims in *Panama: The Whole Story* that the Medellin cartel gave the order to kill Hugo."

Does MacRenato believe that he and fellow rebels did the right thing?

"I was once interviewed for a White House fellowship. One of the questions, which I didn't expect, was 'Do you regret anything in life?' I thought about it and realized that the correct answer was 'I regret nothing,' because there is nothing you can change.

"The fact that we were naïve in certain areas or were betrayed by the Marxists doesn't change the fact that we had to get rid of Somoza and his thieves. The people took care of business and got rid of the Sandinistas, although they are not all out. And to the extent that they remain, creating mischief, the economy will sink deeper and deeper.

"But we made the right move."

20. Those who do not remember the past.

A white sado-socialist leads 1,000 people, many of them black, to a Guyana commune, orders them to commit suicide, and they do it. Nothing like that had ever happened before. Twenty years later, as I discovered, key elements of the story remained obscure. That continues to this day, when many know nothing at all about Jim Jones and his high-profile political supporters.

The Death of God Socialist
Heterodoxy, November 1998

IT WAS LIKE ONE OF THOSE SIXTIES MYTHS, IN WHICH YOUNG PEOPLE FROM THE hinterlands journey to the epicenter of the cultural revolution to find a new identity in the new reality being built there.

If not for the gravitational pull of the New Age, the Reverend Jim Jones might have remained in Indiana, working the spiritual edges of its farming communities with a hardscrabble fervor the way generations of evangelists had done. Instead he journeyed west, to San Francisco, and was born again in the afterglow of the sixties. By the early seventies, he was embedded in the power structure of the City of Love, the People's Temple he had established there more a political than a spiritual presence. He rose in stature, proclaimed a kingdom of heaven on earth, and led his flock into the wilderness. But evil befell them. On November 18, 1978, 913 people, including 267 children, lay dead on the ground in Guyana, the largest known mass suicide in history.

The mass deaths of nearly 1,000 Americans, many of them black, shocked the world and set pundits, professors and shrinks scrambling to explain how such a thing could have happened in modern times. Film producers and documentarians rushed to cash in on the "Guyana cult," but they, like the intellectuals, managed to miss the core of the story.

Today, two decades after the Jonestown disaster, those who hailed Jim Jones first coming are not eager for that story, and their role in it, to emerge. Many others have simply forgotten those events, while few in the Generation X crowd have heard of the Jonestown holocaust. And the historical record hasn't been much clarified by recent media efforts to commemorate the twentieth anniversary.

On October 18, ABC's *20/20* dedicated an hour to the subject, including interviews with two of Jones' sons. One of them, Stephan, said that his father was "a fraud," a tepid enough evaluation given the outcome of his journey into the heart of the Guayanan darkness. Jim Jones Jr., the prophet's black adopted son, was pictured in the crumbling ruins of the New Jerusalem in the jungle, uncovering the vat from which Jones' flock drank the poisoned kool aid that took their lives. It was an indisputably dramatic moment, but the drama was self-contained. Viewers learned little about the forces that had been in play, and why the full meaning of the mass suicide remains a symbol for our time. Like much of the early analysis of Jonestown, the program did not mention the words socialism or Communism. Which was odd because Communism, almost as much as the megalomania that makes it lethal, was the driving force of Jim Jones' life. It was his commitment, as much as the outcome to which they had led, which made Jones a man of his time.

James Warren Jones was born in Crete, Indiana on May 13, 1931, in one of the cruelest years of the depression, and early on showed a cruel streak himself. ("I was read to kill by the end of the third grade," he once confessed.) The young Jones once took to combing his hair to one side and demanded that friends use the password "Heil Hitler" to enter the loft where they played. This was Ku Klucker country and Jones described his own father as a racist redneck. But his own religious inclinations startled his parents. He favored Pentecostalism with its rollicking "holly roller" style of worship, ecstatic reveries, and claims of healings and miracles as part of normal church experience. But Jones managed to combine attraction to the church as an institution, and to the revivalist form of worship, with rejection of traditional Christian theology and what he viewed as its fanciful "sky God." He remained a true believer in the social gospel, not a minority view but a strong trend in Protestantism since the 1920s, a vision of pie on the earth rather than pie in the sky. A vision of sharing, of holding things in common. Jones did not lack dedication to this vision or imagination in carrying it out. For a time he supported his ministry by selling monkeys door to door, at $29 a piece.

One of the influences which helped define the religious entrepreneur was Father Divine, "alias God," a celebrated black cult leader and head of a booming religious empire. Jones supported Father Divine's concerns over segregation and hoped to succeed him one day. The fiery Malcolm X also left a deep mark on Jones, who shared his view that Christianity was a threadbare hoax to keep the black man passive. Jones spent two years in Brazil, where he saw grinding poverty and encountered Marxism in an early form of "liberation theology." The Cuban Missile Crisis spawned the fear that an apocalypse was at hand, and hardened a hatred for his native country, the United States, that Jones had begun to nurture as early as the Korean War.

By 1964, when he was ordained in the Disciples of Christ denomination, Jones no longer believed in the Judeo-Christian God. His fake but effectively staged healings had made him an object of veneration from a growing flock at his People's Temple in Indianapolis, a kind of First Church of Jonesian Socialism. The socialist message did not resonate with the Bible-toting Hoosiers, who preferred the old-time religion of salvation from sin and eternal life an another world. But Jones and his congregation were planning a move to more receptive fields.

In 1962, *Esquire* proclaimed Eureka, California, one of the safest areas in the nation, upwind from every nuclear target. For Jones, who had predicted a nuclear holocaust on July 15, 1967, this cinched the decision to make northern California his home base. He began in Redwood Valley and his congregation hit stride as a member church in the Disciples of Christ, a denomination whose 1.5 million members then included J. Edgar Hoover and Lyndon Johnson, both of whom would have found it odd to be in a religious bed with this darkly charismatic figure.

"The only thing that brings perfect freedom, justice and equality, perfect love in all its beauty and holiness is socialism. Socialism!" the prophet spoke. He baptized members in the Temple's swimming pool "in the holy name of Socialism," a creed Jones believed he personally embodied. Jones portrayed himself as the fulfillment of Isaiah 7:20 "I come shaved with a razor," he said. "I come with the black hair of a raven. I come as God Socialist." He continued to put down the "sky God" of the Bible and to tell his flock that "I your socialist worker God, have given you all these things." On another occasion it was: "What is your god? Communism!"

Jones growing flock cheered wildly at such pronouncements, but being a member of the People's Temple involved more than being dazzled by God Socialist. It meant being subjected to him, and God Socialist was a jealous god, especially demanding of the inner circle he called, in good socialist style, the "Planning Commission." At meetings, Jones would challenge their bourgeois sexual conventions. This, of course, meant that he liberated many Temple women by claiming them as his personal sexual property. He bragged that he could "fuck for seven hours," and that this was part of his duty as a socialist leader. He ridiculed his followers for sexual inadequacies and preached that bisexuality was a revolutionary virtue and test of commitment.

During one meeting, Jones forced a white man to prove he was not a racist by performing oral sex on a black woman in the midst of her period. Rather than let her leave the meeting to relieve herself, Jones forced a woman to defecate in a can. Jones urged all good socialists to seek deep self-knowledge. Practically speaking, this meant that all good socialists had to be sodomized, a task for which he volunteered, telling the men that it was for their own good. At a Los Angeles church service Jones took aside a Vietnam veteran.

"Son," Jones said, "if you want me to fuck you in the ass, I will." The startled vet said that wasn't exactly what he had in mind. Jones replied, "just so you know I'm here if you want me."

One man wrote a confession about the therapeutic effect of his encounter with Jones: "Your fucking me in the ass was, as I see it now, necessary to get me to deal with my deep-seated repression against my homosexuality. I have felt resentment at being fucked even though I knew your motives were utterly pure."

It was only a matter of time before Jones' progressive, multi-racial congregation drew attention in San Francisco. He met Dr. Carlton B. Goodlett, a mainstay of the black community there since 1945. Tim Stoen, a graduate of Stanford Law School, became one of Jones' lieutenants and signed a statement that Jones had fathered his child, John. Stoen became assistant district attorney for San Francisco, where Jones set up a branch of his People's Temple in a yellow brick former synagogue on Geary Boulevard. The ministry grew by leaps and bounds, to a membership of some 3,000, with an additional thriving congregation in Los Angeles at the corner of Hoover and Alvarado. But it was in San Francisco where Jones gained the highest acclaim, in spite of what should have been fatal lapses.

On December 3, 1973, at Westlake Theatre across from MacArthur Park, then playing *Dirty Harry*, an undercover policemen went in the men's room to find the 42-year-old Jones advancing aggressively toward him while masturbating. The officer arrested Jones for lewd conduct. His public relations machine sprang into action and a doctor sympathetic to the Temple floated a story about urinary trouble. Then as now, in a city of revolutionary sex where the personal is the political, the zeitgeist did not disqualify someone arrested for lewd conduct from community leadership, nor even from praise. For the most part, Jones' socialist politics were politically correct, so the liberal luminaries of the time were disposed to overlook rumors about questionable activities at the Temple.

Jones' revivalist radicalism made him a perfect fit for Bay Area Communists like Angela Davis, for whom the People's Temple held rallies. Black Panther Huey Newton considered Jones a comrade, and the Temple received ringing endorsements from Laura Allende, Salvador's sister, and Dennis Banks of the American Indian Movement. Jones also cultivated the Black Muslims, who in 1976 joined him in a "Celebration of Brotherhood" featuring Los Angeles mayor Tom Bradley. Angela Davis, San Francisco District Attorney Joe Freitas, and California Lieutenant Governor Mervyn Dymally. At the event,

Jones said he wished Wallace Muhammad was running for President of the United States.

Jane Fonda was so impressed with the People's Temple that she wrote a thank-you note praising Jones as a man who had "redefined the role of the church. . . I also recommit myself to your congregation as an active and full participant, not only for myself but because I want my two children to have the experience."

A sign of Jones' arrival in the middle of the San Francisco power structure came when mayor George Moscone appointed him to the city's Housing Authority on October 18, 1976. The meetings soon became Jones' private forum, policed by a squad of Temple guards Jones called his "angels." After newspaper and magazine articles emerged citing abuses at the Temple, Moscone stonewalled requests for an investigation. Likewise, the state attorney general twice declined to investigate the Temple, despite reports that children were being abused there.

In the fall of 1976, at the dedication of Carter-Mondale headquarters, Jones gained a place on the platform with Rosalyn Carter, who sent a letter to Jones thanking him for his views on Cuba. On September 25, 1976, assemblyman Willie Brown, Mervyn Dymally, George Moscone, Angela Davis, *San Francisco Chronicle* city editor Steve Gavin, and leftist lawyers Charles Garry and Vincent Hallinan, joined many other luminaries in a tribute to Jones, who received approval from the state senate and San Francisco board of supervisors.

"Let me present to you what you should see every day when you look in the mirror in the early morning hours," said master of ceremonies Willie Brown, now mayor of San Francisco. "Let me present to you a combination of Martin King, Angela Davis, Albert Einstein, Chairman Mao." Jones stood to a thunderous ovation.

Walter Mondale praised the People's Temple for defending the First Amendment. Joseph Califano, secretary of HEW, praised his "commitment and compassion, your humanitarian principles. . . furthering the cause of human dignity." Sen. Hubert Humphrey said "The work of Reverend Jones and his congregation is a testimony to the positive and truly Christian approach to dealing with the myriad problems of our society today." Other tributes came from Sen. Warren Magnuson, Bella Abzug, Ron Dellums and Roy Wilkins. In 1975 the Foundation for Religion in American Life named Jones one of the 100 outstanding clergymen in America and in 1976 the *Los Angeles Herald Examiner* hailed him as "Humanitarian of the Year."

Jones had arrived but he had not left behind his paranoia, siege mentality and apocalyptic fantasies. Beneath all the praise from the Democratic Party machine, he continued to maintain what amounted to a private reign of terror, punishing dissenters, including children, and using sex and fear to maintain control over his flock.

Under Jones' reign, the People's Temple in the mid-1970s became part of a Bay Area radical stew that included revolutionary gangs such as the New World Liberation Front, the Black Liberation Army, Venceremos, and the Symbionese Liberation Army. Jim Jones also had a military dimension to his personality, stockpiling hundreds of weapons and maintaining an elaborate security system. Convinced that America was Babylon the doomed and that the CIA was out to get him, Jones looked for a place to build his kingdom.

He had visited Guyana in 1963 on his way back from Brazil and was impressed when in 1966 that nation won independence from Britain and soon elected a black socialist government. When Jones went back in 1973, leftist Guyanese leaders proved receptive to his plan for a settlement. Four years later, Temple members were arriving in Jonestown, their own socialist state, where their revivalist songbook included this refrain:

We are Communists today and we're
Communists all the way
Oh we're Communists today and we are glad.

Being lord of his own police state fed Jones' god complex. Away from prying reporters and politicians he proved that absolute power corrupts absolutely and that no tyrant is worse than the one who indulges his cruelties in the belief that they advance the cause of progress and social justice.

Jones forced people to prove their loyalty by signing false confessions and blank power-of-attorney forms. He continued to order the beatings of men and women and continued to coerce them into having sex with him in private and with others in public. Jones worked his members like slaves, which they in fact were. When some complained, his squad of "angels" dumped them into a trench, nine feet deep and nine foot square. Children were also beaten, thrown into the trench, tortured with electric shock, and had hot peppers stuffed into their rectums and even made to eat their own vomit. By one account, the screams of the children were amplified for others to hear.

It was supposed to be a police state walled off by solitude, but even from the jungle word began to leak out. Relatives of Temple inmates began to complain and some made trips to try and persuade family members to leave. These overtures, coupled with key defections, inflamed Jones' siege mentality. When members came back from the United States, they had to confess sins such as spending money on Big Macs, sold by rapacious corporations. Jones also taught his followers to hate their own relatives back in "Babylon." He ordered the entire community to file before a microphone and describe what torture and deaths they would recommend for their families. An elderly black woman said she would build a big church, put her relatives in it, and burn it to the ground. An eight-year-old boy proposed killing his mother, cutting her up and poisoning the pieces, then feeding them to the remaining relatives.

Jones began staging the suicide drills he called "white nights." If they went down, as Lenin said, they would slam the door on an empty house. The also considered moving to an even safer refuge in Stalinist redoubts like North Korea and Albania. But it was the Socialist Motherland that showed some interest, delighting Jones, who punished anyone who said Christ's birth was more important than the Russian Revolution.

The USSR was then on a roll, encouraged by U.S. defeats in Vietnam, and with successful pro-Soviet guerrilla movements in Angola, Mozambique and Ethiopia, and inroads in Latin America. Fedor Timofeyev, the Soviet consul in Guyana, arranged to visit Jonestown.

Jones ordered his followers to spend hours practicing Russian phrases to impress the Communist diplomat for whom they arranged a huge celebration.

"For many years we have made our sympathies publicly known," said Jones. "The United States is not our mother. The USSR is our spiritual motherland." Timofeyev expressed greetings to "the people of the first socialistic and Communistic community from the United States of America in Guyana and the world." Soviet publications made Jonestown the centerpiece of propaganda, but Jones was getting a little too crazy for the Soviets. He was finding it difficult to continue his role as God socialist without chemical support. He drank heavily and consumed drugs such as Demerol, Valium and Quaaludes. A September 25, 1978 letter he wrote to Jimmy Carter showed his state of mind.

"The schemes against us include some of the most devious strategies," he wrote to the president. "I have to leave the church. My wife is going to leave me. But she is attracted to you. Will you please have sex with her?"

Defectors, relatives and a few journalists had raised enough concern about the People's Temple to prompt California congressman Leo Ryan to consider whether Americans were being held against their will in Guyana. Ryan was a Bay Area liberal who had taken up the cause of baby harp seals off Newfoundland and authored the Hughes-Ryan amendment changing oversight of the CIA. In November of 1978 he led a delegation to Jonestown that included press and relatives of Temple members. Several days before they arrived, the riverboat *Cudjoe* delivered a piece of cargo that Jones had recently ordered from Georgetown: a 100-lb. drum of potassium cyanide.

Jones tried to stage his best show for Ryan but panic began when some members made it clear they wanted to leave with the delegation. For Jones it was a sign that the apocalypse was at hand that the CIA, sent from Babylon, was about to converge and despoil his socialist paradise. After his angels gunned down Ryan and three reporters, the real "white night" began. But not all went gently into that good night, not even some of the 267 children, 33 of whom had been born in Jonestown. Thirteen people died in Jones' house, including John Stoen and Kim Prokes, two boys he claimed to have fathered. Jones himself died by a .357 magnum slug to the head but the identity of the gunman remains a mystery. Temple member Annie Moore even shot the commune's chimpanzee, Mr. Muggs, before shooting herself. But before the nearly 1,000 bodies lay in piles. Jones last will and testament was being carried out.

The Temple had amassed more than $7 million in Venezuelan and Panamanian bank accounts and it was the wish of God Socialist to leave this money to the Socialist Motherland. Annie McGowan, the Temple secretary, arranged to transfer the $7 million to the Soviet Union, explaining, "We, as communists, want our money to be administered for the help to oppressed people all over the world, or in any way that your decision-making body sees fit."

Neither that detail, nor Jones' socialist fundamentalism, emerged in most of the early reporting. The public got little enlightenment from *Guyana: Cult of the Damned*, a film shot in Mexico. A CBS documentary depicted Jones as a good man victimized by others, mainly by women and the Father Divine character. These sensational treatments only hindered understanding of Jones and his victims.

The omnisexual Communist sadist who ushered hundreds to their deaths had emblazoned a sign, for all to see: "Those who do not remember the past are condemned to repeat it." That came from *Life of Reason* by George Santayana, who in the same passage wrote: "It is remarkable how insane and unimaginative utopias have generally been." The Jonestown holocaust is parable of the larger truth: no socialism without mass death, no socialism without terror. In an age dominated by the medical model of human behavior, in which sin is replaced by sickness and redemption by therapy, Jim Jones confirms the reality of evil. That is his heritage twenty years after the fact.

The old People's Temple on Geary Boulevard crumbled in San Francisco's last earthquake, but many of those who hailed Jim Jones remain. The stellar reception they gave him during his brief strut upon the Bay Area stage shows how liberals, unwilling to do the heavy lifting, have aided and abetted radicals who have no such qualms. Jim Jones was politically correct, and that was enough for Willie Brown,

Mervyn Dymally, Jane Fonda and many others. And despite the demise of Communism, the ideological superstitions that Jones lived for remain alive and well. The idea of a kingdom of heaven on earth, with wise leaders ordering life for the greater happiness of all, with all needs met, and all anxieties tranquilized, remains incredibly seductive. And in an age when institutional religion has been discredited, its comeback cannot be long delayed.

21. The Man Who Knew Too Much

The Hungarian revolution of 1956 is the first international event I remember with any clarity, a David-versus-Goliath story in which David makes a brave effort but loses for lack of support. Decades later, when working on *Hollywood Party*, I learned about Povl Bang-Jensen from Roy Brewer, the anti-communist Hollywood union boss who had been part of the Dane's support network. If Bang-Jenson wasn't a hero it's hard to say who might be, but as I noted, 30 years after his mysterious death, he was a forgotten man. Even after the end of the Cold War, the Soviets weren't talking but more than 50 years after his death, some people remember Povl Bang-Jensen. According to Wikipedia, "a tombstone was placed in Budapest, in Plot #301 of the New Cemetery of Rakoskeresztur, among those he fought for." And died for, as this piece contends.

An Unsolved "Suicide"
The Spectator, November 18, 1989

On 24 November, 1959, a Thanksgiving Day, the body of a man was discovered in a New York City park. There was a bullet hole through his right temple, a pistol in his hand, and a suicide note in his wallet. His name was Povl Bang-Jensen, a former diplomat whom Dag Hammarskjold, then-Secretary General of the United Nations, had fired. The events surrounding his dismissal and death caused a great stir at the time. Now, 30 years – and a Cold War – later they continue to mystify.

Povl-Bang-Jensen was born in Denmark in 1909 and became the leader of the Danish Liberal Party's youth movement. He was known as a champion of liberty and a staunch opponent of Nazism.

In 1939 Bang-Jensen came to the United States to study international law. He married Helen Nolan, an American, in 1939 and at the start of the World War II joined the Danish embassy in Washington, where he became First Secretary. After Hitler invaded Denmark on 9 April, 1940, the country's puppet government demanded that Denmark's ambassador to the United States, Henrik Kauffman, return home. Both he and Bang-Jensen refused and were tried for treason.

Kauffman set up a government in exile and Bang-Jensen became his key official. One of his biggest coups was the negotiation of a base deal, signed on 9 April, 1941, by which American forces gained access to Greenland, effectively preventing Nazi occupation. He also kept Danish ships sailing under their own flag and, as much as possible, serving the Allied cause. Further, Bang-Jensen took it upon himself to direct the Danish resistance forces.

Bang-Jensen remained with the Danish embassy through 1949 and was instrumental in Denmark's entry into NATO. Although he was anti-communist, he still considered himself a liberal and a strong supporter of the United Nations, then in its evangelical stage.

During the Soviet invasion of Hungary in 1956, a number of Hungarian freedom fighters pleaded with the UN for help but the organization did nothing while the tanks were rolling in. The following year, Bang-Jensen became the Deputy Secretary of the UN's belated Special Committee on Hungary. Exiled Hungarians were at first not cooperative, with good reason: relatives could be executed in place of those the occupational government called "traitors." But when Bang-Jensen, with UN approval, assured the exiles that their identities would remain secret, some came to Vienna and testified. But problems quickly arose.

The UN Secretariat reversed itself by demanding the list Bang-Jensen swore to keep secret. He knew there was a strong possibility that the names would be leaked to the Soviet Union and lead to savage reprisals. Accordingly, he refused to release the information. On 4 December, 1957, a UN official informed Bang-Jensen that by the order of the Secretary General, he had been suspended, but no reason was given for the action. He was told to tell no one and guards evicted him from the building. Such procedures were in complete violation of UN rules. In addition, UN officials leaked to the press a slanderous report that introduced new charges and described Bang-Jensen as an "over-sensitive, highly emotional man given to exaggeration and falsehood, who was driven out of his mind by cruel facts and overwork." The Dane's conduct, the report charged, "departed markedly from normal and rational standards of behavior."

This was only the beginning of a campaign of vilification led by high officials of the UN Secretariat. Bang-Jensen found himself slandered as "disordered," a "McCarthyite," an "alcoholic," a "psychopathic troublemaker," and a homosexual. Rumors were circulated that he had left his government "under a cloud." American Nobel Prize winner Ralph Bunche contended that Bang-Jensen was "hysterical," "mentally ill," and prone to violence.

Many who had known and worked with Bang-Jensen strenuously denied these wild accusations. These included Danish physicist Niels Bohr and a host of other eminent people in America and Europe. But in spite of this, and all Bang-Jensen's invaluable assistance during the war, the United States government sided completely with the UN Secretariat. Eleanor Roosevelt called attempts to defend Bang-Jensen "wicked."

On 24 January, 1958, Bang-Jensen burned the secret list on the roof of the UN building. At about this time, someone offered Bang-Jensen $20,000 to write a book critical of the UN. He refused, still thinking that he would be vindicated through official channels. But during his disciplinary trials before UN bodies he was not permitted to use documents essential to his defense.

On 3 July, 1958, Hammarskjold sacked Bang-Jensen, who got the news in a 19-page letter. Four days later, Hammarskjold made the letter public even though its many falsehoods and unsupported allegations were damaging to Bang-Jensen's reputation. Five days after the sacking the United Nations held a celebration of its 1948 human-rights declaration.

On 29 July, Bang-Jensen returned a UN severance check for $17, 416.65, still holding to the belief that he had acted properly and would eventually be cleared. He eventually found work with a relief agency at a fraction of his former salary. But through it all Bang-Jensen maintained his reputation among Eastern Bloc dissidents as someone who could be trusted.

Potential defectors gave him evidence that the Soviets controlled key UN agencies and also provided information that Soviet operatives were active in both the CIA and State Department. Since they were unwilling to approach either agency, they wanted Bang-Jensen to take their case directly to the President of the United States. He tried, but the highest he got was to Allan Dulles, and nothing came of it.

On Monday, 21 November, 1959, a neighbor gave Bang-Jensen a ride to the bus stop and this was the last time he was seen alive. When he was found dead three days later, many were troubled about the position of the body, which looked as though it had been carefully set in place. It was also neatly dressed and the face cleanly shaved. There were disturbing questions about the time of death and many other details.

The suicide note, for example, was in Bang-Jensen's handwriting and contained a phrase about "the forces I am dealing with," which his wife testified he had first heard from a potential defector, who may well have been a fraud. The police were puzzled by the "6A" which had been inscribed on one corner of the note. It was later revealed that the Hungarian exiles had testified at 6A Wallnerstrasse in Vienna. Moreover, Bang-Jensen had written to his wife that "under no circumstances" would he ever commit suicide. Such an act, he wrote, would be "completely contrary to my whole nature and to my religious convictions," adding that if any note was found to the opposite effect in his own handwriting, it would be "a fake." His psychiatrist, Frederick Freidenborg, contended that Bang-Jensen was entirely normal and positively anti-suicidal.

Many believe that he was a victim of a simulated suicide perpetrated by the KGB. One such case was that of Walter Krivitsky, the former head of Soviet military intelligence in Europe. He was found dead in a Washington hotel, with a suicide note in his pocket, but it was widely believed he had been murdered.

Without the UN's smear campaign to distort judgment, this

explanation seems the most plausible in the Bang-Jensen case. Motive, means, and opportunity all point to the Soviet Union. Perhaps the case could be reopened by the United States, the UN and, in the interests of *glasnost*, the Soviet Union.

And what about Denmark? After several inquiries, I have yet to receive a response from the Danish government as to its official position on Bang-Jensen and his death. It seems they too would rather forget about Povl Bang-Jensen.

22. "I'm glad what I done to you."

To all but the willfully blind, Elia Kazan is one of the great directors of all time, but for the American left he remained politically incorrect because he was a friendly witness before a government committee looking into Communism. He dealt with that subject in *On The Waterfront*, and his autobiography, *Elia Kazan: A Life*. But the Hollywood left still held it against him when he came up for an honorary Oscar. *Hollywood Party* had just come out in 1998, and one editor tasked me to write about the Kazan affair.

Elia Kazan: Feted but not forgiven.
Christian Science Monitor, March 10, 1999

THE CAMPAIGN TO DISRUPT THIS YEAR'S ACADEMY AWARDS HAS WHAT Hollywood calls a "back story." While claiming to protest an honorary Oscar for Elia Kazan, the campaign is part of a longstanding cover story about the major mass movement of our time, communism, and one of its leading characters, Josef Stalin.

Elia Kazan learned his craft in the early 1930s in New York's Group Theatre. In those Depression days, it seemed to many that democratic capitalism was finished, and that the Soviet Union represented the wave of the future.

When Kazan joined the Communist Party in 1934, he thought he had enlisted in "the victorious army of the future." But he quickly discovered that the party, like the Soviet regime that funded it, was a police state that told its artists what to do.

Though Kazan quit the party in 1936, he remained a man of the left. When the House Committee on Un-American Activities began investigating communism in Hollywood in 1947, he was directing

170

"Gentleman's Agreement," for which he won his first Oscar, and was not called to testify. By the time those hearings resumed in 1951, the world had changed.

Through the help of American Communist spies, the Soviet Union had acquired nuclear weapons. Stalin launched a new series of anti-Semitic purges that claimed thousands of writers and artists, including Kazan's mentor Vesevolod Meyerhold. By this time Kazan had become, in his words, "another man," a premature anti-Stalinist.

Kazan believed that Stalinist penetration of American institutions posed a threat to democracy at home and abroad, and that the government had a duty to investigate a political party that dutifully served as an adjunct of Soviet policy. He cooperated with the House committee, named names of former comrades in the Group Theatre. Though vilified by a party whose members avoided or defied the committee, Kazan refused to apologize and defended his stand in a New York Times notice and in the film "On the Waterfront." Accused of "ratting" on his buddies, Terry Malloy (Marlon Brando) shoots back, "I'm glad what I done to you. You hear that?"

Kazan directed "East of Eden" and "A Face in the Crowd," and also wrote novels such as "The Arrangement." By the late 1980s, there were few parallels to his body of work, but those who hand out the awards operated under a double standard that considered "stool pigeons" worse than Stalinists and made heroes out of those who refused to state their true beliefs to the committee.

In 1989, the American Film Institute rejected Kazan for a lifetime achievement award, and in 1996 the Los Angeles Film Critics Association passed him over in favor of Roger Corman, pioneer of low-budget horror flicks such as "Attack of the Crab Monsters."

This year the same group gave a career award to Abe Polonsky, one of Kazan's most bitter critics. Polonsky, screenwriter for "Body and Soul," played a major role in the Communist Party's inquisition of Albert Maltz, a novelist and screenwriter whose crime was to write an article disagreeing with the party doctrine that art must be a weapon. Maltz was forced to publicly denounce his stand and write a humiliating retraction.

This year's announcement of an honorary Oscar for Kazan touched off a protest led by writer Bernard Gordon, co-scriptwriter of "55 Days at Peking," who called the committee hearings a "reign of terror," and revealingly added "we must protest everything Citizen Kazan stood for."

Kazan stood for democracy and openly opposed Stalinist communism when it posed a clear danger to the United States. That is something Stalin's critics have never done, not even after the demise of the cold war and full revelation of Stalin's crimes, a revelation more eager received in Russia than America.

Kazan has been blacklisted by a campaign of carefully fondled hatreds. As actor Karl Malden has noted, the director deserves to be considered for his body of work alone.

The campaign of vilification against Elia Kazan obscures the little publicized reality that many in America remained silent, and even approving, in the face of Stalin's reign of terror. These are the ones who owe the apology, Kazan argued in his 1988 autobiography.

The record of Stalinism in America is something those who will take the nation into the next century need to know. This year's Academy Awards is a good place to start learning.

23. The Greatest Story Never Told

Full disclosure: I knew Herb Romerstein and he wrote a thoughtful review of my *Hollywood Party* book, which he found entertaining and educational. Herb Romerstein knew more about Soviet espionage than just about anyone outside the KGB, but he always resisted the temptation, as he used to say, to start with a button and sew on a coat. He only wrote about what was true, and that is also the practice of M. Stanton Evans on the subject of the late Senator Joe McCarthy. He may have tried to sew on a coat, but he really didn't know half of what was going on. Romerstein and Evans know much more, and handle it with care.

Stalin's Secret Agents Held High Posts In Cold War U.S.

M. Stanton Evans and Herbert Romerstein, *Stalin's Secret Agents: The Subversion of Roosevelt's Government*, Threshold Editions, 2012, 294 pages, $26.00
Carolina Journal, July 1, 2013

THE INTRODUCTION OF THIS TIMELY AND IMPORTANT BOOK PROCLAIMS "THE Greatest Story Never Told," and that is no exaggeration. Indeed, *Stalin's American Government* would also have been on target because his agents achieved massive penetration of the United States government and society during the Roosevelt administrations. Once in place the Stalinist agents wielded huge influence that damaged the United States and left casualties in the millions.

One reason Stalin's agents were able to achieve such success is because President Franklin Delano Roosevelt, whose disabilities had long been concealed from the public, was declining into decrepitude at a time when adulation of Stalin and his Communist regime was at its peak. In this account, FDR is surprised by policy positions to which he had already agreed.

It will also come as news to many that, at Yalta, FDR's concession to Saudi Arabia's King Ibn Saud "was to give him the six million Jews in the United States." This was edited out of the official record but survives in the Roosevelt library and the papers of Secretary of State Edward Stettinius. The authors helpfully show it here and note that the president's statement suggests "a lack of judgment, mental balance, or just plain common sense." The book makes a strong case that that FDR's posture toward Stalin, to say the least, also lacked judgment and common sense.

The policy was to give Stalin, a totalitarian dictator, everything he wanted without asking anything in return. A key architect of that policy, FDR's most powerful advisor, was Harry Hopkins, a social worker and Socialist Party alum who excelled at giving away other people's money. For most of his time in Washington Hopkins held no cabinet post but resided at the White House for three years, giving Stalin the inside track.

The authors show how Hopkins, Moscow's "principle agent" during the war, made sure Stalin got U.S. documents about the American nuclear program, and even a shipment of Uranium-235. Hopkins further wanted Stalin to keep all the Polish territory he grabbed under the Nazi-Soviet Pact, when then-allies Hitler and Stalin invaded Poland in 1939. Hopkins also blocked aid to Polish anti-Nazi fighters and backed Stalin on every demand.

"To read statements about these matters by Hopkins, FDR, and some historians of the era," say the authors, "is to enter a mental world where reality counts for little and delusion is set forth as self-evident wisdom." The authors also find it odd that FDR should single out Alger Hiss, a mid-level State Department employee, as someone who should go to the Yalta conference. *Stalin's Secret Agents* shows how Hiss served his Soviet bosses well.

By WWII Stalin had already murdered millions within the USSR and he wanted to execute 50,000 Germans after that nation surrendered. U.S. Treasury Secretary Henry Morgenthau wanted to help Stalin in that cause. The authors find it strange that the Treasury Department should be involved in such a move, perhaps explained by the reality that three key Treasury advisers were Soviet secret agents. So Stalin's influence was pervasive indeed, and giving him what he wanted had deadly consequences.

Stalin's Secret Agents shows how the western Allies acted as Stalin's enablers by handing over refugees and captives in Operation Keelhaul. "Horrendous scenes ensued as British and American soldiers bludgeoned helpless prisoners, herding them into boxcars and forcing them onto ships that would take them to their fate in Russia." Behind this atrocity the authors see the hand of Hiss and other agents, whose influence extended to personnel decisions.

Russia expert Charles Bohlen said the Soviets themselves took part in the campaign against Robert Kelly, a State Department scholar and expert on the Russian Revolution. His division was eliminated and he was packed off to Turkey. Kelly's ally Loy Henderson, another Soviet expert, was transferred to Iraq. Assistant Secretary of State Adolf Berle also ran afoul of the Hiss group and was sent to Brazil, "and that ended my diplomatic career," Berle said. But the influence did not end with government.

The cast includes media figures such as I.F. Stone, author of a book charging that South Korea invaded the North, a typical inversion of reality. Edgar Snow, who wrote for *Saturday Evening Post*, accepted Communist Party edits on *Red Star Over China,* "an unabashed commercial on behalf of the Communist Mao Tse-Tung and his Yenan comrades." And when the conflict swung to Asia, Stalin's network continued to conceal facts and was even able to rig a grand jury to prevent agents from exposure.

Plenty more here for everyone, including future Senator Alan Cranston of the Office of War Information cracking down on radio broadcasts he deemed adverse to Moscow. But this account is only "part of the Cold War story," say the authors. An historical blackout still exists "in too many places" and the information the authors were able to set forth is "fragmentary and episodic." On the other hand, "there is much more out there still to be tracked down by researchers of the future."

Stan Evans, author of *Blacklisted by History*, is getting into his emeritus years. Herb Romerstein, expert on Communism and author of *The KGB Against the Main Enemy*, passed away in May. So those new researchers need to pick up the torch from these veterans. Left-wing revisionism is surging, and as Orwell put it, those who control the past control the future.

24. PC Sex Ed

In the 1973 film *Sleeper*, set in the distant future, clarinetist Miles Monroe (Woody Allen) meets the poet Luna Schlosser (Diane Keaton), who boasts a PhD in oral sex. Something similar took place in California during the 1980s, with full approval of the state. This is the only piece in this collection edited for brevity.

University of Sex
Heterodoxy, March 1994

I KNOW IT IS GOING TO BE A DISTINCTIVE ACADEMIC EXPERIENCE WHEN THE woman who answers the door at the suburban San Diego house tells me to leave my shoes at the door. I paid $7 to join this "Mark Group" and I am not sure what to expect. Some guy is practically dry-humping a woman on the couch, although the pair attract little attention. Other couples are engaging in spontaneous massage, but it remains uncertain who had come with whom. I keep hearing the phrases: "doing" someone and "getting done by."

I sit across from a robust woman who looks like Tip O'Neill. Men outnumber women by a small margin. A woman who describes herself as "a healer, an actress and a travel agent" says that this is not usually the case in the Mark Groups. We go around the room for introductions, which sometimes digress into short autobiographies. The ages run from about 25 to over 60. There are five masseuses, many real estate people, some brokers and copier salesmen, and one guy with a charter bus business.

When asked why she came, a woman in a tight pink sweater responds: "To get turned on." Others say they wanted to meet people and have fun. "I had nothing else to do," one man volunteers, "and this is better than watching LA Law."

177

On the coffee table lies a book on how to lose weight during sex. Another elegant volume looks like it might contain Ansel Adams prints of Yosemite, but inside are Mapplethorpe-like photos of genitalia, Asian women doing their best Deep Throat imitations, and naked people probing each other's orifices in creative ways.

Finally, an ostensible leader of the gathering—a man named Aubry with limp hair and an overbite—introduces himself and announces the first game: mimicry. People pair off, and one member of each pair has to immediately repeat everything the other says. This, explains Aubry, "will help you focus attention on the other person and help you grow." The starting phrase is: "The last time I felt really free was. . ." For a minute or so the room sounds like a Pentecostal church meeting at full velocity.

Afterwards Aubry asks how people liked it. A few hands go up. Who didn't like it? A rather faded middle-aged woman named Angela raises a hand, "I thought it sucked," she says in a raspy voice.

Aubry announces the rules for the next game, "hot seat." The person so designated must answer all questions, as long as people raise their hands and say thank you.

"Are you rich?" someone asks a man who claims he took pictures of one girl beside his Rolls Royce. "Not really," he says. "Depends what you consider rich."

Someone asks an athletic looking man in a cutoff football jersey why he broke up with his girlfriend. "She said I was conceited, self-centered, and narcissistic," he explains, "but I'm really a naturally loving and giving person."

"How big are your chest and biceps?" someone else asks. He has no idea. Then someone asks about the size of another appendage.

"Twenty-seven inches," he replies.

"Ouch!" says Angela, the faded middle-aged woman who thought mimicry sucked and who, during the introductions, described herself as a "swinger." Then Mr. Jock explains "Twenty-seven inches from the floor." This wins him a laugh.

Now Angela is on the hot seat, and someone asks why she thinks the mimicry game sucks. "I don't like one-on-one," she says. Angela claimed she has had sex with five men at one time, but she doesn't practice S&M. "I like to stay in control," she says, without explaining how she kept control of the eager fivesome.

"Why is this called a 'Mark Group?'" someone then wants to know. It is a legitimate question. Our host, a freckled blond named Donna, responds. "Victor Baranco compares it to carnival barkers. The people they bring in are 'marks.' Everybody is a mark for something and with us it happens to be love."

Victor Baranco, it emerges, is the founder of More University in Lafayette, California, the institution where the hosts of this Mark Group and several of the participants in the session received their professional training. This group in San Diego has not been trying to revive arcane '60s lifestyles, as it sometimes seemed during the meeting, but doing school work, part of More University's recruiting program.

More's courses, the literature explains, include Basic Hexing, Aphrodisia, Mutual Pleasurable Stimulation of the Human Nervous System and A Weekend with Vic. The most unique thing about More is that it grants degrees. As California's official Council for Private Postsecondary and Vocational Education verifies, since 1979 the Golden State has approved More to grant Bachelor's and Master's degrees in the humanities and communications, and Ph.D. degrees in Lifestyles and Sensuality.

According to recent descriptions, More University's founder, Victor Baranco, 59, stands six-foot-two and weighs some 300 pounds. He is currently living in Hawaii where he has faced drug charges. He is not approachable.

"Dr. Baranco talks to people who have the proper requisites and three grand," Jackie Van Sinderen, More's Dean of Instruction, told the *Contra Costa Times*. She was referring to a More University course, Audience with Victor Baranco, which costs a cool $3,000. When *Times* reporter Michael Hytha travelled all the way to "Dr." Baranco's hideaway in Pupukea, Hawaii, he found himself confronted by a barechested bodyguard named Sam, who was polishing a white Cadillac in front of Baranco's purple house and who warned, "Vic doesn't like to speak with reporters." Yet as with the presidents of more conventional universities, Baranco has a curriculum vitae, however much he tries to hide it.

More's founder was born Wilbert V. Baranco in Oakland in 1934, the son of a black jazz pianist and a Jewish woman named Florida Mae. Baranco has claimed he was a gifted child but drummed out of Hebrew school because of "the black thing." He has also claimed he played in the 1954 Rose Bowl, but unfortunately Cal's squad didn't go to the Bowl that year.

Author David Felton profiled Baranco in his 1972 book, *Mindfuckers*, and the portrait was far from flattering. As Felton explained: "Charles Manson, Victor Baranco and Mel Lyman, the superheroes of the following stories, are mindfuckers simply because they have made it their business to fuck men's minds and to control them. They've succeeded by assuming godlike authority and using such mindfucking techniques as physical and verbal bullying and group humiliation." Baranco is the least well known of this threesome, but for all their other achievements, Manson and Lyman never established a school approved by the State of California to grant PhDs in sex.

Baranco earned his administrative credentials by joining the Sexual Freedom League in Berkeley in the 60s. Followers call Baranco Thought "responsible hedonism," but let Baranco explain: "It's like a boat. The woman is the steerer and the man is the motor. And once you can relax, men, and settle down into slavery in the motor room—what a gas! They take care of you sexually, feed you and clothe you. They take care of all your creature comforts and all you gotta do is shovel coal."

Felton portrays Baranco as a wheeler-dealer type, who along with Haight-Ashbury colleagues Robert Kerr and Paul Robbins set up the Institute for Human Abilities (IHA), a real estate corporation, in late 1969. Baranco and his pals bought derelict houses at low prices, got hippies to fix them up, then resold or rented the places at a handsome profit. But there was more to it than commerce.

The partners also published *Aquarius Magazine*, which advertised courses such as Basic Sensuality and A Weekend with Vic Baranco, both $45. Another subject of instruction was masturbation. According to Felton, Baranco and his followers had some doubts about intercourse. In the words of a man named Wayne, it is a "haphazard affair." Instead the institute recommended mutual masturbation as "a surefire way to a perfect orgasm every time. He called it 'doing' the other person, and told us how to do a perfect 'do.'"

The managing editor of *Aquarius* was a guy named Dewey, who ran the operation from a basement closet. Every month, Baranco would send in a taped "parable" for Dewey to transcribe and edit. Dewey said this was his "toughest task."

One parable concerned a woman who for a long time drove by a hitchhiker she saw every day, then finally decided to pick him up. He promptly killed her. ("There was no moral to the story," said Dewey, "but the heaviness was obvious.") Another parable was about "a bunch of wretched characters who lived in a concentration camp surrounded by squalor and barbed wire. There was no toilets, and their food was thrown on the ground with their shit. Every day an executioner would drag one of them to the chopping block and bloodily decapitate him in full view of the others." After several paragraphs of lurid description, it turned out the victims were actually chickens.

By one account, Baranco was influenced by "The Millionaire," a television program from the '50s in which a man of means gives away $ 1 million to a stranger in each episode. Another influence came from the Lloyd Douglas novel, *Magnificent Obsession,* in which a character gives away the family fortune to the needy. Baranco established Turn On To America (TOTA), as Felton describes it. "to collect government and foundation funds for alcoholics, nonplaceable foster children and parolees."

Baranco acquired the 16-acre Lafayette spread that currently houses More University in 1968. The grounds feature a main residence and houses, a studio, a house trailer, some shanties, tennis courts and assorted junk cars. The buildings are all painted a bright purple because that was the favorite color of Baranco's first wife Suzanne, whom he married in 1959. They bore two children then divorced in 1976. Suzanne, however continued to live on the Lafayette property, which neighbors call the "Purple Palace" and journalist have dubbed "Fuck U," a tag that fits in ways other than curriculum.

The campus features a lookout tower and guardhouses at each entrance. Armed guards prowl the property and signs warn: "No trespassing, unless you want your feelings hurt" and "Only cowards commit suicide slowly." Members of More's paying student body arrive in purple Cadillac limousines and get around on campus in golf carts, which travel on paths paved with carpet remains. A 1978 More course catalog explains that the school was established in 1967 to "expand the physical, spiritual and intellectual capacities, with tolerance for all apparent alien encounters." But the prophet of responsible hedonism found that, even in swinging California, tolerance has limits. In 1978, according to the *Contra Cost Times*, the county sued and got a court order that prohibits more than five unrelated people from living on the property. Baranco simply moved classes elsewhere, then moved them back when a court of appeals overturned the ban.

Also in 1978, Contra Costa County health officials reported that a three-year-old girl contracted gonorrhea while on the Lafayette property. No charges were brought, but the parents, who lived on campus, agreed to a $3,500 settlement with the county. That same year, Contra Costa sheriff's investigators said they had evidence that four men sexually molested two girls and a boy and that there had been illegal drug use at More. For reasons that remain unclear, the sheriffs called off the investigation, and there were no arrests or charges.

That same year, during the apotheosis of alternative lifestyles under Governor Jerry Brown, Baranco applied to the California Department of Education for approval, which the state granted in 1979 despite the troubling sexual incidents. More University could now award academic degrees.

According to Darlene Laval, who headed the state council that reviewed More in 1986, all one needed to do for approval at that time was show that they had a certain amount of money and a library, or access to one, "and that was about it." There was no review of the school's faculty, facilities, or curricula. State approval doubtless raised Baranco's self-esteem, even as it enhanced More's recruiting prospects. (Werner

Erhard of EST fame even attended a Baranco class.) But approval did not eliminate the school's public-relations problems.

Dr. Marc Hirsch had been serving as the head of More's Department of Medical Science. In 1980, California's Board of Medical Quality Assurance revoked Hirsch's license on the grounds that he had been prescribing excessive amounts of narcotics and mood-altering drugs. The same year Hirsch married Victor Baranco's ex-wife, Suzanne.

During 1981-82, More filed three lawsuits against the *Contra Costa Times*, which found the university a lively topic. Although all three suits were dismissed, the school's fondness for legal action was not diminished. Court records show that Baranco has been involved in nine lawsuits over property rights, including a long struggle with his own parents. The university recently filed a libel suit against the *San Francisco Chronicle*, which dubbed the school an "Academy of Carnal Knowledge." Still another suit involved Contra Costa County. During this tiff, More lawyer and longtime resident Richard Hyland said, "We'll consider suing everyone."

After the suits against the *Times* were dismissed, More continued its affairs with little publicity. Indeed, few people in the Bay Area know such a place exists, even though it operates a sort of extension campus in the purple More house in San Francisco (although the city at one time shut down Baranco's houses and "sanctuary" programs for code violations). Throughout the mid-1980s, Baranco was building up a faculty for his state-approved operation.

More's chief executive officer is Alexander Van Sinderen, 48, who majored in history at Stanford University, served in the Peace Corps from 1967-69, and did graduate work at Syracuse. Van Sinderen also holds a doctorate in lifestyles from More U. His dissertation was titled, "A Married Couple and a Single Woman as a Social and Sexual Unit." He and his wife live with a woman named Marilyn.

Jackie Van Sinderen, 48, Alex's wife and More's dean of instruction, is also a veteran of Stanford, the Peace Corps and Syracuse. A press account identifies Jackie as a former member of More University's boxing team, which was discontinued several years ago.

Suzanne Baranco Hirsch, 55, received her doctorate in sensuality from More University in 1980. Thus qualified, she has since chosen to pursue a career as dean of More's Sensuality Department. Former sociology major Cynthia Baranco, 40, married Victor Baranco in 1979 and now teaches at More and participates in Bay Area Mark Groups. More boasts a total of 34 faculty members, 15 of whom have doctorates—one from UCLA and 14 from More. The state lists More's chief administrator as Lilyan Binder, 43, a graduate of Hunter College and a former mental health counselor.

Eleven of More's courses were designed by Victor Baranco, who has described the "mutual stimulation" program as "making friends with another crotch." Expansion of Sexual Potential involves "hands-on guidance of agreed-upon, selected members of the Department of Sensuality," who lead couples "in the exploration of the parameters of their sexual response." The course has five prerequisites and costs $16,800. According to state officials, More's entire doctoral program will set a student back $43,200.

Just how much revenue the school brings in is not clear. The *Contra Costa Times* has reported that the various entities housed at More control $1.7 million in East Bay real estate and generate revenues of about $1 million. These "entities" are an interlocking directorate of non-profits including "Turn On To America" and "The Private Sector," which both deal with the homeless. To the Institute of Human Abilities Baranco has added Humore Inc., the real estate company in charge of the East Bay properties. Both Humore and the Institute are run from a property on Purson Lane in Lafayette, one of several residences owned by Baranco. The *Times* has also reported that in 1990 More reported total income of $958,140, though it is not clear what came from where.

Baranco's charitable impulses, some reporters discovered, did not extend to his parents. According to probate records, when Wilbert Baranco Sr. died in 1983, he disinherited his son. And when Victor's mother, Florida Mae, died in 1987, she left everything to Victor's two adult children. "As for our son," Florida Mae wrote, "he put us out of his life about 10 years ago. He didn't come to see his father before he died nor did he attend the funeral. . . he made it clear that he doesn't care about me."

Baranco may have put his parents out of his life, but he could not permanently avoid the scrutiny of the state, which had allowed him to function in loco parentis for years on his Lafayette campus. By the mid-1980s, California had tightened its rules for private post-secondary education. A team of educational inspectors were preparing for their first trip to the purple palace, completely unaware of what they would find.

"It was an eye-opener," says Darlene Laval, who chaired the state's regulatory council for five years and now works for the Department of Education as a consultant. In 1986 she and two colleagues spent two memorable days at More.

"Here were all these old limos and people sitting around in their underwear peeling potatoes," says Laval, who describes the place as "really filthy," to the point that "I would hesitate to drink their coffee." A guy named Jim, Laval says, "came out of a building buckling his pants, followed by a woman, who was followed by a child." One of the teachers also turned out to be a student.

"She said she had gotten her degree in sensuality and was now working on her other degree, for which she would have to spend a week with Vic," says Laval. "I said we need to talk to Vic, only to learn that he was 'too busy.'"

To maintain approved status, schools must send in a lengthy self-study. More's version said in one place: "Equipment to take to class: a towel, a mirror, and all body parts." This caused review team member Roz Elms, who earned her Ph.D. at U.C. Berkeley, to crack, "Doesn't that discriminate against the handicapped?" When she learned of the "Weekend with Vic" course, Elms asked, "Is there a weekend with Vickie?"

The inspection team wanted to see the classrooms and attend sessions. They were told they couldn't. In fact, says Laval, "They said none were being held. They said the classes were in Oakland." Aware of past complaints against the school, the team wanted to see the nursery. They were told that it was closed that day because a child had fallen and was "on the verge of dying." But a staffer did let them see one building that contained a state-of-the-art video studio with a gynecological table as its centerpiece.

"My mouth dropped," says Laval. She and Elms, imaginations running wild, asked about the purpose of the table. They were told that this was where Vic "did his sessions" in front of the student body. As Laval recalls, "They had a library of tapes of things like 'Vic's birthday party.' There were hundreds of tapes, in order and labeled. This was the only library we found at the place." Neither was there any required reading.

The team asked to see financial records. Such information was not available, they were told. "There was not one verification for any of the faculty," says Laval, "not one qualification for anything, let alone their speciality." The team then asked to read some theses and were handed a cardboard box containing eleven.

"Most were handwritten and none was bound," says Laval. "One woman wrote that Vic had kept a stimulation of a student going for seven hours and why couldn't her boyfriend do this? This was her thesis."

Roz Elms read a dissertation about sexual encounters titled "Recollections of a Married Couple and a Single Woman" and pronounced it "not original research." The paper was for a Ph.D, in Sensuality. Another paper was about pregnancy and contained nude photos.

By now the state review team was finding it "hard to be professional," as Laval puts it, and feeling dirty to boot. "They stuck us in this one-room shack, and there was no way for us to talk without them hearing us. They made phone calls with a hand cupped over the receiver, like some B-movie." But the visitors had seen all they needed to see.

More failed 108 out of 111 points of evaluation and the team recommended that approved status be denied. The council agreed, but More's lawyer showed up at the hearing and threatened Elms with a lawsuit for "lying" about the school and performing a "hatchet job." The school's advocate also charged that Laval "didn't know what she was talking about." More University appealed and won.

California was then in the process of changing its regulatory system, and the procedures used to review More were never officially adopted. While new regulations were being drafted, California grandfathered in More and a number of other schools with questionable qualifications.

More duly expanded its operations to New York, Philadelphia, Chicago, Atlanta and other cities.

The Lafayette campus maintained an uneasy truce with neighbors until the university started to house the homeless in the early 1990s. One family whose property borders More reported constant noise and garbage, including hypodermic needles, being dumped over the fence. Yet when neighbors complained, More said that it was a witch-hunt caused by the longstanding activism of Baranco and others at the university on behalf of the homeless.

"They are hiding behind the politically correct stuff," says a woman who asked not to be identified. "Nobody wants to be against the homeless." Morehouse attorney Richard Hyland had learned another PC trick. He pointed out that Baranco was of "black and Jewish heritage," and therefore the complaints were "based in racism." But, as it turned out, the homeless issue provided journalists with an opportunity to penetrate the purple curtain that had veiled More's inner doings for so long.

On May 27, 1992, Donna Hemmila and Carolyn Leider, two reporters for the *Contra Costa Times*, showed up at More claiming they needed a place to stay. A man named "Joe without hair" let them in. They registered at Waipuna Lounge, a 24-hour diner for guests, and here their discoveries began.

At More, the reporters learned, only first names are used. "Do you want clean underwear?" someone asked. Leider, who has examined the records of More's nonprofits in Sacramento, explains that More receives generous donations from corporations, including Jockey. The reporters also discovered that the campus had been upgraded since the 1986 site-review visit. It now boasted a closed-circuit television system. On that evening's "news," the top story was a series of party scenes with a potbellied man dumping ice cubes down a woman's bikini, followed by safe sex tips and gossip. In another feature, a woman sang an off-key version of Peggy Lee's "Fever."

Those described as the campus "elite" lived on the hill, and the reporters were warned not to get too close. But they did learn that the elite enjoy the service of female servants dressed in skimpy costumes, which they wear sans drawers in spite of Jockey's largesse. In addition to fashion, the faculty was also sensitive to non-homeless visitors. "They let them in but videotape their every move," Leider says. The communards are also sensitive to communication.

"You don't have any rights here," a More staffer named Tom barked when a homeless guy asked to use the phone. "So don't even think that you do."

The reporters were the only female visitors in a room full of guys they didn't know, many smoking and drinking beer. The pair spent most of the night playing cards and bailed out early the next morning.

John Koopman of the *Contra Costa Times* followed up on his colleagues' discoveries by attending a Basic Sensuality course with three other students: a dentist, an engineer and a veterinarian. The teacher was Joe Hills, who had the class talk about male and female genitalia and masturbation. He also asked them to strip and use mirrors to take a "visual inventory of [their] bodies." Homework questions asked whether they would have sex with men, midgets, paraplegics and animate. The course included a "do date," which, Koopman wrote, "usually consists of one person masturbating the other."

When Dan Reed of the *San Francisco Chronicle* went to the More campus, they ushered him into a room with a conference table across from the Van Sinderen *ménage a trois*. More staffers videotaped the entire interview, during which one of the scantily clad maids brought in water.

Reed discovered that More uses its own currency, called "scrip," which was once old Pall Mall cigarette packs embossed with the university seal, but which now resembles Monopoly money and is called "Karma Molecules."

Allan Steele, a hypnotherapist from Coral Gables, Florida, who treats sexual disorders, said he and his wife Rochelle paid $47,500 to the university for doctorate courses. "While I was living on campus there was encouragement to use illegal drugs, including the availability to purchase illegal drugs," Steele wrote in an April 5, 1992, letter to the California Council for Private Postsecondary Education. "They also engage in prostitution," Steele added, "that is, sex for money, with quotas [of conquests], which if not met results in threats of physical violence and exclusion."

Dan Reed reported that in late May 1992 the State Council demanded a response to the accusation but received none from More, which filed a $120 million libel suit against Steele. The hypnotist won't talk but stands by his allegations. More has also sued the *Chronicle* for libel, but the paper stands by its stories and has published no retraction. More's well-known litigiousness may have scared off "A Current Affair," interested in a story but wary of a prolonged legal wrangle.

The agency currently charged with protecting Californians from educational fraud is the Council for Private Postsecondary and Vocational Education (CPPVE), established in 1991. As its "fact sheet" says, the council certifies "that an institution meets minimum statutory standards for integrity, financial stability and educational quality, including the offering of bona fide instruction by qualified faculty and the appropriate assessment of students' achievement prior to, during and at the end of its program." Further there are "tuition refund formulas" should "the institution breach its contract with the students."

The state considers the task of protecting consumers from educational fraud so important that it pays the council's director, Kenneth A. Miller, a handsome $82,000 a year plus benefits. Other professional staffers earn in the $60,000 range. As those who try to contact them will verify, these people spend a lot of time away from their desks or flying around the country to conferences. But although it has taken stands on issues involving race, and gender and multiculturalism in other institutions, the CPPVE has, to date, done nothing about More.

"California is much more tolerant than the rest of the United States," explains the council's Ken Miller. "If something is legitimately new and innovative, they let it go ahead." Miller is vaguely aware of the sexual nature of the courses but allows that there has been "lots of research with Masters and Johnson." He has not visited the campus.

Nor has the council's official in charge of More, Dr. Betty Sundberg, who, like Miller, was unaware of the 1986 report of state investigators Elms and Laval. Sundberg says that More University recently applied for renewal of its approved status, which must be recertified every five years. Another inspection team will soon be scheduled. Miller concedes that the process will be "interesting."

Roz Elms is currently an administrator at the University of Northern Colorado. When she was told that, eight years after her site-review visit, this '60s time capsule continues to grant degrees with the state of California's approval, she reacts with stunned disbelief and anger.

"I'm appalled," Elms says. "I can't believe they didn't close that place," which she ranks with academic bottom-feeders such as acupuncture schools and "a guy who was granting doctorates out of a two-bedroom apartment."

California educrats have made life difficult for a number of private schools, particularly religious schools, even those whose academic achievement is unquestioned and whose faculty boast impeccable credentials. And yet the state has allowed More to thrive since 1979—fifteen years—for the most part undisturbed. But bureaucratic indifference and ineptitude alone cannot explain that longevity. An institution like More University could only thrive in the kind of society the '60s helped to create.

Note: "California eventually eliminated the category of postsecondary institution to which More University belonged," explains the current website for Lafayette Morehouse. "While we no longer award degrees, we continue to offer all the courses that comprised our degree programs. New courses are added to our curriculum as our ongoing research of pleasurable living continues to develop."

25. Exceptional Anti-Americanism

Back in the day I found Oliver Stone's *JFK* so ludicrous I thought I might get tossed from the theatre. Many of Stone's movies share a common villain, the United States. That also proved true in his 2012 book, in which the great director plays the part of an historian.

Oliver Stone, Peter Kuznick Book Recycles Stalinist Talking Points

Oliver Stone and Peter Kuznick, *The Untold History of the United States*, Gallery Books, 2012, 750 pages, $30.
Carolina Journal, April 1, 2013

"WE DON'T FOCUS ON MANY OF THE THINGS THE UNITED STATES HAS DONE right," explain Oliver Stone and Peter Kuznick. "We are more concerned with focusing a spotlight on what the United States has done wrong," what the authors call the "darker side of U.S. history."

From the outset the authors reject American exceptionalism and, as in Oliver Stone's movies, the United States is always the villain. From the Spanish American War through World Wars I and II, the Cold War, Central America and the Middle East, the authors show the United States in the worst possible light. None of it us "untold" and from start to finish one can hear the barrel being scraped. The prose style runs a heavy fever. For example, "Venezuelan dictator General Juan Vincente Gomez's brutal and rapacious regime made his country a favorite of American and British oil companies."

The authors profess to find nuclear weapons troubling but only in context. By setting off atomic bombs in Hiroshima and Nagasaki the United States, "once again, proved itself unready to provide the kind of leadership a desperate world cried out for."

Jimmy Carter gets some points as "marvelous ex-president" but catches heat for national security adviser for Zbignew Brzezinski, "an obsessed anti-Communist." The chapter on the Reagan years is subtly subtitled "Death Squads for Democracy." George H.W. Bush is "among the very worst presidents in U.S. history, if not the absolute worst" and his son no better. Even Barack Obama does not emerge unscathed.

Overall the United States emerges as the flywheel of fascist imperialism, headed by warlike racist buffoons eager to back murderous regimes by any means necessary. The authors never ask a key question: compared to what is the United States an evil empire? Consider their treatment of the Soviet Union, Stalin and Communism, America's major rivals in the past century. Here, in particular, does *Untold History* stand in need of stool-softener and a polygraph test.

The Nazi-Soviet Pact of 1939, which effectively started World War II, was an "unsavory deal" Stalin struck with Hitler because he feared a "German-Polish alliance" to attack the USSR. As noted in the *Black Book of Communism* and Timothy Snyder's *Bloodlands,* Stalin's USSR was a death squad, ruling by terror and murdering countless millions. For all its bulk *Untold History* lists only two atrocities for Stalin, the massacre of Polish officers in the Katyn forest and "having the Red Army stop on the banks of the Vistula while the Germans put down the Warsaw uprising." This is the moral equivalent of holocaust denial. The authors even include a photo of Russians mourning Stalin, whose death in 1953, some 50 years too late, was a cause for celebration.

Here the Soviet Union gets full credit for winning World War II and afterwards "had no blueprint for postwar Sovietization of Eastern Europe and hoped to maintain friendly and collaborative relations with its wartime allies." Further, the Soviets "had gone out of their way to guarantee West Berliners' access to food and coal from the eastern zone or from direct Soviet provisions." So with the USSR essentially a peaceful regime, no need for the heroic Berlin airlift touted in American schools.

Despite the occupation of half of Europe, the crushing of reform in Hungary and Czechoslovakia, and the invasion of Afghanistan, the "picture of a hostile, expansionist USSR," from CIA director William

Casey "didn't accord with the facts." And in the1983 KAL 007 shoot-down, the Soviets "mistakenly took a Korean Air Lines passenger jet for a spy plane." In the lexicon of neo-communism, the peaceful Soviets make "mistakes" and are evaluated by their aspirations. The militant United States commits crimes and is evaluated on the worst of its record.

In *Untold History* American Stalinists get off easy. Julius and Ethel Rosenberg, for example, are responsible for giving nuclear weapons to Stalin, the worst mass murder in history. Here they are only "accused atomic spies." For the real story see *The Rosenberg File*, by Ronald Radosh and Joyce Milton.

Stone and Kuznick predictably tout "three thousand brave American volunteers" who "went to Spain to battle the Fascists. . . the legendary Communist-backed Abraham Lincoln Brigade." For the real story of this sorry Stalinist militia see Cecil Eby's *Comrades and Commissars* and *Between the Bullet and the Lie*.

The star of *Untold History* is former vice-president Henry Wallace, the Progressive Party candidate in 1948 and portrayed here as a kind of American Mikhail Gorbachev, an endorser of the book along with Daniel Ellsberg and Bill Maher. The authors tout Wallace's "Century of the Common Man," but fail to note that, as one observer put it, Wallace's Communist backers confused the Common Man with the Comintern (the Communist International, the Soviets' agency for managing national Communist parties).

The book mentions the Hollywood Ten but does not chart how the Communist Party USA set the tone for politics in the American movie industry. After revelations of Stalin's crimes, the Soviet Union ceased to be a model for emulation but the anti-American demonology remained, mindless and sulfuric as ever. As Richard Grenier observed, Hollywood leftists charge that America is bad and capitalism is evil except for their three-picture deal with MGM, except for their fat bank accounts, except for their Malibu mansion, except for their Mercedes-Benz and Ferrari. So despite everything in *Untold History*, even Oliver Stone believes in some form of American exceptionalism.

26. "We are going to get you."

Bert Corona is a brave labor and civil rights leader, a champion of immigrants and the downtrodden, a man to be mentioned in the same breath as Cesar Chavez and Martin Luther King Jr. That was the politically correct line on Corona, but the reality proved different. My research revealed a hatemongering old-line Stalinist with a fondness for violence. As I noted in this article, educator Robert Cervantes discovered the same thing by direct experience.

Ethnic Politics Gets Nasty
Heterodoxy, October, 1999

"WE ARE GOING TO GET YOU, *PINCHE CABRON*," SAID THE VOICE ON THE phone, in the threatening manner of some ripped-off customer who was after the punk who had failed to pay off on a drug deal or gambling debt. But the recipient of the call was no small-time hood. He was Robert Cervantes, a former California assistant superintendent of education, with a Ph.D. in educational psychology. And he hadn't ripped off anyone. Quite the opposite, in fact. In the course of his duties as overseer of adult education programs, Cervantes had discovered that a group of so-called Community Based Organizations (CBOs) could not account for how they had spent millions in federal funds. Some of these funds, slated for English classes, had gone toward such educational items as jewelry and Mercedes-Benz automobiles. Those on the receiving end of the millions did not appreciate the publicity, and Cervantes was soon to learn that those threatening him were not just puffing wind.

Colleagues tipped him off that a former National Guardsman was being paid to find out where Cervantes lived. Gang types began hanging around his residence, and the houses on either side of Cervantes burned to the ground, with arson the probable cause. A graying, soft-spoken man who could pass for a high-school guidance counselor, Cervantes began to be very "security conscious." But these were only part of his woes. His revelations ultimately got him fired, a political decision yet to be reversed, even though he has been vindicated.

In July, California's state auditor, Kurt Sjoberg, confirmed every-thing Cervantes had said in a report that got little ink from a sleepy capital press corps and brought no comment from either Democratic governor Gray Davis or State Superintendent of Education Delaine Eastin. Both Eastin and Davis had good reason to keep the issue quiet, because what the state's press corps had missed was a story that re-vealed the dynamics of the ethnic politics increasingly dominating the state and tapped a vein of California history barred from discussion under the current regime of political correctness. The back story, and its key player, a man named Bert Corona, stretched all the way to the 1930s, to the heyday of the popular front. It confirmed that Democratic Party funding of the left is not history but news. And it was a case study of how a career path on the farthest reaches of the left can expect abun-dant rewards within the system.

The revelations of the July audit came larded in bureaucratic boil-erplate that failed to identify the groups in question, even though they were matters of public record and, in some cases, the subject of on-going FBI investigations. The ten CBOs involved are a kind of inter-locking directorate, with some serving as little more than front groups. The executive director of CBO number six, for example, is also on the board of CBO number one, and in their articles of incorporation, the addresses of the two organizations are conveniently the same.

CBO number one is the Mexican National Brotherhood, a nation-wide organization usually referred to by its Spanish name, *Hermandad Mexicana Nacional*. The Immigration and Naturalization Service once allowed Hermandad to conduct citizenship interviews but stopped the practice when misconduct came to light. The group was the key player in a 1996 voter-fraud scandal surrounding the narrow defeat of Republican Robert Dornan by Loretta Sanchez. Hermandad registered

721 people who were not American citizens, and 442 of them voted illegally.

The executive director of Hermandad, at the center of the CBO storm, is Bert Corona, occasionally referred to as Humberto Corona, hailed as a Latino leader, a colleague of Cesar Chavez, an advocate for immigrants, and a friend of Bill Clinton who keeps a residence in Washington.

Corona was born in El Paso, Texas, in 1918, and recalls that the high school there was integrated, including its sports teams. "I don't recall any racial tensions that accompanied playing at El Paso High," Corona told his biographer Mario Garcia. Still, some teachers "held racist versions of the Alamo." Though born in the United States, Corona did not think of himself as an American or even a Mexican-American. "We as Mexicans also had a historic and rightful claim to El Paso and the Southwest," he has said.

Corona recounts with delight stories he was told as a child of Pancho Villa's raiding party into New Mexico in 1916, recalling "how yellow the Americans had been, of how they had begged for their lives, how they had shit and pissed in their pants, crying '*No me mates, no me mates, yo soy amigo de los mejicanos.*'"

In the mid-1930s, Corona came to the University of Southern California on a basketball scholarship. Although he dropped out of USC, he learned to drive to his left. "Socialism could solve many of the problems created by capitalism," Corona told his biographer. "The Communist Party always stressed the example of the Soviet Union and of the significant progress there since the Bolshevik Revolution."

After leaving college, Corona worked with Harry Bridges, longshore boss and secret Communist, as the Venona intercepts of Soviet intelligence traffic confirm. Corona is unapologetic about his Party affiliations: "It is important to understand that a strong relationship existed between Mexican-American activists and the Communist Party in the 1930s." Further, "the Communist Party contained many dedicated people . . . not solely interested in promoting the Party but committed to advancing the cause of working and poor people." As an organization, he says, the CP played "a positive role in trying to build a democratic

196

trade-union movement that would be controlled by the rank and file."

Corona's beat was the Congress of Industrial Organizations (CIO), then solidly Communist in leadership. "The CIO developed a very important relationship with the growing number of Mexican youth gangs in the barrios," notes Corona. "While some delinquency and crimes were associated with gangs, many gangs served as mini-communities for youth." Corona would later cultivate similar relationships of his own.

By all evidence, Corona stayed the course during the Nazi-Soviet Pact, when the Party picketed the White House, called Roosevelt a warmonger, and Party-backed CIO unions struck American defense plants such as North American Aviation in Inglewood, California. Roosevelt called in the troops. Max Silver, a longtime Party boss in Los Angeles, identified Corona as a CP member before World War II, when Party members were given a leave of absence to be patriotic. Corona served on the board of directors of the Los Angeles Communist School with Party stalwarts LaRue McCormick, Eva Shafran, and Leo Gallagher.

After the war, the mass revolutionary upheaval many Communists had been expecting failed to materialize in America, but Corona continued organizing along the lines pioneered by Saul Alinsky. The strategy was based on the community service organization as a kind of front group, like the ones the Communist Party developed during the 1930s and '40s. Corona helpfully notes that ANMA, the Asociacion Nacional Mexico-Americana, was involved with both the longshoremen and the Mine, Mill, and Smelter Workers, a CP-led group that backed the making of *Salt of the Earth.*

Khrushchev's revelations about Stalin made things difficult for CP organizers during the 1950s, when the CIO joined with the anti-Communist American Federation of Labor. But the following decade turned things around for Corona, who kept the faith through hard times.

He busied himself running the Mexican American Political Association (MAPA), the successor to ANMA. In 1965, California Governor Edmund "Pat" Brown, Jerry's father, appointed Corona to the California Civil Rights Commission. Corona's Stalinism was to provide public-relations problems for Cesar Chavez, with whom he marched.

During the '60s, Corona threw MAPA's support to the Brown Berets, a Chicano militia styled after the Black Panthers, with its own "minister of information" and education, and which had begun in Los Angeles as "Young Citizens for Community Action." Corona organized the National Chicano Moratorium, to oppose U.S. involvement in Vietnam.

In 1968, Corona gave a nationally televised address to the Democratic National Convention in Chicago, urging the seating of the "Texas irregulars," a group that included Chicano militants. The following year Corona founded Hermandad Mexicana Nacional to work for the interests of immigrants, a new vanguard he exploited for other causes, bragging that "we also organized them in protest against the war" in Vietnam.

During the 1970s Corona broke with the Democrats and worked with the separatist La Raza Unida party based on the irredentist concept of a paradise lost called Aztlan, the occupied Chicano nation in the southwest that needs to be wrested from Anglos "by any means necessary."

Though he lacked a college degree, he secured a job as a part-time professor in the Chicano Studies Department at California State University-Los Angeles, where he taught for more than a decade, survived an attempt to fire him for liberal grading policies, and got many of his fellow activists hired. Described in a May 24, 1982, *Los Angeles Times* story as "an energetic man with a booming voice and a Marxist-Leninist viewpoint," Corona told Robert Cantu, a legitimate scholar about to gain tenure, to get out of the department because his retention in a tenured post would mean fewer part-time hires.

Cantu recalls that Corona surrounded himself with a "bunch of thugs," one of whom threatened the professor. Cantu held his ground but five days after he got tenure his car exploded into flames.

"What happened to your car is nothing," Cantu says Corona later told him. "We can get rid of you by getting the community against you. You may have tenure but you are not going to have peace."

Corona also opposed Professor Hector Soto-Perez, who found his tires slashed and brake cable cut. Corona blamed the attacks on the police, but after he left campus, the violence stopped. Corona went on to teaching stints at Cal State Northridge, UC Berkeley, Stanford, Yale, and Harvard. His message involved support for the increasingly unstable Communist regimes of Eastern Europe. "Renewed class struggle in these societies will lead to new forms of social arrangements," he said. "The workers of East Germany, for example, aren't about to give up easily many of the supports they had under socialism, such as low rents and free education for their children."

In 1996, the Southern California Library for Social Studies and Research, a legacy of the CP heyday in Southern California, honored Corona and his Hermandad troops. The sponsoring committee comprised an honor roll of the left wing of the Democratic Party, including Assemblyman Gil Cedillo; Antonio Villaraigosa, now California Assembly Speaker and aspiring mayor of Los Angeles; Tom Hayden, the New Left oracle and state senator; "Dobie Gillis" alum Sheila Keuhl, now head of the California Assembly's lesbian-left caucus; along with filmmaker John Sayles, Marxist professor Rudy Acuna, actor Ed Asner, and emeritus Communists Dorothy Healey, Paul Jarrico, and John Randolph.

By the time of that gala event, Hermandad, under Corona's helmsmanship, had become a kind of domestic Third World dictatorship, in style, tactics, and fiscal policy.

Corona had prevailed on the *Los Angeles Times* to stop using the phrase "illegal alien," which gave way to "undocumented." When the *Los Angeles Times* wrote about Hermandad registering non-citizens to vote, the group rushed a mob of 300 protesters to the paper's offices in Costa Mesa, demanding a boycott of the publication. It didn't work and, for all his leverage, Corona was unable to block the *Times* reporting on Hermandad's financial woes.

By 1997, despite receiving a staggering $35 million in grants during the previous decade, Corona's Hermandad was $8 million in debt, including $4.2 million on its new Los Angeles health clinic. In 1995, Hermandad was evicted from its North Hollywood office and sued for

$400,000 in back rent. Rank-and-file employees complained they had not been paid, but the lifestyle of Bert Corona did not suffer. Neither did that Orange County Hermandad boss Nativo Lopez, a Corona crony.

"The whole Hermandad organization is a money-making situation for him," said Al Chavez, a member of the Democratic Central Committee in Orange County. "He's very much building a political machine, and for some reason, very few people are willing to speak up about it." And there was lots to speak up about.

Hermandad used its employees' withholding taxes to pay bills, a violation of state and federal law. The U.S. Department of Health and Human Services demanded the return of a grant for $404,248 but no charges were filed. Corona's years of experience had tapped into multiple pipelines, and the group proved equally creative with federal funds received though California's Department of Education. CDE officials had long been aware of improprieties with Hermandad, but the group deployed strategic point-men within the department, tasked with keeping the money flowing.

Hermandad requested funding for a stupendous 22.4 million student hours, including one million in the same county as CBO 6, The TODEC Legal Center of Perris, its Siamese twin. The CDE approved all but 760,000 hours. CBO 6 produced records, obvious fabrications, showing every student attending every weekday from August 1997 to April 1998, including Labor Day, Christmas, New Year's, and Thanksgiving. One student was shown attending 3,406 hours in five classes, a Stakhanovite schedule that would have required a nine-hour class day. These were cons a high-school student could have conceived and which an Inspector Clouseau on downers would have spotted in an instant. And besides overlap among the groups, there is obvious duplication.

The services Hermandad, One-Stop Immigration and Education Center (CBO number two in the report), and others offer are widely available at other sources such as public schools, often free or at low rates. The entire flow of money was unnecessary, except as a gift to Corona.

Through the CDE, Hermandad received 23 grants, from $428,000 in 1994-95 to $3,500,000 in 1997-98, the largest funding to any CBO during those years. The department continued the funding even though Robert Cervantes noted concerns and Hermandad provided no documentation.

"There were no controls," says Cervantes. "It was the worst I had ever seen." The volcanic, white-maned Corona, lawyer and personal goon squad in tow, threatened Cervantes, accusing him of being a traitor to his people. Corona told Cervantes he did not want anyone snooping around his books and that he intended to put a stop to it.

State Education Superintendent Delaine Eastin, a former Bay Area Democratic assemblywoman, is the candidate of choice for the California Teachers Association, a Democratic Party stronghold. Eastin styles herself a tough advocate of accountability, but during the height of the misconduct her Department of Education gave all the CBOs a clean bill of health and took until June of 1998 to demand repayment of $4.3 million from Hermandad.

Corona took up the issue with Richard Polanco, telling the Democratic state senator from Los Angeles that Cervantes needed to be stopped. He was. Delaine Eastin had Cervantes fired, claiming, in classic bureaucratic style, that it had nothing to do with his work exposing the corrupt CBOs. Likewise, the state controller's office, under Democrat Kathleen Connell, reprimanded Alan Cates, who worked with Cervantes to uncover the fraud and is now with the FBI.

Though his organization was bankrupt, Corona found money to bus protesters to Sacramento, and won back most of a $2.1 million grant that had been denied in February of 1997. And despite the problems, the Department of Education awarded grants to Hermandad including another $3.5 million in October of 1997. For that year, Hermandad's request for 2.5 million student hours for citizenship classes was almost seven times the hours it reported in the previous year. None of the $4.4 million has been recovered and Corona, with full impunity, has openly defied the order to repay.

Some of the smaller organizations admitted misconduct and attempted to give some money back, but the California Department of Education refused to accept it. They took this as a license to spend it as they chose, and in one case, a woman used the federal funds to purchase a Mack 18-wheeler for her husband's trucking business. The total amount in the scandal, some auditors estimate, exceeds $50 million.

The Department of Education's response to the July 1999 audit, a true collector's item, said CBOs are "passionate about the work they do for their community," and "well intentioned about keeping accurate records." The CDE is not funding Hermandad for 2000 but the group should not be counted out. Bert Corona is a political Elfego Baca, with more than nine lives, and still livin' la vida militant after all these years. He knows the Republicans are out of power and fail to understand political combat even when in power. Better still, he knows that the Democratic Party establishment prefers not to know what its far-left hand is doing. Already, Corona's allies in the legislature are taking steps to keep the money flowing.

Assembly Bill 33, introduced by Nell Soto, and co-authored by, among others, Gil Cedillo and Tom Hayden, contains the "Tom Hayden Community-Based Parent Involvement Grant," which apportions money for "training courses for parents," with funds "directed to non-profit community-based organizations through a grant program administered by the State Department of Education" and conveniently channeled through school districts. State officials remain reluctant to place the CBO case where it belongs, with Attorney General Bill Lockyer, a liberal Democrat who claims to detest white-collar crime.

A small business owner who admitted in print that he used employee withholding to pay bills could expect to serve time, pay a heavy fine, or both. Likewise, the IRS does not accept "good intentions" as a defense in tax-fraud charges. Had the CBOs been linked to white separatists or the "religious right," groups that are also passionate about their work, the groups would have been shut down long ago and the ringleaders jailed. But no charges have yet been filed or arrests made, leaving Cervantes and other auditors baffled.

Despite an abundance of damning evidence, the investigations have dragged on for years. A member of a federal agency now looking into Hermandad downplays the fraud as a petty and typical matter, describes Corona as a "nice guy" and a hero to his people, a man who walked shoulder to shoulder with Cesar Chavez. The impression, clearly given, was that such a person, whatever they might have done in this case, couldn't possibly be charged with a crime, and that lack of funding in future might be sufficient punishment. If a case of this magnitude, with a clear paper trail, fails to produce charges or convictions, that will give the game away.

But the game is not over for Robert Cervantes, who has no regrets, stands by his work, and is going after the Department of Education in court over his firing. But he is now aware that being an auditor is a dangerous job, part of the violence inherent in the system.

"We're going to get you, *pinche cabron*," he repeats what his anonymous caller said. They are still trying. In late August, assailants deliberately sideswiped a car in front of his house.

Cervantes has learned that trying to do your job in an era of ethnic politics is truly quixotic.

27. A Vietnam Memorial

Full Disclosure: Like many others of my generation, I opposed the Vietnam War, spouted slogans and handed out antiwar propaganda. In 1987 while attending the Second Thoughts Conference with former leftist radicals, I happened to visit the Vietnam Memorial. On panel 10E, row 36, I found Marine Corps PFC Richard W. Billingsley of Glendale, California, killed in Quang Nam province on August 25, 1966. He was 22 years old. If anybody can see that memorial without breaking down, I certainly don't want to hear their problems.

C-SPAN's Book Notes recently provided another Vietnam Memorial when host Brian Lamb interviewed Lee Ellis. He had been shot down over Vietnam and served a stint in the infamous Hanoi Hilton. The tortures there were bad enough but a couple of Americans made that stay much worse. For many readers, Ellis' account will serve as a realistic introduction to Vietnam, Tom Hayden, and Jane Fonda.

Grim Account of Life in Infamous Hanoi Hilton Yields Leadership Lessons

Lee Ellis, *Leading with Honor: Leadership Lessons from the Hanoi Hilton*, FreedomStar Media, 2012, 233 pages, $18.95.
Carolina Journal, March 31, 2014

NAVY LT. PORTER HALYBURTON WAS A WHITE PILOT WHO HAILED FROM segregated North Carolina. His Communist captors put him in a cell with Maj. Fred Cherry, a black American pilot from segregated Virginia, hoping to exploit racial strife back in the USA. Instead, for six months Halyburton "completely attended to Cherry's every need."

Lee Ellis tells that story and many others in *Leading With Honor*: *Leadership Lessons from the Hanoi Hilton,* a place he knew well.

In November of 1967 Ellis was shot down on a mission to destroy the guns that protected the Quang Khe ferry that supplied the Ho Chi Minh Trail. Ellis was taken to the Hoa Lao prison, which American POWs dubbed the Hanoi Hilton. The author provides detailed drawings of the place but many readers know little or nothing about North Vietnam and its systematic torture of American POWs.

The North Vietnamese tortured more than 95 percent of American POWs including eight tortured to death. A full 40 percent of POWs remained in solitary confinement for more than six months, 20 percent for more than a year, 10 percent for more than two years, and several for more than four years. Pilot Ernie Brace spent five years in a cage in Laos and North Vietnam, where one of the regime's favorite tortures was the "Pretzel."

"After the prisoner's legs were tied together," Ellis writes, "his arms were laced tightly behind his back until the elbows touched and the shoulders were virtually pulled out of joint. Then the torturer would push the bound arms up and over the head, while applying pressure with a knee to the victim's back. During the torture, the circulation is cut off and the limbs to go sleep but the joint pain continues to increase as the ligaments and muscles tear. When the ropes are finally removed, circulation surges back into the 'dead' limbs, causing excruciating pain." *Leading With Honor* includes a sketch of the practice by POW Mike McGrath.

The Vietnamese Communists also strapped Ken Fisher to a stool in leg irons and kept him awake for 21 days. Others were kept awake more than two weeks then beaten. The North Vietnamese also used handcuffs that could be ratcheted down tighter and tighter until they cut off circulation, even cut into the muscle and on some men, "deep enough to expose bone." But the torture wasn't all physical.

The captors piped in propaganda and, Ellis explains, "the afternoon broadcasts were especially disheartening because they featured Americans spouting words that could have been written for them in Moscow and Hanoi." American Tom Hayden "was a regular speaker," later joined by his wife "film star Jane Fonda." For this pair, the American POWs were war criminals and their reports of torture were lies.

Ellis explains how POWs communicated with a tap code used by prisoners in the Soviet gulag and mentioned in Arthur Koestler's *Darkness at Noon*. They memorized literature, music and languages. Navy Lt. Denver Key taught a class in differential calculus, writing problems on the floor with a piece of brick. Ellis spent ten hours a day imagining the operation of a 40-acre farm. Lt. Dan Glenn designed a home and made a scale model of the place. Charley Plum was well on his way to making a radio when his captors intervened.

The POWs joked and laughed even though beatings and torture could easily follow. Ellis draws leadership lessons from the ordeal and challenges the notion that most Vietnam veterans are "societal failures." On the contrary, Ellis' fellow captives learned their lessons well.

"In the POW camps they chose courage over compromise, commitment over comfort, and pain over shame," Ellis writes. "Their character, refined in the fires of captivity, propelled them to success in a wide range of endeavors." From Ellis' POW group came 16 generals, six admirals, two U.S. ambassadors, two college presidents, two U.S. senators, one U.S. representative, several state legislators and assorted doctors, attorneys, corporate CEOs and diplomatic officials.

Some readers may wonder what happened to those who subjected American POWs to beatings, death by torture, and years of solitary confinement. Ellis leaves that theme unexplored, but by all indications the torturers have never been called to account. Neither have Tom Hayden and Jane Fonda, who were not "anti-war activists" but propagandists for the North Vietnamese regime.

Jane Fonda even partied it up with a North Vietnamese anti-aircraft squad. But unlike "Axis Sally," Mildred Gillars, who served jail time for broadcasting Nazi propaganda, "Hanoi Jane" suffered not at all. Fonda's money and prestige helped Tom Hayden, whose propaganda broadcasts so disheartened American POWs, gain public office in California.

The war in Vietnam continued after the United States pulled out in 1973 and in 1975 South Vietnam fell to the Communists. Hayden and Fonda celebrated the victory and remained uncritical of a Stalinist regime more repressive than its Soviet sponsors.

Leading With Honor deserves a wide readership, particularly in Washington DC where "leading from behind" is in vogue, and where the Vietnam Memorial bears the names of more than 58,000 Americans who gave their lives there.

Beyond the leadership and history lessons from that conflict, Lee Ellis guides readers to many valuable resources. They include James Hirsch's *Two Souls Indivisible: The Friendship that Saved Two Lives in Vietnam*, the story of Fred Cherry from Virginia and Porter Halyburton from North Carolina.

28. Fidelity to Fidel

In the course of writing "Half-Priced Hispanics: CBS and the Writers Guild Make a Barrio in Hollywood" for the April 1994 *Heterodoxy*, I came to know a small group of Cubans working in the entertainment industry. These included Orlando Jimenez-Leal, who made the documentary *8A* about Fidel Castro's show trial of General Arnaldo Ochoa. I also corresponded with Cuban cinematographer Nestor Alemendros, whose *Improper Conduct*, a collaboration with Jimenez-Leal, documented Castro's repressions. The views of actual Cubans on Fidel Castro's Communist dictatorship stand in stark contrast to those of American New Left icon Tom Hayden. He first visited Cuba in 1968, the same year Jean-Paul Sartre denounced the Castro regime, and has remained a fan ever since. In late 2014, when Barack Obama moved to normalize relations with Cuba, Hayden, a former California legislator, whooped it up in the *Sacramento Bee*.

"After the fall of the Soviet Union," he wrote, "there was a decade of American triumphalism based on the mistaken belief that the Cuban state would collapse like East Germany." Further, "The Cuban Revolution has achieved its aim," he wrote, "recognition of the sovereign right of its people to revolt against the Yankee Goliath and survive as a state in a sea of global solidarity." And so on. The *Bee* was kind enough to run my response offering a different perspective from actual Cuban friends.

Books, Movies by Cubans Offer a Different Take
Sacramento Bee, December 28, 2014

FORMER CALIFORNIA LEGISLATOR TOM HAYDEN CONTENDS THAT KEY EPIsodes in Cuban history are "best recalled" through "The Godfather:

Part II" ("50 years later it's time for closure and moving on"; Forum, Dec. 21). Those who seek actual knowledge of Cuba will find it in two films by actual Cubans.

When Cuban Gen. Arnaldo Ochoa returned from his military campaign in Africa, "8A," a play on his name, began to appear on walls all over the island. Cubans believed the popular general was the only one with a chance to topple Fidel Castro's communist dictatorship. Castro knew it, too.

He held a show trial for Ochoa and put it on satellite television. Cuban filmmaker Orlando Jimenez Leal taped it and made the documentary "8A." Viewers can see the regime's lawyers demanding that their clients get the death penalty.

Castro agreed and on July 13, 1989, duly carried out the sentence by firing squad, just like back in the day. No appeal process, and no more threat from Arnaldo Ochoa and others.

In "Improper Conduct," Jimenez Leal and cinematographer Nestor Almendros portrayed the Castro regime's repressions against political dissidents, journalists, poets and homosexuals. The New York Times called the film "convincing," and former Castro supporter Susan Sontag said, "The discovery that homosexuals were being persecuted in Cuba shows how much the left needs to evolve."

Hayden has written a new book, "Listen Yankee! Why Cuba Matters." Sounds fascinating, but readers might want to compare it to books by actual Cubans.

In "Against All Hope," which has been compared to Arthur Koestler's "Darkness at Noon," Cuban dissident Armando Valladares charts 20 years in Castro's prisons, and the violence he and other political prisoners suffered. Arrested in 1960, Valladares was not freed until 1982, through the efforts of French President Francois Mitterand and human rights organizations.

In "Family Portrait With Fidel," Carlos Franqui charts the Cuban Revolution from 1959 to 1964. Franqui broke ranks over Castro's shift to Soviet communism, after which "nothing worked." The privations of the regime get extensive treatment in Heberto Padilla's novel, "Heroes are Grazing in My Garden."

In "The Longest Romance," Humberto Fontova calculates that between 65,000 and 85,000 people have died trying to escape Cuba, 30 times the number of casualties at the Berlin Wall. Cuba's prison population includes Eusebio Penalver, "the world's longest suffering black political prisoner."

Hayden has written a great deal about himself but recently showed up in "Leading with Honor: Leadership Lessons from the Hanoi Hilton." Author Lee Ellis was shot down over North Vietnam, imprisoned and tortured. Americans were kept in cages with their legs tied together and arms laced behind the back until the elbows touched and shoulders pulled out of joint.

Some were kept awake for two weeks and beaten, but the treatment wasn't just physical. As Ellis explains, the guards piped in propaganda broadcasts by Hayden, a "regular speaker" who supported the regime and said the reports of torture were nothing but lies.

Hayden issued an apology of sorts, but his worshipful public relations for the Cuban regime questions his sincerity. That regime remains a one-party military dictatorship and massive violator of human rights. So Amnesty International reports will also serve as helpful companions to Hayden's new book.

29. Domestic Terrorists SLAy Innocents

During a bank robbery in April, 1975, the Symbionese Liberation Army killed Myrna Opsahl, an innocent woman. It took some 25 years to catch one of the perpetrators but that was hardly the only remarkable feature of the case. This feature headlined the final issue of *Heterodoxy,* where my work about "political correctness and other follies" had appeared since the early 1990s.

Remembering the Revolution
Heterodoxy, January/February 2001.

THE THREE WOMEN ENTERING THE CROCKER BANK IN CARMICHAEL, California, a Sacramento suburb, on a warm Monday morning in April, 1975, thought it odd that a foursome entering at the same time should be so heavily dressed, as though for hunting. Once inside, it became clear that they were indeed hunting. The four pulled masks over their faces, drew guns and the leader, a woman, began screaming.

"Down on the floor you motherfuckers! Get those noses on the carpet!"

Startled patrons and bank workers dropped to the floor as fast as they could but the shrieked commands left Myrna Opsahl, one of the three who had come to deposit funds from her church, in shock. She was a 42-year-old mother of four, married to Trygve Opsahl, a physician with whom she had worked in a medical mission in Trinidad. Before she could join her companions in the prone position, one of the heavily dressed bank robbers leveled a sawed-off double-barreled shotgun at her and rocked the woman with a blast that ripped open her torso. Mrs. Opsahl crumbled to the floor, her life bleeding away, as the foursome began looting the bank in Bonny-and-Clyde style, while one kept time with a wristwatch.

"Where's the traveler's checks?" demanded one, in a southern drawl, before methodically emptying the cash drawers, including two at the drive-through window. In the process, a pregnant teller received a kick that sent her into premature labor.

When Myrna's companions craned to see if she was still alive, the robbers kicked them and told them to stay down. They grabbed $15,000 and fled, leaving a trail of 9mm casings, and Myrna Opsahl. An ambulance sped the victim to American River Hospital, where her husband Trygve worked as a surgeon. He rushed to the operating table but by the time he got there Myrna was dead.

At first, few realized the bank hit was the work of the Symbionese Liberation Army (SLA). The group, whose symbol was a seven-headed cobra, assassinated Oakland school superintendent Marcus Forster, engaged in a series of robberies, and kidnapped Patty Hearst. As it happened, the newspaper heiress, now SLA soldier "Tanya," had been assigned to one of the get-away cars that day. According to Patty's later published account, the four SLA soldiers looting the bank were Kathy Soliah, Jim Kilgore, Michael Bortin, Bill Harris and Emily Harris, the "operations officer" who gunned down Myrna Opsahl.

"She's dead but it doesn't matter," said Emily Harris, back at the T Street safe house. "She' a bourgeois pig. Her husband is a doctor."

The four were jubilant that all the buckshot from the shotgun blast, fired by Emily Harris, had been absorbed by Myrna Opsahl, saving Jim Kilgore, who had been standing next to her, from injury. In full agreement was Kathy Soliah, an accomplished actress and Emily's sometime lover, whose manly garb and performance had convinced bank employees that all but one of the robbers were men, including Tanya herself. Neither she nor her SLA accomplices knew it at the time, but Soliah would one day qualify for full membership in the bourgeoisie as Sara Jane Olson, the hygienic wife of a wealthy Minnesota doctor.

Though doctor's wife and soccer mom were among the fugitive Soliah's best disguises, an "America's Most Wanted" program would make her a news item more than 20 years later and leave her waiting for trial after her long imposture. Soliah's case, finally on its way to court, reveals the staying power of a murderous ideology, double standards and ineptitude in American justice, and a left wing still blinded and bigoted after all these years.

As one who had been picked up scores of times for muggings and assault, Donald DeFreeze did not differ from a thousand common criminals, except that all his victims were black. DeFreeze also gained considerable expertise with firearms, which he at one time sold to Ron Karenga's United Slaves, rivals of the Black Panthers. While doing time for robbery and assault in Soledad prison, DeFreeze shoplifted his ideology through the Black Cultural Association, a prison support group, where he became a disciple of the George Jackson school of social change through violence.

DeFreeze escaped from Soledad and made his way to the Bay Area, a petrie dish in the late sixties for a variety of revolutionary groups. There his female comrades would be white middle-class women who aspired to full revolutionary status. One of them penned a poem:

Is it real to load a magazine of dreams?
No!
We say fire power to the people
Against the hire power of the ruling class
Who chained our hired hands, feet and genitals
Our grip on the gun grows stronger
And they will no longer see day
They'll feel what's real
From a magazine of steel

The group that hatched under DeFreeze-Cinque's incubation was the Symbionese Liberation Army, which DeFreeze pronounced "SymBIOnese" and was based on the concept of symbolism. The group's symbol, the seven-headed cobra that looked like a bad tattoo, was based on the principles of Kwanzaa, as outlined by Ron Karenga. DeFreeze took the *nom de guerre* of Cinque, after Cinque M'Tume, a Mendi chief given a number by Portuguese slave traders.

Cinque's army included Angela Atwood ("Gelina"), Bill Harris ("Teko"), Emily Harris ("Yolanda"), Nancy Ling Perry ("Fatizah"),

Camilla Hall ("Gabi"), Patricia Soltysik ("Mizmoon" and "Zoya") and Willie Wolfe ("Kojo"). These comrades were all deracinated middle-class whites, whom Field Marshall Cinque put through their paces in rigorous training exercises. The group survived by looting Goodwill boxes and lived in communes with names like Peking House, in a level of filth below the standards of the time. At one of their hideouts, the SLA kept a poster bearing smeared paint and two words: REVOLUTION and NIGGER.

Field Marshall Cinque sometimes forbade the troops to have sex but at other times freely partook of Patricia Soltysik, which infuriated Camilla Hall, an overweight activist lesbian, who had staked a claim of her own. Cinque also coupled with Fatizah and Yolanda, after getting drunk on palm wine, saving the bottles for use as Molotov cocktails. While the whites were pleased to have Cinque in command, other radical blacks dismissed DeFreeze as a promoter of "jive-ass adventurism."

Early on, the SLA's practice targets bore a sketch of Marcus Foster, the first black superintendent of the Oakland School District, then plagued by gangs and drug dealers. Foster planned to issue identity cards as a way to keep the dealers out. The plan even met with approval from local Black Panthers but the SLA considered it oppression. They marked Foster, whom they called a "honkie," for assassination. They put cyanide in the bullets because, as one comrade explained, "when you sure-kill shit you demoralize the establishment."

On November 6, 1973, election day, Cinque, along with SLA gunmen Russell Little and Joe Remiro, ambushed Foster, shooting him in the back seven times after a shotgun blast from the Field Marshal. Little and Remiro had painted their faces dark, a kind of militant minstrelsy, part of a Manson-like plan to have the hit blamed on black criminals.

The assassination of Foster was the SLA's debut act of terrorism and drew denunciations from the Bay Area left, but attracted neither the press coverage the SLA wanted, nor the police attention they did not want. At the time, the police were occupied with the Zebra killers, militant Black Muslims who were randomly assassinating whites. Cinque avoided police shakedowns of black men by dressing in drag.

Early the next year the SLA grabbed newspaper heiress Patricia Hearst and began issuing their communiqué:

"If any citizens attempt to aid the authorities or interfere with the implementation of this order they shall be executed immediately. This court hereby notifies the public and directs all combat unites in the future to shoot to kill any civilian who attempts to witness or interfere with any operation conducted by the people's forces against the fascist state. Should any attempt be made by authorities to rescue the prisoner, or to arrest of harm any SLA elements, the prisoner is to be executed. DEATH TO THE FASCIST INSECT THAT PREYS UPON THE LIFE OF THE PEOPLE."

Hearst came to sympathize with her captors and, as "Tania" took part in bank heists. She issued a communiqué of her own that the robbery "forced the corporate state to help finance the revolution" and described herself as a "soldier of the people's army."

Even though the SLA never had more than a dozen members, the police began to get tips and traced them to Los Angeles. On March 17, 1974, Field Marshal Cinque, Nancy Ling Perry, Patricia Soltysik, Angela Atwood, William Wolfe and Camilla Hall died in a shootout and fire. For the Bay Area left, the inferno conferred a kind of martyr status, but to join the SLA after it had been revealed as a homicidal gang took a special kind of person. One of the eager walk-ons was Kathy Soliah, who had been well trained for the position.

The oldest of five children, Soliah hailed from a middle-class family in Palmdale, a high-desert town north of Los Angeles, where she was a Girl Scout and churchgoer. She earned an education degree from UC Santa Barbara, where she fell in love with James Kilgore, later to become the SLA's chief bomb maker. In 1972 they moved north to Berkeley, where Soliah took night courses in radical politics. By day she worked at the Great Electric Underground restaurant, in the Bank of America building in San Francisco. There she attempted to organize restaurant workers, denouncing management as "agents of the ruling class." But she also showed an artistic side.

At the Company Theatre in Berkeley she played Hedda in *Hedda Gabler*. Her radical restaurant colleague, Angela Atwood, played

Thea. Producer Jerry Roth called Soliah an "excellent actress." Soliah and Atwood later created *Edward the Dyke*, a one-act play strong on foreshadowing.

Soliah operated the SLA's propaganda arm, the Bay Area Legal Collective. On June 2, 1974, the 27-year-old activist-actress organized a rally for the SLA in Berkeley's Ho Chi Minh Park, complete with plum wine bottles lined up in memory of Donald DeFreeze. Soliah claimed that "500 pigs in LA" had attacked and murdered her six comrades.

"Tania, Emily and Bill, you have made your message clear. Keep fighting. We are with you. I am with you," said Soliah. "I am a soldier of the SLA."

With her hair long, Soliah would not have been out of place among those who followed Charles Manson. But as her FBI wanted poster shows, she also sported a pert, short-and-sassy look, like Olympic skater Dorothy Hamill. And Soliah was now "with" Emily Harris in a literal sense.

The two became lovers and wanted to live separately from the men, in the women's collective with Wendy Yoshimura, Patty Hearst, and Kathy's sister Josephine. Under this regime of gender apartheid, the SLA's "jive-ass adventurism" took a feminist tack. The SLA sisters called sexism the "primary contradiction" and issued a statement that "out of the Women's Movement we see emerging the potential leadership of white people in the coming revolutionary struggle." That struggle involved robbing banks where actual working people put their money.

The remaining SLA troop set up shop in Sacramento, where the anti-war movement and counterculture revolution never gained much traction. During their January 1975 robbery of the Guild Savings and Loan, Soliah sat in a coffee shop across the street and timed the police response. The women insisted that they be given a leading role, to be showcased in the Carmichael robbery, where the SLA claimed their second murder victim.

Undisturbed by the murder of an innocent woman, the SLA gang launched a campaign to murder policemen and veterans. The group bombed the Marin County Civic Center and attempted to plant "anti-personnel" bombs packed with nails in a veterans' convention. In August of 1975, Los Angeles prosecutors believe, Soliah slipped two pipe bombs under a police car, part of a revenge attack.

Meanwhile, back in the Bay Area, Soliah worked as a waitress at the Plate of Brasse, under the revealing alias of Kathleen Anger. She joined her sister, former boyfriend James Kilgore, and Patty Hearst painting apartments in Pacifica, a non-union job. By some accounts, Soliah set up the New Dawn Collective with the New World Liberation Front, connected to at least 70 bombings, and which put out a death warrant on then-San Francisco mayor Dianne Feinstein.

The police eventually bagged Joe Remiro and Russell Little, killers of Marcus Foster, and bank robber Patty "Tania" Hearst. Also arrested were the Harrises and Kathy's brother Steven. Kathy's desire to be a soldier of the SLA did not including doing hard time. She fled east, changing her name to Sarah Jane Olson, after Sara Jane Moore, who tried to assassinate president Gerald Ford.

Olson is a common name in Minnesota, where many are of Scandinavian descent. The Opsahl family, as it happens, is of Norwegian background. The fugitive would soon add another touch of irony as she starred in what would become the major role of her life: wholesome, progressive doctor's wife, bearing three children, active in the community, and taking part in local theatre.

St. Paul, Minnesota, was a long way from the crime scene and accomplices. Better, from Soliah's point of view to be straddling a wealthy doctor in posh suburbia than to couple with Emily Harris in a stinking San Francisco safe-house, with her brother and Patty Hearst listening in the next room, guns on the table, and maybe the cops about to crash in. What Fred G. Peterson, an esteemed local physician, saw in the thespian fugitive remains unclear. Even then she bore a gaunt, hard look, with none of the physical charm of Patty Hearst. But Olson-Soliah had little trouble leveraging the good doctor into the bourgeois convention of marriage. The couple soon enjoyed an upper-class lifestyle in the exclusive Highland Park section of St. Paul.

For Olson-Soliah, it was the best safe-house ever, and as she doubtless considered, good forever. Under this cover, the bisexual adventuress could easily slip away for secret meetings with old comrades. Her former lover Emily Harris is living under a new name in southern California, where she works with computers. Bill Harris is a private investigator in the Bay Area. Michael Bortin, married to Josephine Soliah, Kathleen's sister, is living in Portland, Oregon. Brother Steven lives in Berkeley. Wendy Yoshimura, one of the drivers for the Carmichael heist, is now an artist in Oakland. Soliah also could have met with former boyfriend James Kilgore, a fellow fugitive also wanted on explosives charges. But like Kilgore, Soliah had not been forgotten. The FBI sought her for an offense similar to that of Timothy McVeigh, possession of a destructive device with intent to commit murder.

The actress-fugitive got her own segment on "America's Most Wanted." Though the doctor's wife now bore more than a passing resemblance to actor James Woods or rocker Edgar Winter, the genuine item was still apparent enough for an alert Minnesotan to make the connection. On June 16, 1999, the cops came knocking for Kathleen Soliah and found her. Doubtless stunned at being busted, Olson-Soliah quickly launched herself into a new role, victim, with guaranteed high ratings and an eager support network that helped raise $1 million in bail, a kind of Symbionese Alibi Armory that included leading Democrats.

Sandy Pappas, a St. Paul mayoral candidate for whom Olson-Soliah raised funds, attacked the FBI for tracking her down. "Don't they have any real crimes to fight?" she said. Andy Dawkins, also a candidate for mayor, defended her in a television appearance.

"We all support her and hope she will be acquitted with the love of God," said a member of the Minnehaha United Methodist Church, where Olson is a member. Twenty members of the church came to California for her arraignment. In Berkeley, the city council made Soliah the subject of a resolution:

"Whereas, over the past 23 years Sara Jane Olson (AKA Kathleen Ann Soliah) has married, raised three daughters, and become a productive civic-minded member of her community, all of which is being disputed by the resurrection of these decades-old charges."

The Berkeley council invoked causes from Sacco and Vanzetti to the Black Panthers and said that the prosecution of Olson would be a campaign to "punish political ideas."

Weatherwoman Bernadine Dorhn, who emerged from the underground of bombing campaigns to respectability in the legal profession without so much as a by-your-leave, also chipped in: "It was the particular responsibility of white radicals from privileged backgrounds with education, to hurl themselves into the struggle and to not have other people always paying the cost of struggle. What we have here is a kind of re-growth of prosecutor-police discretion determined to make this a massive show-trial of the violence of the 60s."

Olson has attempted capitalize on the publicity by posing, as one account had it, as a cross between Mother Teresa and Martha Stewart. But the cookbook she wrote, *Serving America's Most Wanted Recipes*, suggests how repentant she is.

In the book, she claims her daughters have suffered from anorexia, blaming this on the "symbolic and psychological values" America attaches to food. So American society is still evil. She poses alongside the clenched fist of the black power movement. American society should still be changed by any means necessary. "What bothers me the most is that she plays the victim," says Jon Opsahl, who was 15 when the SLA gunned down his mother. "Her actions were callous and willful. Her attitude hasn't changed, no remorse. She tries to get people to think she's a victim."

Jon Opsahl tells anyone who will listen that the SLA murdered his mother and should not be allowed to get away with it. He has written to California governor Gray Davis and maintains an exhaustive knowledge of the case. The police not only have a palm print of Soliah from the SLA's Sacramento garage but other evidence has come to light, including matching shell casings and bills from the robbery.

Despite the evidence and several accounts, including Patty Hearst's, placing Kathleen Soliah in the bank, the Sacramento District attorney Jan Scully, a Republican woman who ran on a law-and-order ticket, says that the case "continues to be unprosecutable." The Los Angeles authorities, by contrast, have pleaded with Sacramento to prosecute the case themselves, even as they pursue the conspiracy and explosive charges against Olson-Soliah.

That case will come to trial in April, the same month the SLA gang murdered Myrna Opsahl. Patty Hearst, who had her own sentence commuted by Jimmy Carter, will likely testify, a prospect that disturbs Olson. She had not been speaking to the press but when Bill Clinton, in one of his final acts, pardoned Hearst, it set the SLA veteran off.

"Just because Clinton pardoned Patty Hearst does not mean her story is true," she huffed. "Money, access to power and friends in high places have once again, as with her earlier commutation, influenced presidential prerogative in favor of Patricia Hearst."

Ever the dramatist, Soliah plays in the melodrama featuring Pampered Patty, the favorite of power, versus poor Sara, woman of the people. Actually Hearst became, like her captors, a bank robber. Soliah became, like her gang's victim, a doctor's wife. But the real play within this play is one involving the sixties and its enduring view of America. Soliah and her supporters on the reprobate left believe that the freest and most prosperous society ever to exist is really a bastion of oppression, that efforts to change it through violence were justified during the 60s and '70s, that innocent victims such as Marcus Foster and Myrna Opsahl were bourgeois pigs who deserved what they got, and that the relatives of the victims are unenlightened types who don't understand what it was like back then, and who should just quit their complaining, shut their mouths, and go away. To maintain that vision involves a loss of humanity, which makes Kathleen Soliah more of a female impersonator than a felon masquerading as a soccer mom. Other revelations may well be in store.

Ordinary Americans have little tolerance for terrorism, whatever the causes the gunmen and bombers espouse. And as the last election showed, ordinary Americans, particularly those on the conservative side, have shown themselves more willing to hit the streets in protest, a welcome and long overdue development. While Sara Jane Olson, aka Kathleen Ann Soliah, aka Kathleen Anger, plays her victim routine for an audience of jurors in a Los Angeles courtroom, outside in the streets there could well be protesters bearing signs reading, for all we know: JAIL THE TERRORIST INSECT WHO PREYS UPON THE LIVES OF THE PEOPLE.

NOTE: In October, 2001, Olson-Soliah pleaded guilty to two counts of attempting to ignite an explosive. In January 2002 she was sentenced to 20 years to life, later reduced by the parole board. In 2003 Olson-Soliah pleaded guilty to second-degree murder and was sentenced to five years to life. She gained release in March of 2009.

30. "I mean, look, shit happens."

When I first wandered around California, "with no particular place to go," as Chuck Berry said, the governor was Ronald Reagan. Some years later, when I moved the family to California, the governor was Jerry Brown, son of former governor Edmund "Pat" Brown. A consort of Linda Ronstadt and a serial presidential candidate, Jerry Brown needs no introduction. At this writing, Brown is in his fourth and final term. Biographer Chuck McFadden couldn't wait that long but, as I discovered, his account manages to miss just a bit more than Governor Moonbeam's last four years in office.

Brown Happens

A new biography overlooks key episodes in the California governor's career.

City Journal California, May 23, 2013.

CALIFORNIA GOVERNOR JERRY BROWN HAS BEEN IN THE PUBLIC EYE FOR more than four decades, shifting with the tides of public opinion, beguiling his friends and outsmarting his foes at almost every turn. For many Americans, he'll always be "Moonbeam." But there is far more to Brown's story than an old Mike Royko nickname. *Trailblazer: A Biography of Jerry Brown*, by longtime Associated Press writer Chuck McFadden, serves as an entertaining primer—even if the author ignores important aspects of the governor's career.

Edmund G. "Jerry" Brown, Jr. grew up in a five-bedroom house in the comfortable Forest Hills section of San Francisco, where he attended the best schools. The man who would one day refuse to live in the governor's mansion went on to buy a house with a swimming pool in upscale Laurel Canyon and, years later, a $1.8 million "live-work loft" in Oakland. Brown's Jesuit training, writes McFadden, "instilled in him a certain amount of intellectual arrogance, a liking for austerity, and a sense of righteousness that has manifested itself throughout his political career." His father, Edmund G. "Pat" Brown, became governor when Jerry was still a student, and the son made the most of it. Even before passing the bar, Brown "breezed into a clerkship" for a state supreme court judge.

Brown "internalized his father's ferocious ambition" and tapped his extensive political network for campaign funding. Houston Flournoy, his Republican opponent in his first race for governor in 1974, told him, "If your name was Jerry Green you wouldn't be here today." McFadden credits the Patty Hearst kidnapping saga, which began that year, for "lessening coverage of the campaign and helping Brown with his built-in advantage of name recognition." He beat Flournoy by 2.9 percentage points and got to work on collective bargaining for farmworkers and state employees.

California homeowners fared poorly during Brown's first term. Property taxes increased 120 percent between 1974 and 1978, and people worried that they might lose their homes. Worse, "no one in Sacramento seemed to be listening," including Brown. Enter Proposition 13, which amended the state's constitution to limit the growth of property taxes—appropriately enough, as the state was running a budget surplus. McFadden fails to point out that Prop. 13, though perennially blamed for California's financial woes, did not raise state spending or government employees' pay, mandated no new state hires, and created no new state agencies. Legislators and special interests saw to that. Brown attacked Prop. 13 as a "fraud" and a "rip-off," but it passed with 65 percent of the vote. "Instantly Jerry Brown performed one of the most dazzling flip-flops in the history of American politics," McFadden writes, and proclaimed himself a "born-again tax cutter."

Of course, Prop. 13 wasn't the first or last time Brown found himself at odds with the people. In a move that some saw as evidence of his rebellious streak, he appointed his University of California at Berkeley chum, Rose Bird, to the state supreme court. Voters rebelled, booting the stridently anti–capital punishment Bird off the court in 1986, along with fellow Brown appointees Cruz Reynoso and Joseph Grodin, "the first justices to be removed by voters in a retention election." In the late 1970s, Brown appointed actress Jane Fonda to the California Arts Council. Fonda had earned the lasting ire of Vietnam veterans and millions of Americans for making a friendly visit to North Vietnam during the war. McFadden ignores this episode, as well as the controversy surrounding Dennis Banks, a founder of the American Indian Movement. Banks was convicted of riot and assault for a 1973 courthouse gun battle in South Dakota. He fled to California, and Brown refused to extradite him.

McFadden does note that Mario Obledo, Brown's first health and welfare secretary, was a "poor administrator" known for "unfairly favoring Hispanic job applicants." That kind of discrimination, along with admissions quotas at the University of California, led voters to pass Proposition 209, which forbids racial, ethnic, and gender preferences in state employment, education, and contracting. Brown was not in public office in 1996, when the initiative passed, but he opposed Prop. 209 from the beginning. Later, as attorney general, he filed several court briefs against it. McFadden ignores Brown's record on the issue.

While still a novice as governor, Brown made his first run at the presidency. He would try three times in all, once even making a conservative flat tax part of his platform. In 1982, he also lost a bid for the Senate to Pete Wilson, who later became California's governor. Brown then brushed up on his Zen and spent time with Mother Teresa before making a successful comeback as mayor of Oakland, where he pursued sensible education and crime policies. With him throughout was longtime confidant Jacques Barzaghi, the French filmmaker, sailor, and Algerian war veteran who "put the frost on the California flake," as a *New York Times* writer explained. It was Barzaghi who famously said, during Brown's final presidential campaign in 1992: "We are not disorganized. Our campaign transcends understanding."

The book's lengthy account of the 2010 California governor's race, in which Brown defeated former eBay CEO Meg Whitman, is freighted with quotes from familiar pundits but short on analysis. McFadden's narrative takes the reader up to the 2012 elections, allowing him to address Proposition 30, the measure that gave California the nation's highest tax burden—yet he barely touches on Brown's tireless evangelism for the sales and income-tax hike. McFadden does note the contrast with Brown's second inaugural address as governor in 1979, when he intoned: "False prophets have risen to advocate more and more government spending as the cure." Back then, Brown argued that government must live within limits. He proposed that Sacramento cut jobs for the first time since World War II, calling a reduction of 5,000 state workers "reasonable and attainable." What happened to the "born-again tax cutter" and his flat tax? What measures might Brown have pushed in lieu of Prop. 30? McFadden doesn't speculate.

Unfortunately, McFadden's book went to press before it could chronicle Brown's response to seismic-safety issues on the new $6.4 billion span of the Bay Bridge, plagued by years of cost overruns and delays. Asked about problems with shaky rods, bolts, and welds, Brown responded: "I mean, look, shit happens." It certainly does. A fitting epitaph? Not necessarily. Brown's term is not finished, and the odds are strong that he'll run for reelection next year. So Chuck McFadden or some other scribe will have more to chronicle in this remarkable Californian's career.

31. "They were all bad."

"I suppose nothing hurts you," says Jehnna, a character in the 1982 film *Conan the Barbarian*.

"Only pain," replies Conan, played by Arnold Schwarzenegger, an actor most noted for the prize-winning physique he showcased in *Pumping Iron*. He added "I'll be back" in *The Terminator* (1984) but topped that in the 1994 *True Lies* as Harry Tasker, supposedly a salesman but uncovered as a spy. His wife Helen, played by Jamie Lee Curtis, wonders, "Have you ever killed anyone?"

"Yeah," Harry explains, "but they were all bad."

That too got big laughs, and *True Lies* may have been Arnold's best film. Even so, nobody in the audience imagined that this same Arnold Schwarzenegger would wind up as governor of California. As in the movies, he talked a good game, but one can make a case that, as a governor, he belongs in the "all bad" category.

Partial Recall
Arnold Schwarzenegger omits a few facts from his new book
City Journal California, October 11, 2012

IN HIS NEW MEMOIR, *TOTAL RECALL: MY UNBELIEVABLY TRUE LIFE STORY*, bodybuilder, businessman, movie star, and politician Arnold Schwarzenegger tries his hand as a critic, reviewing his own six-year stint as California governor. "We made a hell of a lot of progress, and we made a lot of history," he exults. "Workers comp reforms, parole reforms, pension reforms, education reforms, welfare reforms, and budget reforms. . . . We made our state an international leader in climate change and renewable energy; a national leader in health care reform and the fight against obesity." That's quite a roster of accomplishments, but it falls well short of the truth.

Schwarzenegger is hardly the first politician to put a fine gloss on his time in public office, but the former governor's attempts to chart his unalloyed success are neither believable nor complete. He positions himself as a latter-day Progressive. "We put in place the most significant political reforms since Hiram Johnson," he writes, referring to the early-twentieth-century California governor. "And we accomplished all this while dealing with the greatest economic disaster since the Great Depression." Well, not quite. Schwarzenegger's best efforts at sweeping reform came well before the recession, when he still believed—in spite of all reason—that he could deal with the legislature and buck the public-employee unions. "I wasn't familiar with the cast of characters in Sacramento," Schwarzenegger admits. That is, he didn't understand that the unions effectively run the place. He called for a "year of reform," posed for photos with a broom, and promised to clean house. "I had declared war," Schwarzenegger writes, "on the three most powerful public employee unions in the state: the prison guards, the teachers, the state employees."

But the former action hero couldn't take the heat. He retreated from reform and became a strategic ally of left-wing Democrats. For example, after Bay Area voters decided not to reelect State Senator Carole Migden, a *do-you-know-who-I-am?* Democrat whose antics included verbally abusing her own staff, Schwarzenegger appointed her to the state's waste-management board at $132,000 a year. (This from the man who had once promised to "blow up the boxes"—the maze of boards and commissions that serve as soft landing spots for washed-up politicians.) Not a word about that appears in *Total Recall*, a book replete with politically correct boilerplate, such as "Republicans had been stupidly alienating women." Which women—or which Republicans, for that matter—Schwarzenegger does not specify.

The Democrats were happy for Schwarzenegger's help but less inclined to reciprocate with genuine compromise. Take the bipartisan Commission on the 21st Century Economy, which Schwarzenegger mandated by executive order. The commission recommended lowering the number of personal income-tax brackets from six to two, with a new tax rate of 2.75 percent for taxable income up to $56,000 and 6.5 percent for all taxable income above that amount. These changes would have reduced the amount of income tax that Californians paid by 29 percent. The corporate tax would have been eliminated, along with the general-purpose sales tax, and replaced by a business net-receipts tax capped at 4 percent. The commission also wanted the state's "rainy day" reserve fund to get 12.5 percent of general-fund revenues, up from a current target of 5 percent, and it recommended restrictions on "the government's ability to use reserve assets so that the reserve is available to help fund services during recessionary periods." Implementing the commission's recommendations would have helped California solve many of its financial problems, especially the feast-or-famine budget cycle. Democrat Karen Bass, the Assembly Speaker at the time, promised a vote on the proposals but failed to deliver.

So preservation of the status quo wasn't entirely the governor's fault, but it was the first of many disappointments in his tenure. Another involved embryonic stem-cell research. When the Bush administration failed to fund that research, Schwarzenegger backed Proposition 71, a 2004 initiative sponsored by real-estate tycoon Robert Klein II, a prominent Democrat. The measure promised to use $3 billion in bond money for embryonic stem-cell research that would turn California into a vast Lourdes, overflowing with miraculous cures for deadly diseases. Alas, *Total Recall* doesn't mention that the California Institute for Regenerative Medicine, the state agency that Prop. 71 created, has spent most of its money without producing a single cure or therapy. And Schwarzenegger the self-described fiscal conservative fails to point out that CIRM remains off limits to state oversight and beset with conflicts of interest.

The former governor does recall former assembly speaker Fabian Núñez, a "smart ex-union leader" who would become "one of my closest allies among the Democrats." The pair worked together on AB 32, the California Global Warming Solutions Act, which the former governor calls "our boldest policy leap." He continues to claim, in the face of all evidence, that AB 32 is good for California's economy. Though he doesn't say so, Schwarzenegger's relationship with the L.A. Democrat didn't end there.

In 2008, Núñez's son Esteban was involved in the fatal stabbing of college student Luis Santos and eventually sentenced to 16 years in prison for manslaughter, avoiding a possible life sentence for murder. Núñez the elder tried to get the sentence reduced, but a judge refused. Not to worry, because on January 2, 2011, during his final hours as governor, Schwarzenegger commuted Esteban's sentence to seven years. The governor failed to notify the victim's family. "We are totally outraged," Fred Santos, the victim's father, told reporters. "For the governor to wait until the last day in hopes it would fly under the radar is an absolute injustice." Judge Lloyd Connelly called the governor's action "distasteful and repugnant."

Now back in the movie business, Schwarzenegger laments the "absurdity of Sacramento" and of its legislature, which has "less turnover than in Austria's Hapsburg monarchy." But as his incomplete memoir makes clear, Arnold Schwarzenegger added several chapters of his own to the state's absurdity.

32. Save the Pigs, and More Dollars from the People

I first visited Berkeley in the summer of 1968, a year after the Summer of Love. Down on Telegraph Street fellow hippies were still singing tunes like "Suzanne," by Leonard Cohen, with a jar for donations. Everybody was reading the *Berkeley Barb* and the cops rousting people everywhere. That was the heyday of the Black Panthers and around the University of California campus, activists were chanting "power to the people!" "off the pig!" and such.

Several decades later I happened to be on campus with my friend and colleague Pamela Riley, a genuine early 1960s Berkeley radical. That day no anti-war protesters or Black Panthers were present, but we did witness a rally for animal rights. As we observed, the outcry was now "save the pigs!" In the ensuing years, I discovered, Berkeley continued to show progress on the political correctness front.

Berkeley's Recycling Reactionaries
CalWatchdog, May 18, 2011

WHEN CITIES OUTSOURCE SERVICES TO SAVE MONEY, THEY OFTEN TAKE HEAT from workers. It's different in Berkeley, where a revolutionary plan to "insource" services to the city drew the wrath of recycling reactionaries.

Berkeley's progressive pretensions cannot prevent economic woes and the city recently found itself with a deficit of more than $4 million in its solid waste department alone. Unlike the federal government, the city cannot print money to stimulate the local economy. The city duly sent a Request for Proposal (RFP) for solid waste consultants to help eliminate the deficit.

The respondents included Sloan Vazquez LLC of Irvine, a company experienced in solid waste management and recycling, and which had recently completed a similar project for the city of Santa Monica. Kim Braun, solid waste manager for Santa Monica, called the Sloan Vazquez recommendations "productive" and "very helpful." She told CalWatchdog that collection route changes had resulted in savings for the city of more than $450,000 on overtime costs and $334,000 on alley cleanup. Santa Monica laid off no workers as a result of the report and is "still implementing" other recommendations, Braun said.

After an interview process, Berkeley selected Sloan Vazquez to conduct the review. The company set out to examine everything in the purview of Berkeley's solid waste management system. If not a model of fiscal rectitude, it did showcase the city's commitment to diversity.

The city itself handles residential and commercial garbage collection and manages its own transfer station for the waste. The city also manages some franchised haulers serving the commercial sector and contracts with the non-profit Community Conservation Center (CCC) to process the residential and commercial recyclables. The non-profit Ecology Center (EC), collects recyclables from residential areas, but that is not all they do.

The Ecology Center runs a Climate Change Action program, with services "to both prevent and prepare for rapid climate change." The center also offers climate change workshops and with its carbon calculator "you can quantify your 'carbon footprint,' quantify the change in your carbon footprint when you shift your habits, and connect with others in Berkeley who are doing the same."

The Ecology Center describes itself as "a community-based non-profit that depends on the generous support of our members and donors." The "many ways" to support the Ecology Center include donations of money, donations of stock, and "sell your house using Green Planet Real Estate." The non-profit also enjoys a steady revenue stream from Berkeley, and occupies a special place in the city's municipal waste system.

Richard Nixon was president and Ronald Reagan governor of California when the Ecology Center began collecting recyclables for Berkeley in 1973. In all that time, nearly 40 years, the city has never put out that service to bid. Waste management services are deemed "public health and safety" concerns, so cities are not required to bid them out. Yet most municipalities do bid out or renegotiate such service contracts every seven to 10 years, in an effort to keep costs down.

Berkeley's recycling costs remain high. Sloan Vazquez found that Berkeley residents paid 50 percent to 60 percent more than neighboring Bay Area communities. At the time of the RFP, Berkeley was paying the Ecology Center an annual $3.2 million to collect residential recyclables, which EC picks up with six trucks, all painted white. The EC mission states:

The Ecology Center facilitates urban lifestyles consistent with the goals of ecological sustainability, social equity and economic development. We seek to make these goals accessible by *providing people with the information they need*, the alternatives they seek, and the infrastructure necessary to make sustainable practices possible on a large scale. We aim to make the visionary mainstream. (emphasis added)

When Sloan Vazquez sought the information it needed for its report, however, EC was not forthcoming, unlike all the other groups, including the city of Berkeley itself and the CCC, also a non-profit. The non-profit that offers to quantify one's carbon footprint was not willing to quantify their own recycling business in any detail.

Sloan Vazquez proceeded with their review, based on the Ecology Center's $3.2 million – by other accounts $3.7 million – annual charges to Berkeley, and compared those to the city's known operating costs. Based on this comparison, they recommended that the city "internalize," that is, take over, the recycling collection service performed since 1973 by the Ecology Center in what can only be described as a sweetheart deal of incredible endurance.

Joe Sloan of Sloan Vazquez calculated that such insourcing to the city would reduce costs by about $1.5 million, even though he found that a single solid waste worker costs Berkeley an average of $113,000 a year in salary, benefits, and other costs. The Ecology Center didn't like the plan, but Berkeley City Council member Gordon Wozniak called the Sloan Vazquez report "a success" because it had motivated proposals for cutting costs. City Council member Laurie Capitelli was also supportive of the Sloan Vazquez report. According to news reports, so were some union people, who had come up with a similar plan.

Some Berkeley city workers are members of the Service Employees International Union (SEIU), and in City Council meeting they praised the Sloan Vazquez report. Ricky Jackson, an SEIU shop steward, said the union's own report had "some of the same ideas."

Andrea Lewis, an SEIU member and city worker, told the council that the Ecology Center has a $3.7 million contract, and "that's not peanuts." The contract, she said, "has got to go to bid! . . . Why is this contract so different?"

Likewise, Berkeley City Council member Susan Wengraf wondered "why this 3.7 million dollar contract is not bid competitively?" She wanted answers, but none emerged in the meeting. A labor rift offers one explanation. Berkeley is a strong union town, but to paraphrase George Orwell, some unions are more equal than others.

The GuideStar profile of the Ecology Center, based on their 2007 and 2008 IRS 990 forms, shows 21-100 full-time employees and 11-20 part-time employees. The Ecology Center is a union shop and its workers are represented by the Industrial Workers of the World (IWW), known as the "Wobblies," a paleo-left group that peaked in the 1920s, even before the Stalin Era. The most famous current IWW member is Noam Chomsky, the American leftist icon touted by Hugo Chavez and Osama bin Laden alike.

"Solidarity Forever," is a famous Wobbly song, but in March, when Joe Sloan presented his report to Berkeley's Zero Waste Commission, an IWW mouthpiece accused him of being responsible for "all that is wrong in America today," and for pitting labor groups against each other. Ecology Center boss Martin Bourque charged that "the end of nonprofit recycling in Berkeley" would lay off more than 35 union employees. That struck a chord with Berkeley City Council member Linda Maio. She said that the city's job is to balance the budget and that "our goal isn't to have anyone laid off from their job."

EC boss Martin Bourque earned a masters in Latin American Studies and Environmental Policy from UC Berkeley. He has served as executive director the Ecology Center since 2000. Before that he worked for the Institute for Food and Development Policy, also known as Food First. The group is "committed to dismantling racism in the food system" and believes in "people's right to healthy and culturally appropriate food produced through ecologically sound and sustainable methods, and their right to define their own food and agriculture systems—at home and abroad."

Bourque talked trash about Sloan Vazquez to anybody who would listen, and proved himself an adept community organizer. He tapped politically correct local PhDs to criticize the Sloan Vazquez report, which some critics said was "incomplete." That was true in several ways.

The report had not included a detailed breakdown of how the Ecology Center spends the nearly $4 million it gets from Berkeley every year. The report did not include a salary schedule for Ecology Center employees, its board, and executive director Martin Bourque. In an email, CalWatchdog asked Bourque if his Ecology Center makes available that financial and salary information. Mr. Bourque's belated email response did not answer those questions. Costs and salaries are of considerable interest in this case, but Sloan Vazquez didn't need that data to perform the job Berkeley wanted.

"We simply looked at what they [the Ecology Center] charge the city to perform the service versus what it would cost the city to do it themselves," says Joe Sloan. "It was very straightforward." Sloan says that the Ecology Center "wants to change the terms of the debate, obfuscate, and bluster." He stands by the report and says that none of Bourque's local experts "could withstand the scrutiny of an open, public debate on the service issues and costs."

The controversy would be understandable if Sloan Vazquez had recommended that the city of Berkeley take services they were currently performing and outsource them to some non-union for-profit multinational company headquartered in New Jersey, with possible oil company connections. But that was not what happened.

Rather, the very consultants Berkeley selected, from many candidates, offered the city a way to save money by insourcing recycling services. Despite support for the Sloan Vazquez report from the SEIU

and various City Council members, Berkeley has not insourced the recycling service as the report recommends. A more likely outcome is a
rate hike, from rates already substantially higher than those in nearby
Bay Area communities.

In the end, Sloan's long experience in recycling and waste management had not adequately prepared him for the conflicts inherent in
the system, specifically Berkeley's longstanding protection racket. In
Berkeley's scale of values, cutting costs takes a back seat to maintaining the recycling status quo, the sweetheart deal with a politically correct, environmentally orthodox non-profit. Observers could be also be
forgiven for thinking that Berkeley would rather jack up the rates than
do anything less than worshipful of the IWW, Noam Chomsky's union.

"Power to the people!" used to be the rallying cry in Berkeley. Now
it's "more dollars from the people."

33. White Coat Syndrome

In California, an environmental zealot like Coastal Commission boss Peter Douglas can gain control over vast territory and secure a steady flow of money from Sacramento, without any need to face the voters. California also allows a clever operator to gain his very own $3 billion state agency and run it for his own financial benefit and that of his cronies. He can do this while remaining off limits to legislative oversight, and without producing any promised benefits. To pull this off, one simply cloaks the scam in the white coat of medical science and promises miraculous, life-saving cures down the road. And this lucrative caper is even possible under a Republican governor, Arnold Schwarzenegger, a former action hero who promised to "blow up the boxes" of bureaucracy. They don't call it the Golden State for nothing.

Scam Cell
California's embryonic stem cell research institute fails to deliver
City Journal California, March 14, 2013

THE CALIFORNIA INSTITUTE FOR REGENERATIVE MEDICINE (CIRM), THE $3 billion state stem-cell agency, has failed to follow recommendations from a December report by the Institute of Medicine (IOM), a division of the National Academy of Sciences. The IOM report failed to convey the magnitude of CIRM's failure but it did confirm that the agency is better described as Conflict of Interest Research Money.

Almost all members of the CIRM board, IOM noted, "are interested parties with a personal or financial stake in the allocation of CIRM fundings." In fact CIRM directed a full 91 percent of its research funding to institutions with representatives on the CIRM board. In similar style,

236

CIRM's own scientific reviewers twice rejected a proposal to fund a for-profit company represented by CIRM founder Robert Klein. But the CIRM board went ahead and gave the money to the for-profit anyway. That kind of wealth redistribution was likely what Klein had in mind from the beginning.

Klein is the wealthy real-estate developer who created the California Housing Finance Agency, (CHFA) in 1973 on the grounds that he was unsatisfied with HUD under president Nixon. Klein deployed the same strategy when George W. Bush declined to back embryonic stem-cell research. In 2004 Klein launched Proposition 71 seeking $3 billion in bond money for embryonic stem cell research. Governor Arnold Schwarzenegger backed the measure and the shameless promotional campaign featured actors Michael J. Fox and Christopher Reeve promising life-saving cures for a host of diseases.

Yet, CIRM has been a scientific bust. It played no role in medical-scientific advances such as the construction of a new windpipe for a Colombian woman, and the near-total restoration of sight to a man whose eyes sustained chemical damage in 1948. Those were triumphs of *adult* stem-cell research. A ballpark figure for the number of promised life-saving cures and therapies CIRM has achieved is zero, something the IOM report failed to note. At a meeting of the Little Hoover Commission attended by this writer, a Commission staffer said CIRM was "getting money out the door," as though this was a marker of success.

CIRM was always more about the money than the medicine. Klein cleverly wrote Prop. 71 to install himself as the institute's chairman, and he freed it from almost all legislative oversight by requiring a 70 percent supermajority of both houses to make any structural or policy changes. He awarded whopper salaries such as president Alan Trounson's $490,000, and provided a comfortable landing spot for Art Torres, a down-at-the-heels former state senator and ex-Democratic Party boss. In 2009, CIRM board member Duane Roth, a San Diego businessman with an extensive background in biotechnology, offered to serve as vice chair for no salary. Instead of accepting this offer, CIRM opted to make Roth co-vice-chair along with former state senator and Democratic Party boss Art Torres, who is a lawyer, not a medical scientist. Almost at once CIRM tripled

Torres' initial salary from $75,000 to $225,000. This largesse came during tough budgetary times for the state. Chairman Klein did not take a salary until 2008 when he began collecting $150,000 a year.

By 2009, the Obama administration had authorized federal embryonic stem-cell research, undercutting CIRM's reason for existence. Prop. 71 gives CIRM until 2017 to find other funding to replace the bond money Californians approved nearly nine years ago. As Klein pitched it then, life-saving cures and therapies would generate significant royalties for the state, and CIRM would eventually be able to fund itself. But no life-saving cures means no revenue. Out of the original $3 billion, CIRM has $859 million left. Before stepping down as chairman of the governing board in 2011, when his six-year term expired, Klein said that he wanted another $5 billion for CIRM. It's not out of the question that Klein and other CIRM loyalists would float another bond measure. And judging by their recent performance with Proposition 30, California voters might fall for the same promises. No billionaires appear eager to pay for another campaign, though, and despite Governor Jerry Brown's assurance that "California is back," the Golden State has no money to burn.

For CIRM's conflicts of interest alone, Californians should think twice before keeping it in business. Jonathan Thomas, Klein's successor as CIRM chairman, says the board will vote March 19 on a new policy that should satisfy most of the IOM's concerns. But once started, government agencies are practically impossible to stop, even if they're ineffective and wasteful. Hearings on CIRM are unlikely in a virtual one-party state addicted to spending, where the governor greets news of hidden millions with a "Hallelujah!" and where the attorney general declines even to consider whether laws were broken. But perhaps something good could come of California's stem-cell calamity.

CIRM is a vivid example of how much one clever insider can get away with in California. At a minimum, CIRM's record should prompt reform of the initiative process. As long as politicos can create ballot measures that remain off-limits to oversight, while channeling money to themselves and their cronies, other self-dealing proposals are sure to follow.

34. Gun Store to the Rescue

As Peter Balakian showed in *The Burning Tigris*, the Ottoman Turks disarmed the Armenians, which made it easier to loot, torture and murder more than a million of them. In similar style, the Nazi regime disarmed those they sought to exterminate, as Stephen M. Halbrook showed in *Gun Control in the Third Reich: Disarming Jews and "Enemies of the State."* So all people, Americans included, have good cause to resist government attempts to disarm them, particularly of military-style weapons. Gun control crusaders and Second Amendment advocates alike might note the use of such weapons in this story.

Store-Bought Protection
Reason, August/September, 1997

WHEN TWO HEAVILY ARMED BANDITS GRABBED $350,000 FROM A NORTH Hollywood bank on February 28, the ensuing shootout with Los Angeles police resulted in a prime-time TV special and prompted politicians to call for stricter gun control. Lost in the shuffle, though, is how the outgunned cops ended their battle with robo-robbers Larry Eugene Phillips and Emil Matasareanu.

The pair deployed five fully automatic rifles, each of which was illegal long before the current outcry against so-called assault weapons. During the heist, they sprayed anything that moved, including news helicopters, with rapid fire. Police-issue 9mm pistols are hardly a match for fully automatic firepower. So as the bullets flew, the outgunned cops headed not to the local precinct but to nearby B&B Sales, a private gun store.

The owner recognized some of the officers as previous customers and, overlooking the 15-day waiting period a typical civilian would face before being able to legally obtain firearms, quickly supplied them with four 5.56mm Bushmaster XM-15 semi-automatic rifles with high-capacity magazines and two Remington shotguns with rifled slugs. Once the officers were on a more equal footing, they plunged back into the fray, taking down the bad guys with no loss of innocent life. The LAPD offers no comment on the officers' use of these privately obtained weapons during the onslaught, as it has been sued by the robbers' families for refusing to give the crooks medical attention after shooting them.

35. 007 Forever

The early James Bond movies were rated "Adult Entertainment" but for baby-boomer adolescent males they were, as they say, a "must see," right from the famous title sequence. Bond was the embodiment of cool as he battled sophisticated villains with high-tech gadgets in exotic locations. On the big screen, in living color, Honor Blackman tells Bond: "My name is Pussy Galore." That was in 1964, no less, and one could say that "Pussy Galore" pretty much summarizes the whole series. I have seen every James Bond film, some many times, but never got around to reviewing one until 2013.

There'll Always Be an England, and Apparently James Bond as Well
Carolina Journal, January 1, 2013

THE SCENT AND SMOKE AND SWEAT OF A CASINO ARE NAUSEATING AT THREE IN THE morning. Then the soul-erosion produced by high gambling — a compost of greed and fear and nervous tension — becomes unbearable and the senses awake and revolt from it. James Bond suddenly knew that he was tired.

That's where it all started, with Ian Fleming's 1953 *Casino Royale* novel, long since made into a film like the others, beginning with "Dr. No" in 1962, staring Sean Connery as James Bond. Fifty years and nearly two dozen films later comes *Skyfall*, worthy of attention for many reasons, not all cinematic. As a movie it breaks some new ground while preserving, as one character says, some of "the old ways."

In 1983, when Sean Connery had another go as James Bond in "Never Say Never Again," Johnny Carson joked that 007 would need a cyanide suppository. That quip might apply to the high-tech *Skyfall*. Judy Dench, here called "Mum" rather than M, is every bit as gray as Desmond Llewellyn, the original Q. As a British spy boss, Ralph Fiennes bears some resemblance to Pete Townshend. Daniel Craig, the latest Bond, also is showing his age, slightly resembling a recently retired linebacker.

On the other hand, the new Q, Ben Whishaw, sports a Harry Potter look. The elegant Naomi Harris has much more to do as Eve Moneypenny than the original, Lois Maxwell, who passed away at 80 in 2007. *Skyfall* also brings in Kincade, the gamekeeper at Bond's ancestral home, played by Albert Finney, not exactly a novice.

As for story, somebody inside terrorist organizations has a list of MI6 operatives and is releasing the names. He must be stopped, but so far he's too smart for M and her crew. Enter James Bond, thought to be dead after a long initial action sequence that combines the X-Games, Ninja Warrior, motocross, and martial arts. The revived Bond must pass tests to confirm his fitness as an agent, then hunt down the villain and stop him.

On that quest, the story is more "what else?" than "what next?" The movie packs more bang-bang than kiss-kiss, and Bond doesn't get to have as much fun as he did in *Goldfinger* or *Thunderball*. No real equivalent here to, respectively, Honor Blackman (Pussy Galore) or Luciana Peluzzi (Fiona Volpe.) That may please feminists, but for politicos, *Skyfall* is something of a moving target.

The left derided the Bond movies as Cold War cartoons but the villains usually were from some criminal organization such as SPECTRE, playing the West and the Soviets off each other. It didn't help that Bond collaborated with the CIA. He still does, but in *Skyfall* the villain turns out to be a renegade MI6 agent with a grudge against Mum. Viewers can judge whether Silva (Javier Bardem) measures up to Blofeld, Dr. No, Auric Goldfinger, or Drax in sophisticated malevolence.

Sylva mocks Bond as a failed agent, and his computer tricks overwhelm MI6. All will depend on James Bond, who like Paul Simon leans on old familiar ways, including a certain tricked-out Aston Martin DB5. But there's more to the film's respect for the past.

"There'll always be an England," as the 1939 song said, and England is the most consistent reality in the Bond films. Bond remains an employee of an elected democratic British government, with established and respected authority that goes back to the Magna Carta. M may be a powerful spymaster but she must face the music in government hearings, where she recites Tennyson. The new M headquarters are in Winston Churchill's old bunker, and a British bulldog figurine, wrapped in the Union Jack, holds vigil on her desk.

In *Skyfall*, as in all the Bond films, there is no question this is all worth defending, and such defense involves espionage, exotic weapons, and secret agents like James Bond. Long before Silva, traitors in British intelligence such as Kim Philby sold out to enemies of democracy such as Joseph Stalin. So perhaps another Bond film will explore that theme in more depth.

A more recent Bond, Pierce Brosnan, said that Sean Connery once came on the set and spoke words he has never forgotten: "Are they paying you enough money?" That raises an economic issue.

Skyfall grossed more than $100 million in the United States alone on its first weekend, and may earn $1 billion worldwide. It is, as they say, a hit, and creators of hits — along with the wealth they create — are worth defending, too.

Money and generally favorable reviews aside, the film has caused some to proclaim Daniel Craig as the "best" James Bond. Sorry, but it's still Sean Connery, and the *Skyfall* theme song by Adele can't hold a candle to Shirley Bassey in *Goldfinger*. Maybe they'll do better next time. As the filmmakers say, James Bond will return.

36. "You can't fight an enemy you don't acknowledge."

I lost a friend in the terrorist attacks of September 11, 2001 and since then have taken special interest in the subject. So I duly took notice when Rudy Giuliani, mayor of New York on 9/11, showed how political correctness makes terrorism even more dangerous.

Tsarnaev, Hasan, and Dangerous Political Correctness
Frontpage Magazine, July 12, 2013

ON WEDNESDAY DZHOKHAR TSARNAEV PLEADED NOT GUILTY TO 30 COUNTS in the Boston Marathon bombings and jury selection began in the case of U.S. Army Major Nidal Hasan, accused of murdering 13 at Fort Hood, Texas, in 2009. The Hasan and Tsarnaev cases emerged the same day in testimony before the House Homeland Security Committee, where the first witness, Rudy Giuliani, said that political correctness hinders efforts to stop terrorists before they strike.

Giuliani, mayor of New York during the September 11, 2001 terrorist attacks, told the committee, "You can't fight an enemy you don't acknowledge." To confront the terrorist threat effectively, "we have to purge ourselves of the practice of political correctness when it goes so far that it interferes with our rational and intellectually honest analysis of the identifying characteristics that help a discover these killers in advance."

Giuliani said that a reluctance to identify violent Islamic extremists could have played a role in the FBI's failure to track Tamerlan Tsarnaev, Dzhokhar's older brother, who last year returned to Dagestan for six months. "There would have been a much greater chance of preventing Fort Hood, and possibly — and this I emphasize is possibly — the Boston bombing," Giuliani said, "if the relevant bureaucracies had been less reluctant to identify the eventual killers as potential Islamic extremist terrorists."

In the 2009 Ford Hood case, Major Nidal Hasan is charged with killing 13, more deaths than in the first attack on the World Trade center in 1993, a year before Giuliani became major of New York.

"The elevation of political correctness over sound investigative judgment certainly explains the failure to identify Maj. Hasan as a terrorist," Giuliani told the committee. "That political correctness has been extended so far that the current administration describes his act as 'workplace violence.' This isn't just preposterous. What we fail to realize is, this is dangerous."

The next witness, Michael Leiter, former head of the U.S. National Counterterrorism Center, denied that political correctness was hindering U.S. efforts against terrorism. Such a claim, he testified, "is simply beyond me." No member of the committee asked Leiter to explain what dynamic might lurk behind the "workplace violence" explanation. Committee members did explore cases where government agencies had failed to communicate, particularly with local law enforcement.

The hearing was called to examine intelligence breakdowns in the Boston Marathon bombings, but any threat from Islamic extremism failed to emerge in the statement of ranking member Bennie Thompson. He cited the Southern Poverty Law Center about a growing domestic threat from right-wing groups.

That theme emerged in *Challengers from the Sidelines: Understanding America's Far Right*, a recent report from the Combating Terrorism Center at the U.S. Military Academy. The report links white supremacists, Aryan Nations, skinheads, the Ku Klux Klan and such with those who "espouse strong convictions regarding the federal government, believing it to be corrupt and tyrannical, with a natural tendency to intrude on individuals' civil and constitutional rights. The groups also support civil activism, individual freedoms, and self-government." As Mark Tapson noted, "that pretty much describes every conservative I know."

Meanwhile, a military judge on Wednesday entered a not-guilty plea on behalf of Nidal Hasan, whose court martial trial is set to begin

August 6. Also on Wednesday the *New York Times* reported mounting evidence that Tamerlan Tsarnaev, Dzhokhar's older brother, participated in a gruesome 2011 triple murder in Boston. The bodies were discovered on September 12, 2001, a day after the tenth anniversary of the 9/11 attacks. Victims Erik Weissman and Raphael Teken were Jews and some Jewish publications consider the murders a hate crime.

According to the *Times* reporters, some law enforcement authorities "contend that if the local murder investigation had been more vigorous it could have led to his [Tamerlan's] apprehension well before the bombings left 3 dead and more than 260 wounded — in short, that the bombings might never have happened."

37. Eastwood Fires Back

Audiences loved *American Sniper*, which broke box office records coast to coast. Normally that would bring it praise in Hollywood, but here the film has a problem. Though authentic about the nature of warfare, *American Sniper* is not politically correct because it is openly patriotic and unapologetic about the use of American military power.

Eastwood's "Sniper" Returns Fire at Hollywood's Leftists
Carolina Journal, February 2, 2015

Long before he produced and directed *American Sniper*, Clint Eastwood played detective Harry Callahan, who tells the mayor of San Francisco that the murderer he seeks will kill again. "How do you know that?" says the mayor. "Because he likes it," Callahan says. The 1971 *Dirty Harry* was the first movie to talk back to liberalism, then preoccupied with the rights of violent criminals. A similar dynamic is at work in *American Sniper*.

The film shows the modern U.S. military engaging the sort of people they actually fight these days, as opposed to such Hollywood favorites as Nazis, neo-Nazis, neo-fascists, and white supremacists. Even so, the script does sanitize things more than a little bit. Viewers see the 9/11 attacks and hear a news broadcast about the bombing of the U.S. embassies in Tanzania and Kenya, but the term "terrorist" is missing in action. The venue is Iraq and the enemy are insurgents, extremists, and militants but never called Muslims or identified with Islam, apart from a few references to the Koran.

They don't self-identify, shout "Allah is great!" or denounce the United States as the Great Satan. The U.S. soldiers routinely call the enemy "savages," and that proves authentic. One, known as "The

247

Butcher," dismembers people and tortures children with an electric drill. The Butcher gets some threatening lines of dialogue but the chief villain, the elusive sniper "Mustafa," remains silent as Rudolf Valentino.

American Sniper is openly patriotic and unapologetic about the U.S. military fighting in Iraq, both frontal attacks on the Hollywood Left, which believes America is bad and capitalism evil — except for the part of capitalism financing their three-picture deals, Mercedes-Benzes, and Malibu mansions. The patriotism comes through the hero, Chris Kyle (Bradley Cooper), who acts on his belief that the United States is the "greatest country on earth." The film shows the young Kyle hunting with this father, and the family in church, and both come across as positive experiences, violating more Hollywood taboos.

Kyle leaves his fun career as a cowboy to sign up with the SEALs, who put him through rigorous training and pack him off to sniper school. He meets his future wife Taya (Sienna Miller) in a bar, so as legendary film critic Pauline Kael might say, this is in part a "kiss kiss" movie. But soon Kyle is off on his first tour of duty to Iraq, where he becomes "The Legend," picking off the enemy. At one point he has to shoot a child and a woman about to hurl a grenade at Kyle's fellow soldiers. It pains him to do this, but toward the end of the story Kyle makes it clear that his greatest regret is the ones he didn't get, those killing his fellow U.S. soldiers. That also breaks some Hollywood taboos.

American filmmakers are normally big on homage and *American Sniper* might have mentioned Chuck Mawhinney, a Marine with 103 confirmed kills who took down 16 enemy soldiers in a single engagement. Of course, that was in Vietnam, where Hollywood has cast the USA as the permanent villain and U.S. soldiers as wackos.

The *American Sniper* combat scenes are crisply directed and about as realistic as it gets. Kael might say on one level it is a "bang bang" movie, consistent with Eastwood's long experience. There is nothing glamorous about house-to-house combat, with sudden death lurking around every corner. "American Sniper" does not shy away from the toll such combat takes on the soldiers, shown taking bloody hits, absent limbs, and in surgery.

Chris Kyle must deal with this, as Taya remains stateside with their son and daughter. They stay in touch by phone, even when Chris is drawing a bead on the bad guys, something Sgt. York couldn't do. Through it all Chris remains someone the audience will like, and a genuine American hero to boot.

Back in Iraq, the insurgents have put a price on Kyle's head and Mustafa is running up his kill count. The U.S. soldiers will have to take him down, and Kyle is the man for the job. Few viewers will be surprised at the outcome. Kyle makes a dramatic narrow escape and returns stateside, where Taya and family await, along with other perils, as "The Legend" discovers.

Audiences have been cheering and the movie finds favor with critics. Cooper and Miller may bag Academy Awards, but one doubts *American Sniper* will win best picture or Eastwood best director. The industry doesn't like it when anyone, however famous or talented, challenges their prejudices and waves the American flag.

Mercifully, not a single politician speaks or appears in *American Sniper*, but national leaders may derive some benefit from the story. The film hit theatres shortly after terrorists mounted a deadly military operation in Paris. Eastwood, 84, knows that the bad guys are still out to kill Americans because they like it. So odds are that such attacks will take place in American cities.

As Eastwood's film shows, even with all the military spending, intelligence, and high-tech weaponry, victory in key engagements may hinge on one brave man who can shoot straight from distance. So future Chris Kyles doubtless will be needed on the home front. *American Sniper* may inspire them to step forward and volunteer, even under a commander-in-chief who, like the film, fails to identify the adversary precisely.

38. Recalling a Terrorist Massacre

In the early going as a journalist, I learned that newspapers love anniversary stories, and that has continued in the Internet Age. So when one of the worst terrorist attacks turned five, I wrote about it.

Five Years Since the Fort Hood Massacre
Frontpage Magazine, October 23, 2014

ON NOVEMBER 5, 2009, AT FORD HOOD, TEXAS, U.S. SOLDIERS WERE GETting their final medical checkups before deploying to Afghanistan. Major Nidal Malik Hasan, an Army psychiatrist began gunning down the soldiers. His victims, all unarmed, included Francheska Velez, a 21-year-old private from Chicago who pleaded for the life of her unborn child. The Muslim major killed two other women that day along with 10 men, more than twice as many victims as the first attack on the World Trade Center in 1993.

Hasan also wounded 33 others, including Sergeant Alonzo Lunsford, who played dead then fled the building. Major Hasan chased down Lunsford, an African-American, and shot him seven times, including one bullet in the back. Firing a high-capacity handgun fitted with laser sights, Major Hasan shot Sergeant Shawn Manning in the chest and pumped four rounds into Sgt. Patrick Zeigler. Hasan would have killed and wounded more if civilian police officer Kim Munley had not wounded the assailant, who yelled "*Allahu akbar*," as he killed. That familiar cry was hardly the only indicator of Hasan's motives.

Hasan had been emailing terrorist Anwar al-Awlaki about the prospect of killing infidel American soldiers, and the "Soldier of Allah," as he called himself, did everything but take out an ad on the Super Bowl to announce his jihadist intentions. The U.S. security establishment was well aware of the communications but did nothing to stop Hasan, who claimed to be acting on behalf of the Taliban. Anwar al-Awlaki was orgasmic with joy that Hasan had done his duty.

President Barack Obama's first response to Hasan's mass murder was brief, low key, and failed to ascribe any responsibility to Islamic terrorism. "We cannot fully know what leads a man to do such a thing," the president said. Such breathtaking denial soon became official policy. The Obama administration's Department of Defense issued *Protecting the Force: Lessons from Fort Hood*, which contains not a single reference to jihad or jihadists. Its only mention of "Islamic" is an endnote reference to "Countering Violent Islamic Extremism," a 2007 FBI Law Enforcement Bulletin.

The United States Army and federal government did not call Hasan's attack terrorism or even gun violence. Major Hasan killed African Americans, hispanics and non-Muslims, but the government did not call the attack a hate crime. Rather, the government proclaimed the murder spree a case of "workplace violence," an absurdity for the ages with consequences for the Hasan's victims. The refusal to classify Hasan's attack as terrorism rendered victims ineligible for medals and other benefits related to combat.

Hasan remained in the Army, retained his rank of major, and the Army continued to pay his full salary. The Army also took care of the paralyzing injuries Hasan sustained, but Alonzo Lunsford told reporters the army refused to cover an operation to remove a bullet still in his body, and docked his pay when he was undergoing treatment for post-traumatic stress disorder. "We don't get passes the way Major Hasan got passes," Lunsford told the *New York Times*. "Each one of us has gotten a raw deal somewhere down the line." In April, the White House declined Alonzo Lunsford's request to meet with the president and explain how the government mistreated victims of the 2009 attack.

In August of 2013, a panel of 13 military officers handed down a death sentence for Major Hasan, but the sentence may never be carried out. The U.S. military has not executed an active-duty soldier since 1961, a span of more than half a century. The appeal process is lengthy and the final call goes to the President of the United States. The current incumbent is Barack Obama and Major Hasan showcases the opportunities for "Soldiers of Allah" under the Obama administration.

They can join the U.S. Army and still get promoted. They can correspond freely with the most bloodthirsty foreign terrorists, and those conducting the surveillance will do nothing to stop them from killing 13 American soldiers on a U.S. Army base. The Army, government, and president will provide cover by calling this workplace violence instead of terrorism. So the Soldier of Allah escapes with his own life and in prison continues to inspire other jihadists.

The month before Major Hasan's trial, Rudy Giuliani said "you can't fight an enemy you don't acknowledge." The next president, who will also be Commander-in-chief, will have an opportunity to acknowledge the enemy, recognize Major Hasan's massacre as terrorism, and execute the terrorist on day one. As one of his victims said, he doesn't deserve to live.

39. West of the Wall

Erected in 1961, the Berlin Wall became a symbol of the Iron Curtain between Communist states and the West. Ronald Reagan challenged Soviet boss Mikhail Gorbachev to "tear down this wall" and it finally did come down, heralding a new era of freedom and prosperity. Twenty-five years later European leaders celebrated the event, but no surprise that the President of the United States failed to show up.

Writing is on the Wall for Obama
Intellectual Conservative, December 10, 2014

THE FALL OF THE BERLIN WALL IS ONE OF THE MOST SIGNIFICANT EVENTS OF our time and in early November leaders from many nations went to Germany to mark the 25th anniversary. President of the United States Barack Obama did not attend, and that is hardly accidental.

The Berlin Wall was a project of the German Democratic Republic (GDR), a one-party Communist totalitarian dictatorship and the most slavish ally of the Soviet Union, which under Joseph Stalin grabbed half of Germany in the wake of World War II. The November 7 White House Statement on the 25th anniversary, however, did not mention the USSR, Communism, or totalitarianism, and even failed to name the German Democratic Republic.

The GDR erected the wall in 1961 as the *Antifaschistischer Schutzwall*, the "Anti-Fascist Protection Rampart," a familiar inversion of reality. As the late American leftist writer Susan Sontag observed during the 1980s, "Communism is fascism." The GDR was the fascist state, with goose-stepping troops decked out very much like those of the National Socialist regime under the *Nationalsozialistische Deutsche Arbeiterpartei*, the National Socialist German Workers' Party, also known as Nazis.

The White House statement says the wall separated Germans "from family and friends" and that Germans were "trying to escape to freedom." But the president gives no detail on what conditions the brave Germans sought to escape.

The GDR had nothing resembling the private sector in Western democracies. The state ran everything, and its command economy guaranteed that the GDR would be an economic basket case, less consequential to the world economy than Hong Kong. The GDR's crowning industrial achievement was the Trabant, doubtless the worst automobile ever made.

Aware of all this, President Obama remains shrink-wrapped in statist superstition, primarily the belief that government always knows best. In fact, he is on record as having said that the government deserves credit for building businesses, not the actual people who started businesses on their own initiative.

Obama's signature program, Obamacare, passed by only the president's party, represents a takeover of one-sixth of the American economy. The president sold it with lies – "if you like your plan, you can keep it" – and Obamacare stripped Americans of their freedom to choose their own healthcare.

The White House's Berlin Wall statement refers to "oppressive regimes" but gives no detail of how oppressive the GDR actually was. That emerged in John Koehler's 1999 book, *Stasi: The Untold Story of the East German Secret Police*. This "Red Gestapo" maintained massive surveillance on all German citizens and served as the strike force of state oppression.

In similar style, Obama has tasked the National Security Agency to conduct mass surveillance against American citizens. The president has deployed the Internal Revenue Service against groups less than worshipful of big government and high taxes. And he has mounted a surge against even the old-line establishment media, as investigative journalist Sharyl Attkisson contends in *Stonewalled: My Fight for Truth Against the Forces of Obstruction, Intimidation, and Harassment in Obama's Washington*.

None of this should come as a surprise. Obama's mentors include

Frank Marshall Davis, an old-line Stalinist, Weather Underground vet Bill Ayres, and left-wing strategist Saul Alinsky. Even a threefold cord is not easily broken.

Still, after six years in office, Americans know less about Barack Obama than any U.S. president. Should that be doubted, google "what we don't know about Barack Obama." A book that answers those questions might sell a few copies. In the meantime, the writing is pretty much on the wall.

40. American Stasi

Television may be high-definition these days but it's certainly not high content. One exception is C-SPAN, which shows entire government hearings without any commercial interruptions, and without any millionaire "anchor" explaining what you heard, and what you ought to think about it. C-SPAN also pays attention to books and authors, and there I heard Sharyl Attkisson reveal how the Obama administration manages the news, not a popular theme with the old-line establishment media. The Obama administration also cracks down on those who tell the truth to power, in at least one case by taking over their computer, as Attkisson shows in considerable detail. I thought her book deserved a review and kindly editor Rick Henderson of *Carolina Journal* agreed.

Stonewalled a Chilling Tale of Government Snooping

Sharyl Attkisson, *Stonewalled: My Fight for Truth Against the Forces of Obstruction, Intimidation, and Harassment in Obama's Washington*, Harper, 2014, 422 pages, $27.99.
Carolina Journal, February 2, 2015

MANY AMERICANS UNDERSTAND THAT FOR THE MOST PART THE OLD-LINE EStablishment media, especially the television networks, serve as faithful echo chambers for the Obama administration. Former CBS investigative journalist Sharyl Attkisson brings more detail to that story in *Stonewalled*, a timely and courageous book that delivers a lot more than it promises.

Many readers may be surprised to learn that CBS News president David Rhodes is the brother of Ben Rhodes, a top national security advisor to Obama and up to his eyeballs in the Benghazi scandal. As the author notes, CBS hasn't exactly been up front about that connection. Likewise, Joel Molinoff came to CBS after serving the Obama White House as director of the president's Intelligence Advisory Board, and before that Molinoff worked for the National Security Agency. CBS also hired Mike Morell, formerly a deputy director at the CIA and a major figure in the Benghazi scandal. So CBS stories on that theme and others such as Obamacare, as the author explains, might as well have been written by the White House. That was not true of Attkisson's stories.

In *Stonewalled* she outlines her work on "Fast and Furious," a government operation intended to back the administration's belief that American guns cause violence in Mexico. The administration did this by forcing U.S. gun dealers to sell weapons to dangerous criminals, known as letting the guns "walk." The existence of the program was denied by Bureau of Alcohol, Tobacco, Firearms, and Explosives bosses, who used taxpayer-paid public relations flacks to attack Attkisson personally rather than refute her reporting. In the author's experience, many establishment journalists believe the motives of government are always good, and with Obamacare they tended to accept information from the government at face value. Attkisson is not one of those journalists.

She documents how the Obama administration's healthcare.gov website was riddled with "giant security holes." The establishment media passed that off as a mere "glitch," and as with anything they don't like, criticism was dismissed as a "Republican story," "right-wing," "conservative," and so forth.

Attkisson has been around too long to accept the idea that the 2012 attack on the U.S. diplomatic compound in Benghazi, Libya, that claimed four American lives, including that of ambassador Christopher Stephens, was prompted by an Internet video. That was the line repeated by the president, Secretary of State Hillary Clinton, and designated mouthpiece Susan Rice. As the author notes, Rice and her boss, Thomas Pickering, were in the State Department in 1998 when Islamic terrorists bombed U.S. embassies in Kenya and Tanzania, resulting in massive loss of life. Hillary Clinton was then first lady and also well aware of the dangers terrorists posed to U.S. diplomats in Africa. Trouble is, in 2012 that knowledge violated the narrative that the Obama administration had terrorists on the run. So they left American diplomats unprotected, failed to send help, and deployed the video cover story.

Attkisson packs four pages with administration claims and countervailing facts. She also deconstructs Hillary's account in her memoir *Hard Choices*, and recalls that the secretary of state told a relative of one victim that "we'll find who made that awful video." Writes Attkisson: "why not say we'll find whoever killed your loved one?" But as the author learned, being unkind to Obama's designated successor, and less than worshipful of the president, has its own special reward.

Attkisson describes working at her computer when something took over and began wiping out material. She had the presence of mind to grab her phone and shoot a video. She learned that her computer had been infiltrated using spyware proprietary to government agencies such as the CIA, FBI, and NSA, which now are conducting surveillance against all Americans. She also found the intruders planted classified information on her computer. That added "the possible threat of criminal prosecution" to the author's list of delay, denial, obstruction, intimidation, retaliation, bullying, and surveillance from the supposedly transparent Obama administration. The back story here is quite remarkable.

The Obama administration has transformed U.S. intelligence and law enforcement agencies into a force reminiscent of East Germany's Stasi security agency, deployed on the domestic scene. CBS has become one of their false-flag operations, but Attkisson failed to play along. She notes that U.S. snoops had information on the Tsarnaev brothers but did nothing to stop their deadly Boston Marathon bombing mission. She might also have cited Fort Hood mass murderer Nidal Hasan. Government snoops also had Hasan's emails to terrorist bosses but made no move against him. The administration believed a persistent journalist such as Sharyl Attkisson required government action, aided by a massive taxpayer-funded attack machine with powerful assets in the media. The author provides a roster of the players.

In the early going, Attkisson quotes leftist icon Noam Chomsky, who said, "the U.S. media do not function in the manner of the propaganda system of a totalitarian state." But *Stonewalled* makes it clear that, at present, they do, echoing government propaganda and attacking those who challenge government power with facts. In these conditions, one can well imagine what action might be taken against some insider filling in the blanks on everything we still don't know about President Barack Obama.

Stonewalled is not that book, but this important work does confirm that the federal government of the United States is now acting in a totalitarian manner. That is of major concern, and not just for journalists. We're all Sharyl Attkissons now.

41. Political Correctness and Violent Crime.

On April 14, 2013, in Davis, California, a person or persons unknown broke into the home of Oliver "Chip" Northup, 87, and his wife Claudia Maupin, 76, and killed them in way that, as a police report said, manifested "exceptional depravity." The crime took place only minutes from my residence, and the victims were my parents' generation. In fact, Oliver Northup and my father both volunteered for World War Two at age 17 and served on surface ships. And they both liked the same old-time folk music. So I duly took notice, and when the police finally arrested someone, I recalled a previous story.

The University of California at Davis, just down the freeway from the state capital of Sacramento, is famous for its school of viticulture and enology, part of its agricultural emphasis enshrined the schools sports teams, the "Aggies." This was the UC campus that rejected highly qualified Allan Bakke for medical school because he was a person of no color. In recent years the campus shaped up as hotbed of sexual assault. That turned out to be false, but as this piece noted, the murders of Oliver Northup and Claudia Maupin, one of the most horrific crimes in California history, failed to elicit a similar response. This crime was the story that led me to write *Exceptional Depravity: Dan Who Likes Dark and Double Murder in Davis, California.*

Take Back the Night from Whom?
Political correctness and a double murder in Davis
City Journal California, October 31, 2013

Davis, California, an agricultural and university town of 66,000 people just west of Sacramento, arguably contends with Berkeley and

Santa Monica as the most politically correct city in the Golden State. The greens in city hall built a tunnel to enable a toad to cross a major thoroughfare safely, and a few years ago a popular Davis eatery called Murder Burger renamed itself Redrum Burger to satisfy residents unnerved by the original name's "violent" connotations. But a real-life, horrific double murder has revealed some hard truths about Davis, an otherwise low-crime town.

From 1999 through 2011, the city recorded three murders, 33 rapes, 38 robberies, and 41 assaults. The city's violent crime rate in 2011 was far below the national average—a pattern that held for the previous decade, too. Oddly, reports from the University of California at Davis during roughly the same period paint a nightmarish picture of a place resembling early 1990s New York City. Why might that be? For 16 years, a woman named Jennifer Beeman ran the UC Davis Campus Violence Prevention Program, an arm of the campus police department.

In 2011, a Yolo County superior court judge sentenced Beeman to 180 days in state prison and five years' probation for embezzlement and falsification of records pertaining to campus violence. In 2001, for example, Beeman claimed in a federal grant application that as many as *700* Davis students were victims of rape or attempted rape every year. University officials eventually conceded that Beeman "significantly over-reported" the figures, but her fakery drew down four federal grants totaling more than $3 million. Some of that money went to a campaign to "Take Back the Night."

Take it back from whom? UC Davis is as hip and multicultural as any university, which leaves students searching for fanciful monsters to kill. Two years ago, on the morning of an annual Students of Color Conference, somebody found a yellow ribbon tied around a tree, on which some joker had scrawled, "Use me as a noose." A student opined in the campus newspaper that the ribbon was "representative of the hate and bigotry still present across our UC campus." Meantime, a bona fide monster lurked just outside the campus gates.

Daniel Marsh, 16, is currently on trial for double murder. He is being tried as an adult but is not eligible for the death penalty. At a preliminary hearing last month, Davis police detective Ariel Pineda revealed what the boy told him after he'd been arrested for butchering an elderly couple last April. Marsh, Pineda testified, had first fantasized about killing someone when he was ten. Though young and slight of build, he fantasized about slashing the throat of the woman he blamed for breaking up his family. Marsh told Pineda he would think about how he could kill every person he met.

On the night of April 13, Marsh—then still 15—donned a black jacket, gloves, and mask and went looking for victims. Marsh not only confessed to the police but also pointed them to the evidence of his crime, asking to keep the black jacket as a souvenir. He told Pineda how he found a promising house near his own. He slit a screen and crept inside. Marsh entered a bedroom where he found Oliver Northup, 87, and Claudia Maupin, 76, sound asleep. Northup was a founding member of the Unitarian Universalist Church of Davis, a criminal-defense attorney, and a guitarist-vocalist with the Putah Creek Crawdads, a local music group. Maupin was a church pastoral associate.

Pineda testified that Marsh confessed to standing in the room and fantasizing what he would do to the couple. When Maupin awoke and screamed, Marsh stabbed her upward of 40 times, telling the detective "she just wouldn't die." He stabbed each victim more than 60 times, even after they were dead because it "felt right." Then he eviscerated both victims and put a cell phone and drinking glass into the bodies because he wanted to "mess with" the investigators. Marsh confessed that the killings gave him a high for a week; as he told Pineda, after the double murders his next goal was to beat someone to death with a baseball bat. His savagery rivaled anything in *Helter Skelter*.

Marsh's story made *USA Today*, the *New York Daily News*, and the *London Daily Mail*. In Davis, however, the response was subdued. Shocked local politicians wondered how their fair city could become Murder Burg, but for some reason the case did not inspire the same sort of outrage that a yellow ribbon with a bit of doggerel had sparked. At UC Davis, where officials perceive rape, hatred, and bigotry at every turn, the murders created scarcely a stir.

The crime may have been ghastly, but its dynamics apparently did not conform to politically correct orthodoxies. If Daniel Marsh had stabbed to death and disemboweled two students from Tunisia, say, or a gay or lesbian couple, the campus would have erupted in protest. Marsh was doubtless brimming with hatred, but his murders failed to qualify as a hate crime. His innocent and unarmed victims were both affluent white people and not members of any accredited victim group. (Advanced age doesn't count.) The gruesome demise of two innocents did not offer the politically correct an occasion to denounce their enemies or champion their favorite causes. If Marsh had shot Northup and Maupin, perhaps the case would have inspired rallies against "gun violence." And though Marsh had spent time in a psychiatric hospital, his actions weren't enough to prompt demonstrations about mental illness, on which California spends billions of dollars, with few positive results.

In Davis, liberal elites, perpetually in the subjunctive mood, show more interest in fake crime than real crime. If people truly want to "take back the night," they should pay more attention to actual threats and less to the nostrums of the politically correct.

42. From Civil Rights to the War on Terror

As one review says, Richard John Neuhaus was "one of the most influential figures in American public life from the Civil Rights era to the War on Terror" but with his friends and colleagues he was a regular chap. He liked to throw down a few drinks, and actually got more lucid as he did so. Since Neuhaus passed away in 2009 nobody has really taken his place. So I was delighted to review a book that will help people get to know this man.

Author of Naked Public Square Led an Extraordinary Life
Randy Boyagoda, *Richard John Neuhaus: A Life in the Public Square*, Image, 2015, 459 pages, $30.00.
Carolina Journal, May 8, 2015

RICHARD JOHN NEUHAUS WAS VARIOUSLY A THEOLOGIAN, INTELLECTUAL, AC-tivist, ecumenist, writer, editor, commentator, pundit, and pastor. Or, as he put it, "a Canadian-reared, Texas-educated, Missouri Synod Lutheran writing from black Brooklyn where I have lived almost the whole of my adult life." To write the definitive book on such a man is no easy task, but for the most part Randy Boyagoda pulls it off in *Richard John Neuhaus: A Life in the Public Square*. The author describes himself as a "Sri Lankan-Canadian novelist and English professor living in Toronto," and his section on Neuhaus' early life shows great attention to detail, supplemented with photos.

Boyagoda's subject was the seventh child of Ella and Clemens Neuhaus, a Lutheran pastor in Pembroke, Ontario, who raised eight children on a salary of $81 a month. In the early going Richard showed interest in the ministry, performing a dog wedding but also revealed a mischievous side. Some of his early life also emerges in Neuhaus' 2002 *As I Lay Dying: A Meditation Upon Returning*, which readers will want to consult, and the subject of a C-SPAN interview with Brian Lamb. The book bears "Proustian intensity," says Boyagoda, but it was not the work that made Neuhaus a national figure.

After an education in Nebraska and Texas, here thoroughly and theologically documented, Neuhaus wound up at Zion Evangelical Lutheran in Detroit. By the early 1960s, he was pastor of St. John the Evangelist church in Brooklyn, a congregation of blacks and whites. He also ministered in death wards and kept his eye on escalating conflicts in Southeast Asia.

A key player with the group Clergy and Laity Concerned About Vietnam, Neuhaus became a "fast-rising activist on the American Left." He made national news on Oct. 25, 1965, for sharp criticism of President Lyndon Johnson, and his emergence as a national religious leader in a growing antiwar movement dovetailed neatly with the civil rights cause. Neuhaus drew inspiration from Martin Luther King Jr.'s "Letter from Birmingham Jail," and in February 1968 joined King, Ralph Abernathy, and others in the march on Washington.

As Boyagoda sees it, Neuhaus had become a leading clergyman of the American Left, "only to discover that the American Left was moving away from his clergyman concerns." Opposition to U.S. involvement in Vietnam did not mean that Communist forces were the vanguard of peace and social justice, as some in the movement contended.

Neuhaus duly became a vocal anticommunist and natural adversary to what the author calls "liberal Christian groups like the Sojourners." In reality, these were not liberals but strident anti-American leftists who smeared Neuhaus as an "intellectual assassin on behalf of wealth and power." Full disclosure: I knew Richard John Neuhaus a bit and when he was visiting nearby I printed up a business card for him reading, "Intellectual Assassin." We enjoyed some laughs at the notion of the cigar-chomping captains of industry assigning a minister and Luca Brasi to attack the evangelists of "liberation theology."

As Boyagoda notes, in keeping with his faith, Neuhaus believed the poor should be liberated. As a founding member of the Institute on Religion and Democracy, he argued that democratic pluralism was a better liberator than any Marxist dogma. He also believed that a public square shorn of religious values was a barren place. Without those values, as he was fond of saying, there would have been no anti-slavery movement, no women's suffrage movement, and no civil rights movement. He delighted to note that Martin Luther King Jr. was in fact a minister.

Neuhaus joked about calling his signature book *The Naked Catholic Bishops*, but Andrew Greeley had already used that one. So he called it *The Naked Public Square*, and the rest is history. As Boyagoda notes, the book got a boost from Ronald Reagan's 1984 re-election campaign and Neuhaus became a staple on television. In a famous "Firing Line" episode with William F. Buckley, he debated the relative merits of Mother Teresa and Sister Boom Boom, a San Francisco transvestite.

The New Republic grouped Neuhaus with the menacing "theocons" and paleoconservative Joe Sobran slammed him as a "one-man magisterium of the neoconservative crowd." In "The Raid" chapter, Boyagoda recounts how Neuhaus and some groups on the right parted company in rather abrupt fashion. Neuhaus then launched the journal *First Things*, which maintained his influence.

In his editorial after the 9/11 attacks, he recognized a real war, not some metaphorical conflict, as some had it. "Metaphorical airplanes flown by metaphorical hijackers," he wrote, "did not crash into metaphorical buildings leaving thousands of metaphorical corpses." A Roman Catholic since 1990, Neuhaus faulted Barack Obama for not disowning the Rev. Jeremiah Wright and found in the president "boilerplate leftisms of class warfare and what he depicts as a nation of black and white, of seething resentments."

As a pastor in Brooklyn, Neuhaus had married a black-and-white couple, and every year called them on their anniversary. One year no call came and the couple knew something was wrong. So in early 2009 they showed up in the hospital room where Neuhaus lay dying. He was unable to speak but when the woman addressed him, "he opened his eyes and smiled. Soon thereafter he fell into a deep and final sleep." Six years later, this great man remains someone all readers need to know. *Richard John Neuhaus* is a good place to start.

43. So What's Happening?

In the argot of my generation, there's something happening here, and what it is ain't exactly clear to many people. Like Gershwin they wonder, how long has this been going on? Barry Rubin took on these issues in his last book, confirming that the truth tends to emerge near the exit door.

Rubin: 'Third Left,' Rising from 'New Left,' Has Taken Over America

Barry Rubin, *Silent Revolution: How the Left Rose to Political Power and Cultural Dominance*, Broadside Books, 331 pages, $25.99.

Carolina Journal, June 5, 2014

HISTORIAN AND POLITICAL SCIENTIST BARRY RUBIN, WHO PASSED AWAY IN February, titled his last book *Silent Revolution*, a perceptive and powerful work that would have been more accurately billed as Silent Counterrevolution.

The United States began with a successful revolution, but now, Rubin explains, we are experiencing a "break from all American history" and "a different system from the one through which America achieved success and prosperity." The altered approach "was one of an unprecedented degree of statism, an imperial presidency that went far beyond Richard Nixon's dreams: record high levels of government regulation, taxation, and debt." All that, plus indoctrination, political correctness, and the alteration of reality. How had all that come about?

Rubin ties it to the "Third Left," the heir to both the Old Left of the 1920s-'50s and the New Left of the 1960s and 1970s. The Third Left took over liberalism, portrayed its only opponent as reactionary right-wing conservatism, and claimed that their radicalism represents all that is good in America and a correction to all that is evil. The new radicalism also claims a monopoly on truth and a right to transform America fundamentally, which President Obama claims as his mandate.

The Third Left goal was "to convince Americans the exact opposite of what their experience proved: that the country had fundamentally failed and the old leftist solutions were the answer." For Rubin, the timing is significant.

At the very moment in human history when it became obvious that the far left's ideas had failed and that statist, big-government, ever-higher-regulation policies did not work, it became possible for the first time ever to convince Americans that these things were precisely what the country needed. And at the very time in human history when Western civilization and liberal capitalism were so obviously the most successful in history — recognized as such in the Third World and most of all in formerly Communist China — a camouflaged radical movement convinced many of those benefiting from the system that their own societies were in fact evil and failed.

It became possible to convince Americans their society had failed because the Third Left "put its emphasis on infiltrating the means of idea and opinion production." In journalism, reporters "routinely used politically charged language that would have gotten them fired in earlier times," comparing the Tea Party to Nazi Brownshirts for example, and the mass media were out to "protect the image of anyone on the left side."

The Third Left took to education for the possibilities of indoctrination and enjoyed great success by excluding materials celebrating America and hiding the failures of Communism, which "produced far more waste and unhappiness and far less wealth than the American system, not to mention totalitarian oppression."

For the Third Left, wealth was not created by individual enterprise and workers, but instead stolen from poor foreigners and oppressed non-whites. The Third Left declares America evil, "and the people are broken up into warring groups," a "country of castes" in which the reward of individual merit is "overthrown in favor of special privileges."

The Third Left shunned the workers and the factories, but — as Rubin shows — they found reliable allies in government employee unions. Most taxes and regulations directly benefit government workers, therefore shrinking government, boosting efficiency, cutting taxes, and maintaining a powerful private sector is all "against their interests."

As Rubin notes: "The economy would decline, constantly adding to unemployment payments, food stamps, and other government programs, which in turn gave the Third Left more reasons to blame capitalism and the greedy rich for not having met society's needs: to demand even higher taxes; to raise taxes, and to increase government spending."

Barack Obama, Rubin writes, "came to symbolize the silent revolution," but readers will find no conspiracy theories. Obama is "just another product of the ideology and indoctrination that grown-up 1960s radicals had systematically spread to his generation and its successors." By radicals he means people like Bill Ayers, Van Jones, and Bernardine Dohrn, who said that young Americans should "use their strategic position behind enemy lines to join forces in the destruction of empire."

In *Silent Revolution*, the president emerges as the Third Left's self-hypnotized Manchurian candidate, shrink-wrapped in statist superstition like his "progressive" political mentors, hostile to America like his spiritual mentor Jeremiah Wright, and certainly not a liberal. If Obama was a liberal, asks Rubin, "why did he repeatedly denounce the greatest accomplishments of liberals and call for a completely different approach?"

For Obama, "A free market only thrives when there are rules to ensure competition and fair play." As Rubin notes, "But it had always thrived under fewer rules than Obama wanted, while it had plummeted with the level of rules and definition of fair play Obama had imposed during his first term."

And, of course, he won a second term, a huge victory for the Third Left, which does not "expose and correct its own failures." The result "may be a very long-term and even permanent change of the United

States into something else, a nation far less affluent and far less free."

Says Rubin, "The idea that tens of millions of Americans could be, in effect, turned into anti-Americans seemed insane. But it happened, didn't it?" Yes, it did happen, and by any standard that is a counter-revolution. Readers will be left wondering with the author: "Will there be a U-turn?"

44. Afterword: Write On.

THERE'S PLENTY MORE WHERE THAT CAME FROM AND SOME OF IT MAY WIND up in a collection. My output, meanwhile, does not equal the "Niagara" of Malcolm Muggeridge, but it may likewise signify possibilities never realized. I certainly had no shortage of opportunities and maybe I could have been a contender in some other field. But overall, as Marlon Brando explained in *On the Waterfront*, I'm glad what I done. And I'm going to keep on doing it as long as I'm able and despite adverse conditions.

At this writing the jihad of junkthought is mounting a surge. One can choose to run away, like Sir Robin in *Monty Python and the Holy Grail*, or one can choose to throw down. As Arthur Koestler said, write ruthlessly what one believes to be the truth, or else shut up.

33216341R00173

Made in the USA
San Bernardino, CA
19 April 2019